The Oklahoma Publishing Company's First Century

The Gaylord Family Story

The
Oklahoma Publishing Company's
First Century

The Gaylord Family Story

DAVID DARY

The Oklahoma Publishing Company

Oklahoma City, Oklahoma

Copyright © 2003 The Oklahoma Publishing Company

All rights reserved. No part of this book may be used or reproduced in any manner whatsoever without written permission, except in the case of brief quotations embodied in critical articles and reviews. For information, write to The Oklahoma Publishing Company.

The Oklahoma Publishing Company
P. O. Box 25125
Oklahoma City, OK 73125

Library of Congress Control Number: 2003101194
ISBN: 0-9706394-4-9

Except where noted, all illustrations are from the files
of The Oklahoma Publishing Company.
Designed by Jeff Wincapaw
Copyedited by Barbara McGill
Typeset by Marie Weiler
Produced by Marquand Books, Inc., Seattle
    www.marquand.com
Printed by C&C Offset Printing Co., Ltd., Hong Kong

Contents

Foreword

The Oklahoma Publishing Company celebrated its first century of service to the people of Oklahoma in early January 2003. This book tells the story of the Company and the role my family and our employees have played during the last century.

Without the support of the people of Oklahoma, *The Oklahoman* would not have grown and prospered in its service to Oklahoma City and the state. As I read this history it gave me the feeling of genuine pride in the Company and especially in our readers and employees and their loyalty through the years. They have seen the Company grow and have shared in that growth.

It is my hope that the reader will enjoy this history and feel the same pride that I feel in The Oklahoma Publishing Company and the state of Oklahoma.

Edward L. Gaylord
Chairman, Editor and Publisher

Preface

When The Oklahoma Publishing Company celebrated its 95th anniversary in 1998, this writer produced a historical sketch of the company and the three generations of the Gaylord family who have led the company since 1903. It was titled "A Work in Progress" and was published as a supplement to *The Sunday Oklahoman* on November 8, 1998. It was well received and many readers asked that it be published in a more permanent form. So the idea was born to expand the history and publish it in book form to mark the beginning of The Oklahoma Publishing Company's second century early in 2003.

This book tells the story of The Oklahoma Publishing Company through its first hundred years. The story, of course, is closely tied to the Gaylord family beginning with E. K. Gaylord, then his son Edward L. Gaylord, and now his son E. K. Gaylord II and his three sisters. It is impossible to separate the Company's story from that of this unique American family. The story of OPUBCO and the Gaylord family also parallels the history of Oklahoma from its territorial period through the state's first century.

It is my hope that this work not only captures the history and color of The Oklahoma Publishing Company and the Gaylord family, but the Oklahoma that has evolved and matured during the last century. There can be no question that the state has been greatly influenced by the Gaylord family and *The Oklahoman,* truly a state newspaper and one of the last family-owned metropolitan dailies in America.

David Dary

Chapter One

PLANTING AN ACORN

It was late December, 1902, when 29-year-old E. K. Gaylord got off the southbound train in Oklahoma City. This mild-mannered and soft-spoken man wanted to learn for himself whether glowing reports about Oklahoma Territory were true. Young Gaylord already had several years of newspaper experience, but he was dissatisfied with his job as business manager of his older brother's *St. Joseph Dispatch* in western Missouri. He wanted his own newspaper.

While visiting in St. Louis several days earlier, Gaylord spotted Victor Lawson, the well-known publisher of the highly successful *Chicago Daily News,* at Union Station wearing a square stiff-felt derby hat and a spade beard, his trademarks. Gaylord introduced himself to Lawson and they exchanged pleasantries. Gaylord then asked him where he would go to get a start in the newspaper business if he had a small amount of capital to invest. Lawson, who had just traveled by train through Oklahoma Territory, replied, "Oklahoma City." On Lawson's advice, Gaylord soon headed south.

Oklahoma City, founded 13 years earlier, already had 10,037 residents, according to the 1900 census. The business district was confined to two blocks on Main Street and two blocks on Grand Boulevard adjacent to another two blocks on Broadway. There were only four blocks of paved streets in the town. There were no automobiles. Nearly all the business buildings were one- or two-story brick structures. The exceptions were the Lee Hotel and the Culbertson Building, both five-story structures. The four-story Empire Building was under construction when young Gaylord began to walk around the town. On the west side of Broadway, between Grand and Main, he found a section called "Battle Row." Every building but one was either a saloon or a gambling house. The exception was the Saddle Rock Cafe, where you could get a ham sandwich and a cup of coffee for 15 cents.

Gaylord later recalled: "I walked in each direction as far as there were homes, west on Main street to the 900 block, east across the Santa Fe to the 1100 block, and north to 13th street. Beyond 16th street there were farms. South, over the Canadian River, there were perhaps 15 to 20 small houses." Gaylord saw that most of the stores carried good merchandise. He was surprised when he found a music store offering several Kimball pianos and one Steinway. That convinced him there were people of refinement and education among those who settled Oklahoma City. As Gaylord toured the town, he visited with the people he met. Most of them were young. He was impressed with their spirit of adventure, faith in the future, and self-reliance.

Gaylord liked what he saw and decided to investigate buying into one of the town's two newspapers. He visited with a banker and asked him about the town's two papers and who owned them. After the banker talked about their owners, Gaylord asked him if the owners were honest, reliable people. The banker responded, "Yes, I guess so." Gaylord then asked, "Which is the better paper? Which would you want me to buy?" The banker responded, "It doesn't make a damn bit of difference! Neither one of 'em is worth a whoop in hell." Gaylord thanked the banker and left, going first to the *Times-Journal* recalling that it was an evening paper. "I thought I would rather work on an evening paper." He visited with Elmer Brown and his brother Cortez, who owned the *Times-Journal,* but as Gaylord later recalled, "They did not choose to take in a partner" and made their views on the subject very clear.

Gaylord then went to the office of *The Oklahoman* on South Broadway, where he visited with Roy E. Stafford, the publisher, who liked Gaylord's ideas about newspapers. Stafford was very receptive to having a partner admitting that he needed a

LEE HOTEL

The Lee Hotel was later renamed the Huckins Hotel in downtown Oklahoma City. This post-card illustration was taken only a few years after E. K. Gaylord spent his first night there in Oklahoma City late in 1902. (Courtesy Oklahoma Historical Society)

This panoramic view of the future site of Oklahoma City was made on the morning of April 22, 1889. By late afternoon the empty space around the railroad depot was covered with tents. (Courtesy Western History Collections, University of Oklahoma Libraries)

Oklahoma City's first post office was a makeshift affair on April 22, 1889. (Courtesy Oklahoma Historical Society)

business manager as well as more financial support. Gaylord wrote some sample news stories and the two men exchanged references. They agreed to get together again within a few days. Gaylord decided to check out Fort Worth, Texas, where he had heard of a newspaper for sale. He took the train to Fort Worth, but as he later recalled, "I didn't like the town. It was too near Dallas. I thought Oklahoma City would eventually be a better town than Fort Worth."

Gaylord returned to Oklahoma City and came to an agreement with Stafford. Gaylord said he would return to Missouri, settle his affairs there, and return in two weeks to formalize the agreement. Gaylord spent the night in the five-story Lee Hotel (later the Huckins Hotel) and the following day boarded a northbound train for Missouri.

The world of Oklahoma newspapers that E. K. Gaylord was about to enter was anything but calm and peaceful. Hard-hitting personal journalism was the rule in Oklahoma Territory, and editors often used back alley, barroom and gutter-style language in attacking and counter-attacking each other, in criticizing citizens, and most certainly the political parties they opposed. The editors sought to keep emotions high as they exchanged blasts with each other in editorial combat. Politics were covered more thoroughly than any other subject. Papers usually put territorial, national and international news stories on page one, much of it clipped and reprinted from other papers. It was then a common practice for newspapers to trade or exchange their papers for those published elsewhere to obtain material.

Newspapers were businesses. Many a paper survived or died on city and county printing contracts. Editors scrapped for money from any source, and sought to cut costs at every turn. To do this, many papers used ready-prints, sometimes called "boiler plates." These were newspaper sheets pre-printed on one side with foreign and national news plus feature stories and

national advertising. Editors bought ready-prints from printing supply firms, most in Chicago. Since the editors had only one side of a newspaper sheet to print, ready-prints saved them time and money.

Even before the Run of April 1889, which opened the region to settlement, a reporter named B. R. Harrington was working illegally in Oklahoma City, then nothing more than a railroad depot. He wrote stories and sent them to Wichita, Kansas, where Hamlin Whitmore Sawyer set them in type and printed them in a weekly newspaper called the *Oklahoma City Times.* The paper was printed at Wichita and promoted or "boomed" the Unassigned Lands that were about to be opened for settlement. In early January 1889, Sawyer and Harrington boldly moved their press to Oklahoma City. By late in the month their paper was being circulated in every state and territory and even overseas. The Oklahoma City dateline was a novelty

since no town existed around the railroad depot.

But the paper's success came to an abrupt end on February 10, 1889, when U.S. soldiers from Fort Reno closed down the *Oklahoma City Times.* Sawyer and Harrington moved their press from the Unassigned Lands south to Purcell just across the South Canadian River in the Chickasaw Nation and later returned it to Wichita. Still they managed to publish the *Oklahoma City*

Tents dotted the landscape of the new Oklahoma City on April 27, 1889. (Courtesy Western History Collections, University of Oklahoma Libraries)

Oklahoma City some days after the Run in 1889. (Courtesy Western History Collections, University of Oklahoma Libraries)

Times most weeks. Following the run of 1889, Sawyer and Harrington moved the press back to the new and rapidly growing town of Oklahoma City, and on June 30, 1899, began publishing the *Oklahoma City Daily Times.* Only then did they discover that Angelo C. and Winfield W. Scott had started a paper in the new town called the *Oklahoma Times.* The Scott brothers soon changed their paper's name to the *Oklahoma Journal* and continued publishing their paper daily. Meantime, the *Oklahoma City Times* ran into financial difficulties and before 1889 ended, the Scott broth-

ers bought the *Times,* merged it with their *Oklahoma Journal* and created the *Oklahoma City Times-Journal,* a Republican afternoon daily.

In addition, three other daily newspapers were established in Oklahoma City during the town's first year. Frank McMaster, a former reporter on the *Chicago Tribune,* started the *Evening Gazette* which lasted only a few months. McMaster then sold the *Evening Gazette* to W. J. Donovan and George M. Adams, who had started the *Oklahoma Daily Press.* Donovan and Adams combined the papers

A street scene in downtown Oklahoma City in 1893. (Courtesy Western History Collections, University of Oklahoma Libraries)

and created the *Oklahoma Daily Press-Gazette,* a morning paper that claimed to be an organ of the Democratic Party. McMaster turned his attention to magazine publishing and created *McMaster's Magazine* in May 1889. Later the magazine's name was changed to *Oklahoma Today.*

By 1894, there were only two daily newspapers in Oklahoma City; the morning *Press-Gazette,* and the afternoon *Times-Journal,* and both were struggling to survive. Then late in 1894, Rev. Sam W. Small, a Georgia native, established *The Daily Oklahoman.* Before coming to Oklahoma Territory, Small had served as an official reporter for the U.S. Senate, as confidential secretary to former president Andrew Johnson, and as editor of a newspaper in Houston, Texas. Small then joined the staff of the *Atlanta Constitution,* but left that paper to become an evangelist. He soon gained national attention lecturing in favor of prohibition. On one of his trips as an evangelist, Small came to Oklahoma City. He

was warmly received, and met another visitor, Col. William Rockhill Nelson, publisher of the *Kansas City Star.* Nelson told Small that Oklahoma City needed a better newspaper. Small agreed, and he soon had a vision of establishing a great newspaper in Oklahoma City, one that would influence the entire territory and later the state and the whole Southwest. He chose the name, *The Daily Oklahoman.*

William Rockhill Nelson agreed to provide Small with type and two printers from the *Kansas City Star.* Meantime, Small made arrangements with Frank McMaster, who had opened a printing shop, to produce *The Oklahoman.* Unfortunately, McMaster had made many enemies who soon opposed Small and his paper. Small wrote copy for the first issue of *The Oklahoman* while waiting for the printers to arrive from Kansas City, Missouri. The printers, however, were delayed. Small and two of McMaster's job printers set the type and printed the first issue on January 14, 1894. From the start *The*

Oklahoman sought to oust the *Press-Gazette* as the organ of the Democratic Party, something it had proudly proclaimed. Because of this, Small quickly gained an enemy in W. J. Donovan, publisher of the *Press-Gazette*. Then too, Donovan did not like McMaster, who had sold him the *Press-Gazette* for $2,500 and had agreed not to compete in Oklahoma City newspaper publishing. The fact that McMaster associated himself with Small made matters worse.

With each issue of *The Oklahoman,* Donovan's blood pressure climbed and his editorials became more heated. He continually referred to the "C.O.D" —cash on delivery—operation of the paper, and his terms for *The Oklahoman* and Small became more caustic. He frequently called *The Oklahoman* the "Coyote" and the "Cuckoo." He described the staff as the "menagerie" and labeled Small a "fake preacher," "Br'er Psaimuel," and "Psalmuel." By March 1894 Donovan's vocabulary was taxed as he wrote: "It is a ship scuttling piratical craft loaded to the gunwales with a class of conscience-less freebooters who lost standing and credit when they parted company with their integrity and manhood and who now thirst for revenge on the decent and respectable elements of the Democratic party."

Across the nation many large newspapers watched with interest what Small was trying to do with *The Oklahoman*. Unfortunately he was operating on a financial shoe string, and *The Oklahoman* literally ate money. His big paper carried reports from the Associated Press received by telegraph, a Kansas City market report, and a weather forecast for the territory from the weather bureau in Washington D.C. The Sunday edition even boasted a society page. Small also opened news offices and hired correspondents in seven territorial towns—Guthrie, Perry, Norman, Ardmore, Yukon, El Reno and Newkirk. Going after the news in these towns naturally drew fire from their local publishers, and their papers made a point of poking fun at frequent and flagrant errors made by *The Oklahoman*'s untutored correspondents. For example, the editor of the *Perry Sentinel* wrote: "Now that Sam Small has engaged in the newspaper business, instead of dining on Sunday with his brethren, he will be found in the rear end of his office reading duns for paper bills and wondering why he ventured thusly."

A view of the railroad depot and Oklahoma City in the 1890s. (Courtesy Western History Collections, University of Oklahoma Libraries)

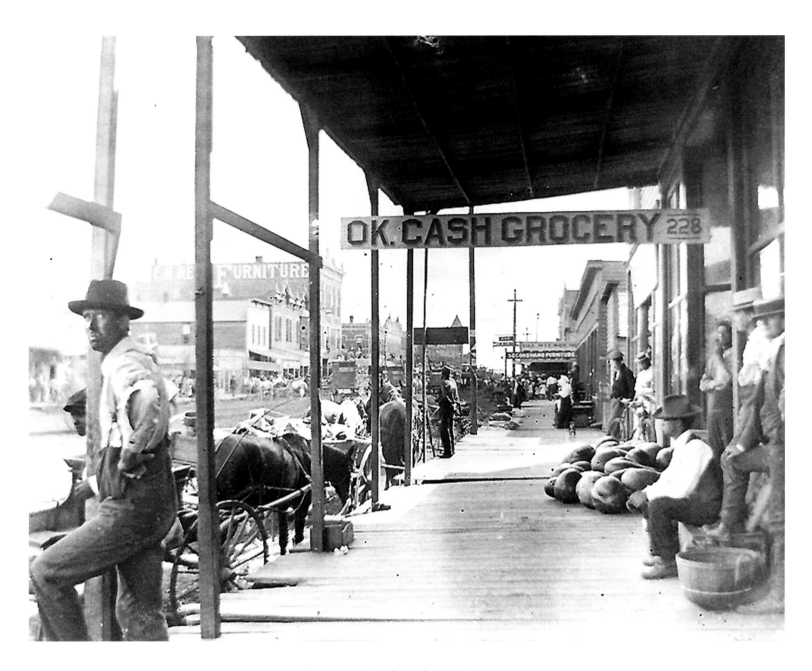

The *St. Louis Post-Dispatch,* which closely followed and chronicled Small's troubles, reported that publishing the Monday paper on Sunday had cost Small the support of his previously large church following. The paper noted that Democrats were leaving his fold rapidly because of his vigorous and very personal bid for party support to nominate him for U.S. senator at one of the many "statehood" conventions held a short time before at Perry, Oklahoma. "A week ago," reported the *Post-Dispatch,* "the funds of the paper began to run low and Small went to Texas to lecture and to preach to get money to run the paper."

Small's trip was the first of several made to raise money. As his absences grew more and more prolonged, Donovan speculated almost daily in the *Press-Gazette* that Small had left *The Oklahoman* to die on the vine. During one of Small's absences trouble broke out among Small's top-heavy staff of temperamental editors. The staff took sides over the question of printing an "apology" to W. C. Renfrow, territorial governor, over an erroneous story. The bitterness over the apology grew until, as the *Atlanta Constitution* reported, "A pitched battle ensued." The Atlanta paper reported: "The feeling is so bitter now that the paper is being issued

with a police officer in charge of the office to keep the peace. It is thought that Small has become so disgusted with the whole outfit that he will not return at all."

The Oklahoman's internal troubles bothered Small, but of greater concern were his financial problems. Many businessmen opposed Small's stand against liquor and refused to advertise, and without advertising dollars, his financial problems grew even worse. In an effort to rejuvenate the paper, Small formed a stock company in Oklahoma City to raise money, but he soon lost control and returned to newspaper work in Atlanta where he died in 1929.

Small's departure from Oklahoma City left the stock company with a large debt. The company was headed by Whit M. Grant, later to be mayor of Oklahoma City, and was controlled largely by the First National Bank. Because Donovan's *Press-Gazette* was having its own financial problems, the city now had two weak voices for the Democratic party. To solve the problem, the stock company bought the *Press-Gazette* and merged it with *The*

Oklahoman in an effort to create one strong Democratic paper.

For a time the stock company kept *The Oklahoman* afloat, but within a few months the paper lost $8,000. The stock company then leased *The Oklahoman* to Charles F. Barrett, who operated it for less than a year. Although Barrett claimed he made enough money to cover the paper's expenses, it never made a profit. When Barrett decided not to continue running the paper, the stock company sold *The Oklahoman* to R. Q. Blakeney, who cut the expenses of the metropolitan operation including the costly Associated Press wire service observing that "many of the expensive features were simply not justified at the time." He published *The Oklahoman* as a modest, small-town paper using ready-prints produced in Chicago, but they contained no local news. Blakeney used the pages he printed for promotion and told readers that *The Oklahoman* had more circulation than any weekly or daily newspaper in Indian Territory or Oklahoma Territory.

While these things were happening, Roy E. Stafford, publisher of the weekly *Champion* in Oklahoma City, was carefully watching *The Oklahoman.* He later said that during this time he believed the paper was "destined to become the leading daily publication of the great southwest." In March 1900, Stafford and W. T. Parker bought *The Oklahoman* from Blakeney. Parker had just returned from a trip to the Klondike gold fields where he found little gold. But while Parker was away, the value of town lots he had purchased in Oklahoma City boomed in value. When he returned, he was a wealthy man by Oklahoma City standards. Stafford approached Parker, who was not a newspaperman, and proposed they buy *The Oklahoman.* Parker liked the idea and provided much of the capital to buy the paper which Stafford wanted to rebuild.

Almost immediately Stafford purchased a new case of type and hired a man to boost circulation. He also bought a Linotype machine to set type and obtained the telegraphic news service called "pony reports" from the Associated Press. They were AP stories received at the local telegraph office and delivered to the newspaper. Stafford also banished advertising from the front page of *The Oklahoman.* When Stafford talked to Parker about buying a second Linotype machine, Parker threw up his hands. Improvements for *The Oklahoman* were costing him too much money. Parker sold his interest to Stafford and left. By February 1902, thrilled with the progress he had made in rebuilding *The Oklahoman,* Stafford bought a new Cottrell flatbed press, and five months later purchased a Cox duplex flatbed press. But *The Oklahoman* still lacked sufficient financial support, and Stafford was not a good money manager.

Less than a year later Stafford agreed to sell E. K. Gaylord an interest in *The Oklahoman.* Gaylord had returned to

St. Joseph, Missouri, settled his affairs, and returned to Oklahoma City in January 1903 ready to become part-owner of *The Oklahoman.* It is doubtful he realized his Oklahoma City investment would be the beginning of a family empire worth billions of dollars a century later.

Chapter Two

THE GAYLORD ROOTS

On a cliff overlooking the Seine River in the Normandy region of France are the remains of one of that nation's most impressive and historic castles. The Chateau Gaillard, today a popular tourist attraction, was constructed in 1196 by Richard the Lion Hearted, King of England and Duke of Normandy, as the key structure of the vast English defense system closing French access to what was then English Normandy. But six years after it was built, Chateau Gaillard was overrun by the forces of the French king, Philip Augustus. More than 200 years later, not long after Christopher Columbus landed in the new world, the Protestant ancestors of E. K. Gaylord carried the Gaillard name from Normandy to England to escape religious persecution. In England they soon spelled their name Gaylord. E. K. Gaylord's ancestors settled in Somerset, England, where Nicholas Gaylord was born in 1499. He was E. K. Gaylord's eleventh great-grandfather. There, several generations of the family lived until Nicholas Gaylord's great grandson, Deacon William Gaylord, came to America in the early 1600s and settled in Connecticut. He was E. K. Gaylord's eighth great-grandfather. From this sturdy puritan stock, a successive line of Gaylords made Connecticut their home. Joseph Gaylord, born about 1720 at Wallingford, Connecticut, was E. K. Gaylord's great, great grandfather. When the War for Independence began in 1776, Joseph, then in his fifties, served in defense of the Connecticut coast and frontier with the rank of Captain. One of Joseph's six sons, Chauncey Gaylord, born at Bristol in 1757, enlisted at the age of 19 as a private in Capt. Jesse Kimball's company and served during the American Revolution at Germantown, Fort Mifflin and Valley Forge. After the war Chauncey married, and in December 1784, he and his wife had a son, Jesse, E. K. Gaylord's grandfather.

By then a new spirit was capturing the young nation following the close of the American Revolution. In all walks of life people enjoyed a liberating sense of freedom, and a restless stream of humanity was beginning to push westward. About 1803, Chauncey, his wife Ruth, and 19-year-old Jesse joined others from the Bristol, Connecticut, area and moved their belongings by ox-drawn wagons about 200 miles to the northwest, where they founded what is today Otisco, near modern Syracuse in Onondago county, New York. The region was then wild and unsettled. In the party was a small, quiet, black-eyed girl with a sunny, thoughtful face. She was 12-year-old Dema Cowles. Her father later died and her widowed mother Lucy married Eliakim Clark from Massachusetts who had fought in the American Revolution. About 1810 they had twin boys named Lewis Gaylord Clark and Willis Gaylord Clark. They were Dema's half-brothers, and she helped to raise them. The boys grew up to become scholars and poets. Lewis edited *Knickerbocker Magazine* in New York City while Willis established a weekly newspaper in Philadelphia and later edited the *Columbian Star*, a weekly religious and literary publication. Both men left their marks on American literature.

As for young Dema, she and Jesse Gaylord became acquaintances, then good friends, and a few years later, in 1817, they married. Jesse operated a nursery business, raising and selling trees and vines. He built a log home for his new wife. The house consisted of one room, a low attic above, and a root cellar beneath. At one end of their home there was a large fireplace to provide warmth during the cold winters. Outside a little way from the house was a well and nearby was a brick oven where all of the cooking was done, even in winter.

About a year after Jesse and Dema were married, they had a daughter named Lucy Ann Gaylord. She was the first of six children. The next child was Leman

Roice Gaylord born in 1820. A second son, Martin Luther Gaylord, was born in 1823, and a third son, George Lewis Gaylord, was born on September 16, 1826. Jesse and Dema had another daughter named Ann in 1830, but she died less than three years later, and their last child was another boy, Willis Edward Gaylord, who was born in 1832.

Jesse and Dema's third son, George Lewis Gaylord, who was E. K. Gaylord's father, grew to manhood and was educated at Otisco, New York. In 1858, when he was 32, he was apparently moved by glowing reports about Kansas and headed west to Atchison, Kansas Territory, where two brothers and a sister were living. George's older brother, Martin Luther Gaylord, a graduate of Amherst College in 1848, was superintendent of schools in Atchison. Martin, who also was a

This photo of George Lewis Gaylord was made in Mathew Brady's New York studio before Gaylord came west in the 1850s.

licensed preacher in the Congregational church, had come to Kansas Territory soon after it was established in 1854. He opposed slavery and supported Kansas as a Free State. In 1856, Martin narrowly escaped being hung by pro-slavery border ruffians from Missouri when he and another man were taken prisoner while trying to reach Lawrence, then the Free State capital of Kansas Territory.

George Gaylord's younger brother Willis was also in Kansas Territory, where in 1857 he became a member of the board of directors of the Atchison branch of the Kansas Valley Bank and later sold railroad land. E. K. Gaylord recalled that Willis "was a promoter type." Lucy Ann, George's older sister, also came to Kansas Territory in 1857 to join her lawyer husband, Samuel C. Pomeroy, an organizer and financial agent of the New England Emigrant Aid Society in Boston. Pomeroy escorted a party of Free State emigrants to Lawrence, Kansas Territory, in 1854 and first settled in Lawrence, but he later moved to Atchison where he became president of the Kansas Valley Bank. Pomeroy also served as mayor of Atchison in 1858 and 1859 and later became a U.S. senator when Kansas became a state in 1861. Pomeroy's wife Lucy accompanied him to Washington where, although in poor health, she helped to care for troops wounded in the Civil War and was president of an organization that established a home for freed orphans and destitute, aged black women freed from slavery by the Emancipation Proclamation. But in July 1863, she died while traveling by boat to Albany, New York, for medical treatment.

When George Lewis Gaylord arrived in Atchison in 1858, he probably felt right at home with two brothers and a sister living there. Pomeroy may have helped George secure a job in a mercantile store at Atchison. E. K. Gaylord recalled in 1968, that his uncle Martin and his father also helped slaves escape through the underground railroad. "I learned from Uncle Martin that before and during the war Martin helped a number of slaves escape who traveled through the woods at night until they got into Kansas, and Uncle Martin helped them on to Nebraska and others helped them to make their way on to Canada. My father never mentioned it, but Uncle Martin told me of times when my father took some slaves, traveling at night, and hiding in the woods during the day, and getting them up to the other underground railroad in Nebraska," wrote E. K. Gaylord.

Soon after the Civil War began George Lewis Gaylord was commissioned as a Captain in the U.S. Volunteers (Union Army) and assigned to Fort Gibson, Cherokee Nation. His commission, dated February 9, 1863, is signed by Abraham Lincoln. He was then 37. Before the year ended, he was making trips to Fort Leavenworth, Kansas, to obtain wagon loads of supplies for Union troops in the Cherokee Nation. In a letter to his brother Martin at Atchison, Kansas, George Lewis Gaylord commented that there were four thousand Indian troops stationed at Fort Gibson, and he described the country around Fort Gibson as very good fruit country, better for fruit and orchards than eastern Kansas.

Gaylord's military records in the National Archives indicate that in 1864 he was named Chief of Commissary of Subsistence in the Field in the District of the Frontier and was stationed at Fort Gibson through 1864 serving under Colonel William A. Phillips, Third Indian Home Guard, Kansas Infantry. Before the Civil War, Phillips had been a reporter in Kansas Territory for Horace Greeley's *New York*

George Lewis Gaylord in the uniform of a Union Army officer at Leavenworth, Kansas, in 1863.

Tribune during the turbulent struggle to make Kansas a Free State. Phillips was also a friend of John Brown, who then lived in eastern Kansas Territory.

Early in 1864 Phillips made a surprise inspection at Fort Gibson and was appalled to find officers in the quartermaster's section "leading a life of idleness." Phillips wrote in a report that the officers "go to work with a very bad grace, and the worthless sorehead's caucus in McDonald's and McKee's store for my removal." Phillips said he had learned that many cattle obtained under a government contract were "contraband," and that "there has been a gigantic swindle by Coffin and McDonald in corn in the [Cherokee] nation." George L. Gaylord was not present when Phillips arrived on his inspection. Gaylord had gone to Fort Smith on business, but in his report, Phillips noted that when Gaylord returns, "I will have to place him in arrest."

When Gaylord returned to Fort Gibson later in January, Colonel Phillips had him arrested and relieved from duty. Gaylord joined other officers already under arrest, which apparently meant they were restricted to their quarters. Colonel Phillips, however, never filed formal charges against George L. Gaylord. He was found innocent of any wrongdoing and later, under Special Orders No. 428, issued August 9, 1865, Gaylord was "honorably mustered out" from military service. That was about four months after General Robert E. Lee surrendered his forces to General Ulysses S. Grant at Appomattox Court House on April 9, 1865.

Years later, E. K. Gaylord recalled, "My father never talked about his experiences in the war except to tell about chasing a contingent of rebel soldiers, as he called them, over into Arkansas and finding a field of ripe wheat which he had his men cut and thresh and added the wheat to his commissary."

After his honorable discharge, Captain Gaylord returned to Atchison, Kansas, and may have briefly joined a government party traveling into western Kansas. A "Captain Gaylord" is listed as a member of a party accompanying Thomas Murphy, superintendent of Indian Affairs for Kansas, and several commissioners of U.S. Indian Affairs from Washington D.C. The party was to negotiate with the Kiowa Indians and the confederate tribes (Comanche and Apache) to permit safe travel by whites over the Santa Fe Trail. The party traveled from Atchison to the mouth of the Little Arkansas River near what is now Wichita, Kansas, in September 1865, about a month after George L. Gaylord was mustered out of the army. The diary of Samuel A. Kingman, who worked for one of the commissioners, contains reference

to a "Captain Gaylord" but lists no first name or initials.

By late fall 1865, George Gaylord was back at Atchison in northeast Kansas. There, while visiting his older brother Martin and his wife Elizabeth, George Lewis Gaylord met Eunice Maria Edwards, the younger sister of Martin's wife. Eunice had come west on a visit. She was a graduate of an academy in Southhampton, Massachusetts, and had attended Mt. Holyoke College for one year. Her family, like that of the Gaylords, came from hardy puritan stock. Her ancestors arrived from Wales in 1640 and several fought in the American Revolution. Eunice Edwards came to Kansas to visit not only her sister but brother Charles L. Edwards. He came to Kansas in 1855 and settled in Lawrence, where he worked for S. C. Pomeroy in the Emigrant Aid Company's office and then taught school. He was elected the first superintendent of schools at Lawrence in 1859 and was one of the first trustees of what later became the University of Kansas, where he was principal of the academic department before the Civil War.

When George Lewis Gaylord met Eunice Edwards in Atchison, he was taken by her charm and beauty. Soon they were engaged, and on July 5, 1866, were married in the Edwards' home at Southhampton, Massachusetts. The newlyweds returned to Kansas where George Lewis Gaylord purchased 1200 acres of farm land about one mile southwest of Muscotah near Atchison. The name Muscotah, written in Indian style as musco-tah, signifies "Beautiful Prairie" or "Prairie on fire." The land had much potential, but to make ends meet George Lewis Gaylord also operated a small store in Muscotah. When the census was taken there on July 14, 1870, George L. Gaylord, reported his real estate was valued

Edwards King Gaylord at age six. This photo was made in North Hampton, Massachusetts, during a family visit.

at $300, and the value of his personal estate at $50. It was there that their first son Lewis Gaylord was born in 1872. A second son christened Edwards King Gaylord was born on March 5, 1873. His first name was his mother's maiden name. About a year after he came to Oklahoma City, in order to avoid questions of legality of his signatures, he had his first name legally changed to Edward.

When George Lewis Gaylord and his wife Eunice celebrated their tenth wedding anniversary in 1876, the Atchison, Kansas, *Champion* reported their "Tin Wedding," observing that friends and neighbors "made one of those social raids, so to speak, which of late have become so common in every village and neighborhood where good society predominates. The guests were cordially received by the happy couple, and most hospitably enter-

tained." The Gaylords went through another marriage ceremony and received many gifts. Everyone enjoyed refreshments.

Within three years, however, things were not going well for George Lewis Gaylord. While his wife and two sons were fine, two years of drought and a grasshopper plague caused George Lewis Gaylord to lose his farm. E. K. Gaylord recalled years later that his father "trusted everybody and while his customers probably were honest, the drought and grasshoppers prevented their paying his bills." While George Lewis Gaylord remained in Kansas to settle his affairs, he sent his family east to visit relatives. When his wife and children returned west, the family took the Kansas Pacific Railroad west to Denver to look for new opportunities. They arrived in Denver in early January 1880, and George bought and ran a small restaurant. But by spring the mining fever hit him.

After only four months in Denver, George Lewis Gaylord moved his family to Pitkin, Colorado's first mining camp west of the Continental Divide. E. K. Gaylord remembered that they took the railroad from Denver to Salida, Colorado, which was then the end of the line. From there they went to Pitkin in a stagecoach over very rough country. The town of Pitkin was less than a year old when George Lewis Gaylord moved his family there in the spring of 1880. Located 28 miles northeast of Gunnison, Colorado, at an elevation of 9,242 feet in an alpine meadow one mile long and one quarter mile wide, the little town was named for Colorado Governor Frederick W. Pitkin.

The year the Gaylord family arrived in Pitkin, the town had just constructed its first school building, and E. K. Gaylord, then seven, attended his first school at Pitkin. He later recalled that his family lived about a mile and a half up the mountain from the town. He and his older brother walked to school carrying their lunches in three pound lard pails. "We sat on split logs with no desks and each child brought his own books and no two kids had the same text books, so the teacher assigned lessons in whatever arithmetic and reader you carried. A lot of arithmetic was taught on the blackboard where we learned to add and subtract rapidly. We small children were on the second floor and there was an outside stairway. There was a well-known legend that the bigger boys used to jump out of the second story windows when there was four feet of snow on the ground. I saw snow there before we left, but never that deep."

For George Lewis Gaylord, the mining fever did not last. The Gaylords soon left Pitkin and moved south to Saguache (pronounced Sa-watch), a

First schoolhouse in Pitkin, Colorado, erected in 1879. This photo was made about 1880 when E. K. Gaylord and his brother Lewis attended the school. Both boys may be in the picture. E. K. Gaylord recalled that during the winter the older boys in the school supposedly jumped from the second story windows into snow banks below.

town of about 300 residents and the northern gateway to the San Luis Valley in South Central Colorado. It was farming and ranching country, and Saguache was the trading center. At an elevation of 7,800 feet, Saguache is surrounded by the Sangre de Cristo mountain range on the east and the San Juan range on the west. The town was founded in 1867 by Otto Mears, who established a mill and general mercantile store, built toll roads to and from the town, and created many opportunities for settlers. Edward Lewis Gaylord apparently was attracted by these opportunities and may have worked for Mears in his general store. What happened next is not clear, but by 1884 the Gaylord family again moved and settled just southeast of Grand Junction, Colorado, near the small community of Whitewater. There George Lewis Gaylord developed a fine fruit orchard. Today, running parallel to and just west of U.S. Highway 50, is Gaylord Street close to where the orchard stood.

E. K. Gaylord remembered: "My brother and I and my father built our second house of adobe. We made the adobe and much of our furniture. I've seen chairs made out of barrels; just cut out and a cushion put in for the seat." He and his older brother walked to school in Grand Junction. At the age of 11, he got a job picking strawberries. Years later, E. K. Gaylord recalled that when he turned in baskets of strawberries, he had them heaped full. The other pickers turned in baskets where the strawberries had been leveled. Gaylord recalled that the man he was picking strawberries for told him, "You are going to be a success in life because you always give full measure."

At 12 years old, Gaylord took a job in a second-hand store, and by the time he was 15, he had so impressed others with his business ability that a man offered to lend him the money to buy out his employer. E. K. declined, saying that he intended to get a college education, no matter whether it benefited him financially, or otherwise. For two or three years he worked on fruit farms, for a railroad company, and for a coal company, but at 18, after having been out of school for two years, he set off to get an education at Colorado College in Colorado Springs. The family pastor at Grand Junction loaned him money for the train trip to Colorado Springs believing he would be successful with an education. E. K. arrived with $17 in his pocket. To make ends meet, he worked for his room and board at Miss Prichard's boarding house. There he stoked the furnace, chopped wood, carried coal, waited on the long boarding house table, cleared, washed and dried the dishes, and swept and mopped floors.

At Colorado College, young Gaylord made time to join the Colorado Collegiate Oratorical Association, a debating club, and to serve as president of the YMCA. He also was business manager of the college paper and later served as both editor and business manager. E. K. Gaylord also excelled academically completing four years of Greek in two years and five years of Latin in three. Once E. K. Gaylord hiked to the top of Pikes Peak, leaving Colorado Springs well before dawn to see the sunrise over the plains of eastern Colorado. He never graduated from Colorado College, but in 1936 was given an honorary degree which pleased him immensely.

At about 11 P.M. on the evening of July 9, 1894, George Lewis Gaylord, age 67, died in the family's Grand Junction home. In reporting his death the *Grand Junction News,* July 14, 1894, described Gaylord as "a man of stern moral qualities and Christian integrity. Some thirty years ago he became a

Christian, but never united with any church till the Congregational church of this place was organized in the winter of 1890, when he united for the first time on confession of faith. For years he has been active in church work, especially in attention to financial matters, having held in different churches the positions of trustee, treasurer and building committee. When financially able he did a great deal both for churches and for the poor and destitute. He was always firm in his convictions and independent in doing what he conscientiously believed to be right. He was one of three officers in his brigade [during the Civil War] who never tasted a drop of intoxicating liquor while in the army, and in all his life he was a man of strictly temperate habits."

There is no question that George Lewis Gaylord passed traits of his character along to his sons Lewis and especially E. K., who returned to Colorado College the following fall, 1895, as a junior. His older brother Lewis, having graduated from the University of Colorado, suggested they buy controlling interest in the *Colorado Springs Telegraph* for $12,000. Between them they had $6,000, but they were able to borrow another $6,000 from a banker in Springfield, Missouri. Lewis Gaylord operated the paper while E. K. continued his schooling at night, studying law, and got a job as deputy clerk in the El Paso County district court at Colorado Springs, then part of the fourth judicial district covering El Paso County and Teller County. In the spring of 1900 a woman named Eva Stanton announced that she had been secretly married to Albert E. "Bert" Carlton, who had made millions in transportation and mining. Carlton filed for divorce and the suit was set for trial in June 1900 in Cripple

Creek. Two judges refused to hear the case and a judge from the seventh judicial district on the western slope of Colorado was brought in to preside. Because the Teller County court clerk, the brother of a county commissioner, had no experience in any court, E. K. Gaylord was made deputy clerk and sent to Cripple Creek.

When Carlton's attorney tried to get Gaylord to call certain persons as jurors for the trial, Gaylord refused. The jurors selected for the trial were then hounded by Carlton's attorney. Gaylord went to the judge and explained what had happened. The judge fined Carlton $1,000 and ordered a grand jury to look into Carlton's actions and those of his associates. Carlton then sought to remove the judge from the bench and to fire Gaylord, whose brother's newspaper in Colorado Springs was covering the whole affair. The judge who handled the case was defeated for reelection because of Carlton's efforts. Later, when a new judge was assigned to Carlton's case, his divorce was granted with no fanfare. Meantime, in December 1900, before the defeated judge's term ended, E. K. Gaylord resigned his position in Cripple Creek and joined his brother Lewis in operating the *Telegraph* in Colorado Springs.

E. K. Gaylord later wrote for the *Denver Post*: "Carlton was incensed at my brother for printing the sensational story in the *Telegraph*. By chance they met in the lobby of the Brown Palace Hotel in Denver. Carlton said, 'I haven't decided what to do with you, but I could have you killed.' My brother replied, 'You could hire somebody to jump out of a dark alley some night and shoot me, but he couldn't get to me if he came to my office. I have a revolver on my desk and the men in the office in front of me cut clippings from newspapers with a Bowie knife. Your assassin couldn't get past them.'"

Carlton apparently decided against physical violence and put up a considerable sum of money to start the *Evening Mail* in Colorado Springs to compete against the *Telegraph*. After a year both papers had lost considerable money. Carlton's people offered to buy the *Telegraph*. The Gaylord brothers decided not to continue the fight and sold their paper and left Colorado Springs.

Lewis Gaylord took a brief vacation in California and then using money from the sale of the paper purchased the *St. Joseph Dispatch* in northwest Missouri. He convinced E. K. to work for him as business manager. But E. K. was now determined to own his own newspaper. Less than a year later Edward headed south to Oklahoma City where Roy E. Stafford agreed to sell him an interest in *The Oklahoman*. Whether young Gaylord realized it or not, he was about to plant his roots deep in Oklahoma.

BUILDING
THE OKLAHOMAN

On January 27, 1903, 29-year-old E. K. Gaylord took charge as business manager of *The Oklahoman*. He set about to build the best newspaper he could, although he had misgivings about the venture. He later recalled: "In 1903, it looked like a forlorn investment, but there was a spirit of hope and ambition in the air. The population was young people, almost without exception. All were earnest, hard working, eager to begin a new life and develop a new city and a new state. An abundance of churches and schools indicated that people were laying the right foundation for a city of honest, hardworking, God-fearing citizens."

The Oklahoman office was located on the first floor of a small building at 18 South Broadway. The office was only 22 feet wide and 65 feet long. The first 16 feet of the building had desk space for Stafford, a circulation manager and one reporter who also served as the telegraph editor. Behind a partition was a job printing shop and the newspaper plant. When Gaylord found there was no space for him, he rented another room in the building for an office. Just outside the front door of the newspaper office was one large roll of paper on the sidewalk. As Gaylord later recalled, "That was a two-day supply for *The Oklahoman*'s entire circulation." He also remembered the mechanical plant was "the dirtiest I ever saw. Paper trimmings and dirt littered the floor and two-foot cobwebs festooned every corner of the room. It consisted chiefly of about a wheel barrow load of type, a couple of Linotypes, a flatbed press and a stove. It was the most magnificent opportunity I had ever seen because there was so much room for improvement," remembered Gaylord, who, being single, got room and board in a house at Third and Broadway. He paid $4 a week— 15 cents a meal, and 85 cents a week for the room.

One of Gaylord's first business decisions was to sell the paper's job printing business so that full attention could be given to publishing the newspaper. While the paper had a flat-bed press capable of printing 3,000 papers an hour, plus two Linotypes, it was "terribly inadequate for a newspaper, and I was ambitious to make it the biggest and best newspaper in the territory," recalled Gaylord.

Two days after Gaylord became the paper's business manager, he and Stafford formalized their agreement with help from attorneys and formed The Oklahoma Publishing Co. Stafford was paid $15,000 for 45 percent of the stock by Gaylord, Ray M. Dickinson, and Roy M. McClintock. Each invested $5,000. Gaylord, Dickinson, and McClintock wanted the controlling interest, but Stafford would not sell it, but Gaylord did get an option to buy more stock. Dickinson and McClintock had been associated with the Gaylord brothers in Colorado Springs, and both had gone to St. Joseph, Missouri, to work on the paper Lewis Gaylord had purchased. Now they had followed E. K. Gaylord to Oklahoma City. Dickinson joined *The Oklahoman* as an advertising man, and McClintock, came as a telegraph editor, reporter and proofreader. Under the new agreement, Stafford retained full control of all editorial policies while Gaylord was to have complete authority in business, advertising and circulation.

The incorporating papers were sent to Guthrie, the territorial capital. On February 6 the secretary of the territory signed the charter which listed Gaylord, Stafford, Roy M. McClintock, C. C. Hudson and C. B. Ames, a lawyer, as the incorporators. Ames and Hudson were both residents of Oklahoma City. The masthead of *The Oklahoman* for February 7 listed E. K. Gaylord as secretary-treasurer and Roy E. Stafford as president. There is no other mention in that issue of the creation of The Oklahoma Publishing Co.

This certificate of incorporation established The Oklahoma Publishing Co. on February 6, 1903.

In 1903 The Oklahoman was in this location at 18 Broadway when E. K. Gaylord entered the business.

Soon after the Company was formed, E. K. Gaylord obtained the services of the Katz Advertising Agency in New York City as the paper's national advertising representative. Gaylord and G. R. Katz became such good friends that Katz became a stockholder in The Oklahoma Publishing Co. in 1912. Later he became a member of the board of directors.

✳

In 1903, Oklahoma City was still something of a frontier town with men outnumbering women, and it bragged it was the best convention town in Oklahoma Territory. E. K. Gaylord recalled: "A few days after I arrived, Oklahoma City hosted a cattlemen's convention and it was a wow! I remember that

Lucille Mulhall rode her horse over a high curb into the Two Jacks saloon in Battle Row and ordered a whisky straight without getting out of the saddle. The bartender and several customers were quite agitated, but the horse and Lucille were unconcerned and turned around and went out as if it was a daily occurrence." To help make the convention a gala celebration, townspeople got a troop of cavalry to come from Fort Sill for a big parade, and dancing girls were brought in from Chicago to help entertain the cattlemen.

The first night of the convention some of the cattlemen got a little free with their six-shooters and a cavalryman was shot. Gaylord was nearby. After getting the facts, he rushed to

The Oklahoman office and gave the story to the city editor telling him to place it on the front page of the next day's paper. He then went home.

When Gaylord picked up a copy of *The Oklahoman* the following morning and did not find the story on the front page or anywhere in the paper, he went to the newspaper office in a furious mood. There he learned that Stafford had suppressed the story because the president of the Chamber of Commerce had told him it would hurt Oklahoma City's reputation if it were known that an army man had been shot while in town entertaining cattlemen. Gaylord then told Stafford that newspapers received by train from Guthrie and even Kansas City, Missouri, had reported the story with large headlines. *The Oklahoman,* he said, should have printed the story.

About two hours later, there was another shooting in an alley behind the newspaper office. "A gambler had his feelings hurt by a man who stepped on his toes in a crowded saloon, and he chased the man out on a sidewalk, knocked him down and shot him as he lay on the sidewalk," recalled Gaylord, who insisted on getting out an Extra, a special edition of the paper. At first the printers objected to being pulled off other jobs to put out the Extra, but they did and it was on the streets by noon. It not only included news of the latest shooting but the earlier story that had been suppressed about the cavalryman who had been shot. It was the first of many Extras to be published by *The Oklahoman.*

Oklahoma Territory in 1903 was still wild and woolly. Disputes were commonplace, and residents took their politics and newspapers very seriously. Many disputes turned violent because weapons were plentiful. Threats of violence against editors were commonplace. E. K Gaylord's slight stature may have given a false impression that as a newspaperman he might bow to threats, but stories of how he refused to be intimidated are legion. The first incident of that kind occurred during his first weeks in Oklahoma City. A prominent young woman from Oklahoma City had been married for a short time to a young man from the Rocky Mountain region when she brought suit to divorce her new husband. The complaint filed at the court house in Oklahoma City read like a dime novel.

As Gaylord recalled: "I wasn't supposed to be an editorial man, but that night with two others I copied a large portion of the divorce complaint and we had a full page story ready for the morning paper." When Gaylord reached his home about 11 P.M., he found anxious friends waiting for him. They said the woman who filed the divorce action had threatened to have her "cowboy brothers" shoot up *The Oklahoman*'s office if the paper published a word about the divorce. Gaylord's friends begged him to suppress the story. He refused to do so because of a threat.

What happened next is told in E. K. Gaylord's own words:

> *Next morning there was a rather tense feeling around the office until about 9 A.M. when a feminine voice on the telephone asked that we please send out 20 extra copies of the paper to her home. We did so with a bill for $1 at 5 cents a copy and she paid it. The cowboy brothers did not show up.*

In another incident some years later, *The Oklahoman* printed a story about a city policeman who had been taking bribes from vice interests in the city and the story carried the policeman's name. About 5 A.M. the day the story appeared, the officer

E. K. Gaylord as he appeared in 1904 less than one year after arriving in Oklahoma City.

came roaring into the newspaper office with blood in his eye. He was told the editor would be there about 8 A.M., so he left. At 8 A.M., the 6-foot-3-inch, 200-pound policeman stormed into the office waving his pistol in the face of the first reporter he found. When Gaylord arrived a few minutes later, he was met by an agitated society reporter who warned him to leave the office at once. Instead he walked into the newsroom and confronted the big, angry policeman.

In a short, scathing conversation, Gaylord informed the disgruntled policeman that the reporter only worked for him and that he, Gaylord, was responsible for the unwelcome and revealing publicity. Gaylord then proceeded to recite the letter of the law to the policeman for brandishing a pistol and threatening people it was his sworn duty to protect. After a few minutes of this, the policeman holstered his pistol and slunk out of the office. He did not return.

Although on the surface Oklahoma City appeared to visitors as just another raw frontier town, it was pretty cultured. The opera house and theaters brought fine dramatic and musical programs to town, and social gatherings were quite genteel. When Sarah Bernhardt accepted an appearance at the Overholser Opera House in 1906, she related in an eastern newspaper interview that she had accepted the booking because she wanted to see "how the raw, crude frontier people lived."

When word of her comment spread through Oklahoma City, Gaylord urged the city's society leaders to appear in formal gowns and their escorts in white ties and tails the night of the concert. They did. "Every seat in the opera house was occupied and the whole play was in French, but everybody was thrilled by Bernhardt's magnificent voice and acting," recalled Gaylord. To the surprise of everyone, Miss Bernhardt accepted an invitation for her and her company to attend a dinner after the show. "The only place to hold it was in the Marquette Club on the top floor of the Empire building, a five story building. . . . Meals at the Marquette Club were normally 35 cents, but the cost of this dinner was boosted to the unheard-of price of $1.50. The cuisine at the party was equal to anything offered in New York City or elsewhere," Gaylord later recalled. All of the elite of Oklahoma City attended, but Gaylord later added, "I imagine Sarah Bernhardt was disappointed that the guests were not in cowboy costume." Gaylord and others never told Miss Bernhardt they were on their best behavior to show her how inappropriate her remarks had been.

E. K. Gaylord recalled another story relating to another Oklahoma Cattlemen's convention about 1905 or '06. Oklahoma cattlemen "invited Texas cattlemen to meet in a joint meeting in Oklahoma City. A man named King was appointed a committee of one to prepare the entertainment. There were more than 1,000 cattlemen from Texas and Oklahoma and a dancer from Chicago was introduced as 'Queenie.' There probably were 50 or more prom-

inent Oklahoma City business men in attendance. Queenie began dancing and presently threw off a cape she was wearing. A little later, shed another garment and the audience sensing what was coming, yelled, 'Take 'em off, take 'em off.' She dropped a skirt—in those days they wore underskirts, took off her waist and finally, one by one, all her garments but the last, and they had to do a lot of yelling before she appeared absolutely nude," recalled E. K. Gaylord.

"The news of Queenie's disgraceful disclosure spread like wild-fire over the entire city. Women whose husbands were not home that night were demanding 'Were you there?' Some of the men, thinking discretion was the better part of valor, claimed they were playing poker with Bill Pettee. Bill had calls from a lot of housewives, asking if their husbands had been playing cards with him last night. Bill was equal to the occasion. 'Why yes, George was here' and another one would call— 'Yes, Roy was here playing with us.' I think Bill alibied for at least 20 or 25 husbands who had gone to the entertainment without any knowledge of the Queenie act."

E. K. Gaylord added, "One man who lived on East 10th street was more candid than cautious. He went home and his wife was asleep so he did not disturb her. When he awoke in the morning, he heard his wife in the kitchen and went out there and found her breaking some eggs to fry in the frying pan. He said, 'Honey, last night I saw a woman take off her clothes one garment at a time—her waist and her skirt and her corset and everything until she dropped her drawers and there she was naked as—' He never finished the sentence. His wife grabbed the frying pan and, wham, those fried eggs went right in his face. It seems that the wives of the Texas cattlemen were the most incensed—they laid the law down to their husbands that never again will you go to Oklahoma City to a cattlemen's convention. In Oklahoma City, Queenie was a fighting word among housewives for many years."

*

The Oklahoman's circulation had reached only 2,500 late in 1903 while the Guthrie *Capital* claimed 20,000. Most towns in Oklahoma Territory were attempting to attract new residents. Years later, E. K. Gaylord recalled: "All the railroads were running monthly excursions, called 'home-seekers excursions' into Oklahoma and most of them to Oklahoma City. There was great optimism on the part of all citizens and nearly everyone claimed to be a 'booster.' If you were not a booster, you were a 'knocker' and would be ostracized. Some enthusiasts claimed that Oklahoma City, in a few years, would have a 25,000 population. Conservatives discounted this but a few more enthusiastic boosters even predicted it would have a population of 50,000."

Early in 1903, E. K. Gaylord knew that if *The Oklahoman* was to be successful, it needed a larger building and new mechanical equipment and other changes. By March 1903, *The Oklahoman* had discarded its Associated Press "pony" service whereby news stories received by Western Union telegrams, one at a time, were hand delivered to the paper from the telegraph office. *The Oklahoman* got its own leased AP wire and was directly receiving national and international news in its newsroom. Gaylord next drew up plans for a new building and contracted to have a two-story building constructed at the northeast corner of California and Robinson. *The Oklahoman* moved into its new and much larger quarters in October 1903, about

10 months after Gaylord took over as business manager.

Gaylord made the paper's mechanical plant the best between Kansas City and Dallas after he purchased new stereotyping machinery, three more Mergenthaler Linotype machines, and a 16-page, two-deck, two-color Goss Perfecting Press costing $15,000. The new press gave *The Oklahoman* the nickname "Red-headed Daily" because headlines could be printed in red ink. Gaylord began printing some headlines in red ink in 1908 after seeing the *Denver Post* using them effectively to attract the attention of readers. Printing front page headlines in red ink, however, was dropped by *The Oklahoman* in 1918.

While Oklahoma City was holding its own with other towns in Oklahoma Territory, Gaylord was determined to make Oklahoma City more attractive for new businesses and as a place where people would want to raise their children. He began a crusade against the city's gambling dives. Initially, the crusade was not popular among gamblers and saloon men and many of the city's businessmen who believed such vice was necessary if Oklahoma City was to retain its reputation as a wide awake town. The competing *Times-Journal,* on the other hand, made fun of *The Oklahoman* for all the fuss and bother it was making. Editorials in the *Times-Journal* pointed out that gambling dens and prostitution had existed in Oklahoma City for 14 years and predicted they would probably remain. The *Times-Journal* was wrong.

Gaylord sought to improve the local news coverage while at the same time making good use of the Associated Press leased wire for national and international news. At the time, one international story concerned relations between Japan and Russia. With the passing of each day the situation became tenser with some observers predicting war between the two countries. During the first week of February 1904, Gaylord had a newsman's "hunch" that war might break out in the Far East. He did not want The Oklahoman to be caught napping, but as the weekend approached, he realized the paper did not publish a Monday edition and would not be receiving AP news service on Sunday. Gaylord contacted the Associated Press and made arrangements to have an AP operator on duty at The Oklahoman on Sunday, February 8, to sit near the telegraphic sounder in the newsroom. When it clattered its code, the AP operator would transcribe the news on a typewriter and then give the typed pages to the telegraph editor.

Gaylord also made arrangements to have a couple of printers and a pressman available should the expected news be received. With Clark Hudson, The Oklahoman's telegraph editor, Gaylord waited. It was late in the afternoon when the news came. The Japanese, not the Russians as expected, made the first overt move by recalling their ambassador to Russia and preparing to attack the Russian fleet at Port Arthur. As the news was received, Hudson wrote a seven-column banner headline and sent it to the composing room with the AP copy. A few minutes later the AP carried another and even more electrifying story from Baltimore. A huge fire was destroying most of the business section of Maryland's major city.

The Oklahoman printed an Extra that Sunday evening with headlines screaming both stories in red ink. Then, capitalizing on his hunch, Gaylord telephoned the Guthrie State Capital and learned it was closed. He then telephoned the Wichita Eagle in Kansas. It was also closed. Neither paper published on Monday so their newsrooms were empty. At 4 A.M. that Monday,

crews from The Oklahoman armed with 2,500 copies of the Extra were on the train heading north for Wichita. Another crew with 1,500 copies was headed for Guthrie. "We doubled or trebled the copy quota for every news dealer in Oklahoma that night. If a dealer handling The Oklahoman ordinarily took 20 papers, we sent him 40 to 60 of the Extra," recalled Gaylord. The news beat put The Oklahoman head and shoulders above every paper in Oklahoma Territory and gave it the reputation of being more enterprising than the others. Sending the Extras into Guthrie was also the first round of a fight for supremacy between The Oklahoman and Guthrie State Capital.

Late in 1904, Roy McClintock, who had come to Oklahoma City with Gaylord and Dickinson, decided to strike out on his own. McClintock sold his stock in The Oklahoma Publishing Co. at a "respectable profit" and purchased a newspaper at Vinita in what is now northeast Oklahoma. Later, after his venture failed, he returned to The Oklahoman as a political writer.

The rivalry between Oklahoma City and the territorial capital of Guthrie continued to build through 1905. In 1906, it came to a head when E. K. Gaylord decided to investigate the claim by Guthrie's newspaper, the State Capital, that it had a circulation of 20,000, far more than The Oklahoman. At the time, both towns claimed 10,000 in population, but in truth neither Guthrie nor Oklahoma City had more than 7,000 residents. Since federal law required a population of at least 10,000 before bonds could be voted for municipal improvements, people in both towns had turned to hotel registers and tombstones to add additional names to the 1900 census. Gaylord later recalled that Oklahoma City apparently had a more diligent crew of tombstone counters because its reported population was 10,037 compared to Guthrie's 10,003.

To try to learn the actual circulation of the Guthrie *State Capital,* Gaylord sent men to Guthrie. "They watched the press run from across the street. Since we knew the speed of the press and the number of papers it could print in a given time, we could arrive at a fairly accurate figure on the number of papers printed," Gaylord remembered. He then contacted a friend in Washington who secured the post office department's figures on second class mail receipts at Guthrie to compare with *The Oklahoman's* guesses on the *State Capital's* circulation.

The evidence suggested the *State Capital's* circulation was not more than 7,000 a day, about the same as *The Oklahoman.* Gaylord then wrote a letter to *Printer's Ink,* a national trade magazine, providing the information. His letter was printed in full. "Of course it raised a stink, but we felt we could prove our figures," Gaylord recalled. When people in Guthrie learned their paper's circulation figures had been falsified, many who had advertised in the *State Capital* descended on its office and demanded refunds. Publicizing the results of Gaylord's investigation caused something of a sensation in advertising circles and laid the foundation for what eventually became The Audit Bureau of Circulation, a national organization which certifies accurate circulation figures for newspapers. Gaylord was one of four newspapermen from across the nation who was asked to serve on its first board of directors. Thus, after a few months in Oklahoma, he had gained national attention and respect in the newspaper industry, and *The Oklahoman* was becoming a business success.

Chapter Four

STATEHOOD AND COMPETITION

By the spring of 1906, *The Oklahoman*'s two-deck Goss Perfecting Press was fast becoming obsolete. Gaylord ordered a new four-deck Goss press, costing $25,000, to double the capacity of the old press. The new press arrived in Oklahoma City on two railroad cars in September 1906. While it was being installed, *The Oklahoman* was printed on the *Times-Journal* press. *The Oklahoman*'s new press was installed about three months after Congress had passed the Oklahoma Enabling Act in June 1906, authorizing a convention to meet at Guthrie to write a state constitution. Although some people had advocated that Oklahoma and Indian territories each become separate states, *The Oklahoman* supported the creation of one state that included both territories.

An election was set to select delegates to a constitutional convention at Guthrie. There the Democrats, who supported one state, won with 98 delegates, while Republicans, who supported two states, saw only 13 delegates elected. One delegate was independent. Charles N. Haskell, a railroad promoter from Muskogee, won the primary as the Democratic nominee for governor by 8,000 votes over Lee Cruce, a Kentuckian and lawyer from Ardmore, and Thomas Doyle. Republicans nominated Frank Frantz for governor of Oklahoma Territory.

The delegates convened on November 20, 1906, and elected William H. "Alfalfa Bill" Murray of Tishomingo in the old Chickasaw Nation as president of the convention. It took the delegates 97 legislative days to draw up a constitution for Oklahoma. The Oklahoma Enabling Act had required that alcohol be prohibited in Indian Territory for a period of 21 years. Since prohibition was a popular social reform at the time, the constitution extended prohibition to the entire state. Voters in Oklahoma and Indian territories approved the constitution by a vote of 180,333 to 73,059 on September 17, 1907. In the same election, Haskell won the governor's race with more than 27,000 votes over Frantz.

When President Theodore Roosevelt approved the constitution and announced he would issue his statehood proclamation on November 16, 1907, *The Oklahoman* published an Extra. In letters six inches tall and in red ink, the headline read: "Proclaims Statehood." The headline covered much of page one. The lead story reported how the proclamation admitting the new state of Oklahoma was signed at 9 A.M. central time that Saturday morning. It added:

> *The president used in affixing his signature to the document a pen made from the quill of an American eagle, which now is alive, in captivity at Woodward, Okla. A quill from the wing of this same eagle was used when the president signed the statehood act. This pen will go to the Oklahoma historical society.*

Since approval of the constitution meant prohibition, at 11:50 P.M. on the night of November 16, 1907, saloons in Oklahoma City and across the new state closed their doors. That day *The Oklahoman* announced it was discontinuing liquor advertisements.

Oklahoma prospered until late in 1907 when a Wall Street panic occurred. Banks folded all across the nation, and the governor closed Oklahoma's banks for one week even though they were in good shape. *The Oklahoman* reassured depositors that Oklahoma banks were sound, and E. K. Gaylord participated in a meeting with city bankers who agreed to issue scrip certificates as money until the crisis subsided. Gaylord then went the extra mile by offering to accept checks in payment for a year's subscription to *The Oklahoman* for $2.95. He later recalled that checks

This is the municipal building at Guthrie, Oklahoma Territory, where the Oklahoma State Constitutional Convention was held in 1906. (Courtesy Western History Collections, University of Oklahoma Libraries)

E. K. Gaylord at his office desk in 1906 about three years after he purchased an interest in *The Oklahoman*.

In 1906 downtown Oklahoma City was already a thriving city, as seen from the sixth floor of the brewery in Bricktown.

The front page of the November 17, 1907, issue of *The Daily Oklahoman*.

THE DAILY OKLAHOMAN

21,040
DAILY AVERAGE FOR OCT.

LARGEST DAILY NEWSPAPER
IN GREATER OKLAHOMA

VOL. 19. NO. 188.

OKLAHOMA CITY, OKLAHOMA, SUNDAY, NOVEMBER 17, 1907--THIRTY TWO PAGES

PRICE 5 CENTS.

OKLAHOMA BECOMES STATE

SALOON DUEL TO CAUSE DEATH

Theft of a Bottle of Whiskey Responsible for Fight

ROBT. JOHNSON DYING

His Assailant, Fred Morris, Surrenders to Under Sheriff Garrison

In a pistol duel in Ed Conleys saloon, 116 West First street, at 8:15 o'clock last night—a little more than three hours before the prohibition law was applied by Sheriff Garrison and the police department—Robert Johnson, bartender, was shot three times and is now believed to be in a dying condition at St. Anthony's hospital.

His assailant, Fred Norris, who formerly owned the saloon in which the shooting took place, is locked in the county jail. He surrendered to Under-sheriff Harvey Garrison 30 minutes after the affray.

Eleven shots were exchanged. A quarrel over the alleged theft of a quart bottle of whisky by Norris is the cause of the shooting.

Norris was not hurt.

The wound that it is expected will cause the death of Johnson extends through the body. It entered the right side and came out at the back. Johnson received two other wounds, one in the right arm, just below the elbow, and one below the left hip.

The only eyewitnesses aside from the principals, so far as known, were E. L. Jones a negro porter employed in the saloon, and John Coleman, another negro.

"It all started over an argument about a quart of whisky," says Jones. "Mr. Norris came in a few minutes before the trouble started. He took a quart bottle of whisky from behind the bar and started toward the rear door with it. Johnson overtook him and took the bottle away from him, put it in his place and sat down. Norris was angry and left the saloon. He returned in a few minutes and Johnson accuses Norris of attempting to steal the booze.

(CONTINUED ON PAGE NINE.)

ROOSEVELT WILL RACE

Afrer a Visit to the President, Boom Is Launched

(By Willis J. Abbot.)

Washington, Nov. 16.—Out of the white house yesterday proceeded three eminent statesmen. They came from Oregon, from Kentucky and from Connecticut. Today two other distinguished senators came out who represented West Virginia and Kentucky. With one accord they declared themselves strongly in favor of the nomination of Mr. Roosevelt for a third term. With equal approval all agreed that he had said no word to justify such a campaign, yet each told the reporters waiting at the gate that his own state would force a re-nomination upon the present. There is a certain significance in this. The silence of the presidence must be qualified by the loquacity of his friends. When a distinguished senator from Massachusetts comes out of the executive offices and tells the reporters that he is convinced that the president should be a candidate for a third term, the cynical correspondent thinks that the senator was looking out for his own future. But when the senator is asked what the president said and says in return that he cannot quote the president's response, the suspicion is aroused and passes very fast that our Caesar does not intend to put aside the kingly crown.

The only active political workers in Washington today are the Roosevelt boomers. Geographically they extend from Portland, Oregon, where Senator Bourne has his habitat, to Wilmington, Delaware, the home of Senator Allee.

CROOKEDNESS IN BROOKLYN BANKS

ATTORNEY GENERAL DECLARES FORGERY AND CRIMINAL TRANSACTIONS PRACTICED.

New York, Nov. 16.—Attorney General Jackson stated this afternoon that, in his opinion, evidence of both criminal and civil liability has been unearthed in the investigation of the Borough bank of Brooklyn and the Jenkins Trust company of Brooklyn and that in the Borough bank of Brooklyn there has been found evidence of illegal over-loans, over-drafts, forged paper and other criminal transactions, all of which will be presented to the grand jury.

In the Jenkins Trust company, the attorney general says there has been found evidence of illegal over-loans. It is claimed by the trustees, the attorney general says, that they knew nothing about these loans made to the president of the company.

The attorney general's announcement contains the statement that the investigation thus far has been confined to the Borough bank of Brooklyn and the Jenkins Trust company.

NEW YORK PATTERNS AFTER GEARY, OKLA.

Geary, Okla., Nov. 16.—The distinction of having the first opera house employing women ushers does not belong to New York city, N. Y., as the Geary opera house has employed women for ushers for the last three seasons, beginning with 1904.

New York City announced to the world the fact that it had the first opera house employing women at play work at the opening of this season, but instead, the distinction belongs to the new state of Oklahoma.

The venture of the Geary opera house has proven highly successful and the patrons are well pleased with the accommodation and attentiveness of the new ushers.

RECEIVERS NAMED FOR SIX BANKS

INSTITUTIONS CRUSHED BY FLURRY NOW IN HANDS OF THE COURT.

Kingston, N. Y., Nov. 16.—Temporary receivers were appointed today for six New York city banks and trust companies which recently suspended payment. The banks are the Hamilton of 125th street, New York; the Brooklyn bank and the Borough bank of Brooklyn, and the trust companies, the Williamsburg and Jenkins of Brooklyn, and International of New York.

Application for receivers was made by William F. Mackey for Attorney General Jackson. Orders to show cause why permanent receivers should not be appointed were granted and were made returnable at Albany, November 20.

WILLIAM CROSS TAKES HIS OATH

BELIEVED THAT NEW SECRETARY OF STATE WILL RECOVER FROM ILLNESS.

William M. Cross qualified for the office of secretary of state in his room at the Saratoga hotel, where he is confined by serious sickness, yesterday afternoon at 10 o'clock. Notary W. A. Smith administered the oath, and the execution of the certificate was witnessed by Attorney E. J. Giddings.

The condition of Mr. Cross was much improved last night, and it is expected that he will soon recover. No visitors are allowed in the room.

COAL MINERS STRIKE IN NEW SOUTH WALES

San Francisco, Nov. 16.—Announcement of a general strike of coal miners at New Castle, New South Wales, said to have resulted in a great industrial American and British Columbia sources of supply. Importers and dealers are looking to the collieries on the coast to increase their output sufficiently to offset the shortage due to the strike.

FIREBUGS STILL TERRORIZE ENID

OIL SOAKED SACKS USED TO FIRE LUMBER YARD—PEOPLE PANICKY.

Special to the Oklahoman.

Enid, Okla., Nov. 16.—A second attempt to cause a disastrous conflagration was made at 3 a. m. today when oil-soaked pieces of gunny sacks were placed in boards in the yards of the Antrim-Todd Lumber Company's yards and ignited. The blaze was discovered and put out before much damage was done.

The lumber yard is in the same block where two of the heavy fires of the previous night occurred.

No clue has yet been found to the fire fiends.

With the coming of darkness there is serious apprehension which may be converted into a public panic if another blaze is started.

FAMOUS CONVENT IS DESTROYED BY FIRE

CATHOLIC INSTITUTION BURNED WITH LOSS OF MORE THAN $200,000.

Bay St. Louis, Miss., Nov. 16.—Fire which started early this morning was swept by a high gail wind through the town, destroying everything in its path and causing damage of about $200,000.

St. Joseph's convent, one of the most famous institutions of its kind in this section of the south, was totally destroyed, also the Catholic church and parsonage.

Other buildings destroyed were the Olsane theater, Hotel Clifton, Cumberland telephone building and the Butler building.

You are overlooking your opportunities if you don't look over the Oklahoman wants.

HOUSE ROBBED IN BROAD DAYLIGHT

WIFE AT CLUB MEETING, HUSBAND AT OFFICE—LOSS IS ABOUT $250.

A daring daylight robbery took place at the residence of F. L. Mulkey, 26 Broadway Circle Friday afternoon while all members of the family were absent, and wearing apparel consisting of skirts, silk waists, cloaks, trousers, and an overcoat, valued at $250 was carried away in a laundry bag. The case was reported to the police last night.

The thief effected an entrance had only to turn the key of the front door which had been left in the lock by Mrs. Mulkey as she left at 3 o'clock to attend a patron's meeting at the McKinley school building. Mr. Mulkey, who is a member of the Hail-Mulkey Investment company, was at his office at the time.

On returning home from the meeting at 5 o'clock and going to her room, Mrs. Mulkey found everything in confusion. Trunks had been opened and their contents scattered on the floor, bureau drawers were lying about on the floor. No person was seen entering or leaving the house during the absence of Mrs. Mulkey.

Eight skirts, six silk waists, two full suits and other women's apparel belonging to Mrs. Mulkey and Miss McDonald, a visitor from Benton Harbor, Mich., and two suits and an overcoat belonging to Mr. Mulkey are missing.

BAVARIAN PRINCE IS DEAD OF DUEL WOUND

Vienna, Nov. 16.—The Neus Weiner Journal asserts that Prince Arnulf of Bavaria, whose death three days ago was officially stated to have resulted from pneumonia, died from a sword wound received in a duel with the Duke of Genoa, brother of ex-Queen Margarita of Italy.

The duel it is declared, was fought at Murano, near Venice.

SCRATCH OF QUILL PEN LETS THE NEW STATE INTO UNION

"That Makes Oklahoma a State," Says Roosevelt, When He Affixes Signature

Special to The Oklahoman.

Washington, Nov. 16.—"There, that makes Oklahoma a state," declared President Roosevelt this morning as he smiled at the spectators in the cabinet room after he had appended his signature to the document admitting Oklahoma and Indian Territory as the forty-sixth state.

The actual signing of the document took place in the cabinet room at 10:16 o'clock in the presence of a number of residents of the new state who are employed in the government service at the national capital, Senator Warner, of Missouri, and Senators Carter and Dixon, of Montana. Secretary Loeb conducted the president to the head of the cabinet table, where the proclamation lay on a large blotter, ready to receive his signature.

As Roosevelt approached the chair where he sat while writing his name Loeb handed him the quill plucked from the wing of an American eagle.

"I've had more requests to use different pens in signing this time than there are letters in my name," declared the president as he wrote his name in large letters, discernable across the room.

As he rose and started to leave the room Albert Hammer, of Enid, Okla., who is a clerk in the government land office, stepped forward and asked the president for a small blotter which had been used in blotting his name. The president handed the blotter to Hammer and withdrew without further comment. He returned to his private office.

CONTINUED ON PAGE FIVE.

GREAT CROWD GOES TO THE INAUGURATION

OKLAHOMA CITY SENDS A BIG DELEGATION TO THE STATE CAPITAL.

Oklahoma City spent inaugural day in Guthrie.

Doctors, merchants, lawyers, laborers—men representing every walk of life—crowded every train bound for the state capital.

Newly elected county officers took their oaths again in order that they might be present at the ceremony which bring to an end Oklahoma and Indian Territory's long struggle against federal domination.

More than 1,000 persons were passengers on the Santa Fe special train engaged by the Chamber of Commerce, which left Oklahoma City at 9 o'clock. The cars were gaily decorated with banners and flags and souvenir badges were worn by members of the delegation. Peterson's State Band accompanied the delegation.

Hundreds of persons from the rural districts came to Oklahoma City to hear the news.

COOVENTION IS NOW DISSOLVED

Special to The Oklahoman.

Guthrie, Okla., Nov. 16.—Declaring that he had never dissolved the constitutional convention, although the impression had prevailed generally that he had so done, William H. Murray today issued a proclamation finally dissolving that body.

"I did not finally adjourn the convention, for I was afraid we might not get statehood," said Mr. Murray. "Now that the president has issued his proclamation, there exists no further reason for holding the convention in existence."

INDIAN TERRITORY AND OKLAHOMA ARE SYMBOLICALLY WED

Thirty Thousand People Attend the Inauwvral Ceremonies at State Capitol

Special to The Oklahoman.

Guthrie, Okla., Nov. 16.—At 9:20 o'clock this morning Governor Haskell received a telegram stating that the statehood proclamation had been signed by the president; at 9:30 o'clock, in his room at the Royal Hotel, with only the members of his family, Senator Robert L. Owen of Muskogee, Thomas H. Owen of Muskogee, Frank M. Canton of Osage, Dr. J. W. Duke of Guthrie, Mark A. Goodwin of Guthrie, A. D. Humbarger of Oklahoma City and J. M. Sandlin, his private secretary, present, he privately subscribed to the oath of office, administered by Leslie Gordon Niblack of Guthrie.

His first official act was to announce the appointment of Frank M. Canton as adjutant general of the state of Oklahoma. His second act was to wire to the sheriff and county attorney of Washington county, orders to prevent, in the name of the state, the construction by the Standard Oil company of a pipe line across the state line.

The union of Oklahoma and Indian Territory in statehood was consummated today in the formal inauguration of the new state's first officials. The weather was warm, the sun shining, and the big crowd that attended, fully 30,000 people, was good-natured and happy. Nothing whatever happened to mar the event and nothing was lacking except the retiring governor of the territory, Frank Frantz, who absolutely refused to participate in the ceremonies. This action by Governor Frantz caused much embarrassment in the final arrangements.

CONTINUED ON PAGE FIVE.

BLOCKS RUSE OF BIG OIL COMPANY

Special to The Oklahoman.

Guthrie, Okla., Nov. 16.—Learning that the Standard Oil company had all preparations made to construct a gas pipe line across the state line in Washington county in the interregnum occurring between the signing of the proclamation and the inauguration of state government, Governor Haskell privately qualified two hours before the public ceremony in order that his first official act might be to direct the county officials of Washington county to prevent the violation of the constitution if it were necessary to put every Standard Oil officer in the county jail. Late last night Governor Haskell had advised that the oil company had the material on the ground and a large party of workmen camped near the state line north of Bartlesville, and that

CONTINUED ON PAGE THREE.

HUNDREDS DANCE MID BRIGHTLY LIGHTED BOWER OF FLOWERS

FIRST INRUGURAL BALL PRESENTS SCENE DAZZLING IN ITS SPLENDOR

Handsome Women, Beautifully Gowned and Chivalrous Oklahomans Enjoy Auspicious Event

Special to the Oklahoman.

Guthrie, Okla., Nov. 16.—The city hall at Guthrie was the scene this evening of a brilliant and auspicious event, the first inaugural ball of the State of Oklahoma.

The perfumed air was raliant with happiness. Every face was expressive of joy, and softened laughter filled the big ball room. Brilliantly lighted by myriads of electric globes half hidden in encircling vines, and filled with gaily gowned women and conventionally garbed men, the hall scene was one of movement and beauty.

From the very entrance down stairs the big building was filled with vines and flowers. All the stairs were entwined with vines, and the big ball room had a lacy wall covering of southern smilax, interspersed with crossed palm leaves.

Against a background of palms and tall cryasr... .me '.e governor, his wife and daughters, and members of the receiving party stood.

A full string orchestra ccupied a corner of the balcony and played a

CONTINUED ON PAGE FIVE.

WOMEN ATTEND BALL WITHOUT THEIR DICKEYS

MAN IN PLAID SUIT ATTENDS INAUGURAL BALL, BUT HE DUCKS.

(BY THE SPORTING EDITOR.)
Special to The Oklahoman.

Guthrie, Okla., Nov. 16.—I would know every horse Jim Keene ever owned, by its canter. I'll beat the champeen pool player of every burg that's got a town pump, and spot him half as many balls as he's got the nerve to ask. I know every pug between Narragansett Bay and Frisco who ever stayed as long as ten rounds. My head is a walking encylo of baseball dope and I'm the candy gazabo when it comes to dishing up gridiron copy. I thought I could trot a heat with any of them at anything—ping-pong barrel.

I can't.

I'm a nine spot—neither high nor low and ain't worth two whoops for game. If you ever hold four like

me in a little game like they played here tonight, take my advice and don't risk any of your small change.

I'm king of the bowling alleys and my credit is good at the bath house, but when it comes to the society game I'm a flounder. I don't shine.

SHOOTS DAUGHTER; COMMITS SUICIDE

PROMINENT CALIFORNIA CAPITALIST PERPETRATES TERRIBLE TRAGEDY.

Santa Cruz, Cal., Nov. 16.—Major Frank McLaughlin, a prominent politician and capitalist, today shot his daughter Agnes in the cimple, the bullet coming out on the other side of her head. Soon afterward he committed suicide. The girl is still alive but unconscious. No hope is entertaine dfor her recovery.

After the shooting Major McLaughlin telephoned to former Lieutenant Governor Jeter to come down immediately to his house.

"I have killed my daughter, Agnes, and I intend to kill myself."

He told Mr. Jeter to bring a doctor. Mr. Jeter and a friend jumped into a buggy and drove to Major McLaughlin's house, where they arrived in time to see him breathing his last. The major had taken prussic acid.

One word, one cent, that is all that an Oklahoman want ad costs.

If there is anything you want just

DEATH BLOW IS DEALT BY LABOR

OPPOSES GOVERNMENT OWNERSHIP THROUGH BELIEF THAT STRIKES WOULD END.

Norfolk, Va. Nov. 16.—The American Federation of Labor by a vote of 154 to 50 today refused to record itself as favoring government ownership of railroads and mines. The question came up on a resolution to include railroads and mines in the action taken at Minneapolis last year favoring "nationalization" of telegraph and telephone properties.

The opponents too kthe grounds that government ownership of mines and railroads would prevent all strikes, no matter how peaceably they might be conducted and that with a federal government opposed to labor it might deal the death blow.

Another important action by the convention was the increasing the salary of President Gompers from $3,000 to $5,000 per annum, that of Secretary Morrison from $2,500 to $3,000 and

The Weather Today: Cloudy; Warmer

I'm goin' to travel agin' an' I'm goin' to have servants who'll call me king an' who'll bow down low when they see me humin', an' say, "Yes, yer majesty," an' "meet grashus king" an' all that kind of stuff, an' I talk to 'em.

We kids had a meeting today an' I 'lected king of the land of Oof. Nun of us know where Oof is, but it sounds like Afrisky an' we're goin' to Afrisky an' find a place what looks like it ought to have a name like that an' we're goin' to name it. An' when I think we've got to the right place I'm goin' to say:

"This is to be my kingdom, varlets, build me a mansion." An' some of the kids'll have to take marbits out of their belts an' cut down trees an' schup'll have to go to the mountains an' carry stone an' others'll have to dig diamonds and preshus jewels an' gold an' make a crown fer me. An' we're goin' to have a take dug clost to the mansion so all I'll have to do when I feel kinda hot is to dive out of the tower in the water an' take a swim. An' we're goin' to put fish in the lake an' raw dads an' turkles an' we're goin' to have ducks.

'Cause I'm king, I won't have to do nun of the work an' enny kid that don't do what I tell him will be to the alligators.

I wuz 'lected king, 'cause I'd traveled an' 'cause I knowed how to kill Indians an' 'cause I'd read 'bout Stanley an' Afraky. I'm goin' to be the real thing. I tell you. I ain't goin' to be one of them putty kings what wears a nappkin 'round his head an' smokes a pipe an' sets on his hanches an' waits for his subjects to bring him things. I'm goin' to hav' a gun an' a hoss an' I'm goin' to ride

fell in the mud puddle. I hope nuthin happens to keep me from bein' king. I always did want to be one.

It'll be cloudy and warmer today. S'long.

THE KID.

The following meteorological record is furnished by J. P. Slaughter, section director of the United States weather station at Epworth University, for the 24 hours ending at 7 o'clock last evening:

Temperature at 7 a. m. 30
Temperature at 2 p. m. 49
Maximum at 2 p. m. 49
Minimum at 8 a. m. 30
Mean temperature 39
Highest actual barometer 30.20
Lowest actual barometer 30.10
Average wind velocity—miles 6
Maximum wind velocity—miles 12
Relative humidity at 7 a. m. 64
Relative humidity at 2 p. m. 44
Dew point at 7 a. m. 19
Dew point at 2 p. m. 27
Precipitation .... .00

Forecast: Sunday, increasing cloudiness, warmer.

Comparative temperature data—Oklahoma City:

Maximum this date last year 72
Minimum this date last year 34
Highest on this date during the past 35 years, in 1905 ....
Lowest on this date during the past

This view in Guthrie made on November 16, 1907, shows the inauguration of Charles N. Haskell of Muskogee, the first governor of the State of Oklahoma. (Courtesy Western History Collections, University of Oklahoma Libraries)

"came in from all over the state. People who were afraid they'd never get the money they had in the bank thought at least they could get a subscription to the paper. They nearly flooded us and circulation went up."

But before 1907 ended, *The Oklahoman* faced new competition from what was then a novelty in publishing, a free newspaper, the first to be published in the United States. Howard and H. H. Tucker Jr. began publishing *The Pointer* carrying advertising and a little local news, but the news it carried was sensational and largely inflammatory. The paper began to gobble the advertising revenue from *The Oklahoman* and the two afternoon papers, the *News* and the *Times*. (The *Times-Journal* had dropped the word *Journal* from its name in 1908.) Gaylord later recalled, "There was only one thing for us to do. We were forced to put out a better 'free' paper to meet the competition head-on." It came in November 1910 when *The Oklahoman* announced it would launch the *Evening Free Press* to be distributed free to every home and

office building in Oklahoma City. *The Pointer* immediately attacked *The Oklahoman* for starting a competing free paper. *The Oklahoman* responded with an editorial noting that the columns of *The Pointer* would in the future "fairly reek with abuse, slander and misrepresentation of *The Oklahoman* and the individuals who publish it. We will be charged with all the crimes in the catalogue; all the designs that the imps of Satan can invent; all the degeneracy that human flesh is heir to."

The Oklahoman editorial then asked, "Why?"

The Pointer responded by accusing *The Oklahoman* of being controlled by "the interests."

To that *The Oklahoman* replied, "If there is an individual in town who believes that *The Oklahoman,* or the publishers of it, are controlled in any degree by the interests, we will gladly stand the expense of having his head bored for samples." *The Pointer* then began publishing the *Examiner,* a free morning paper heavy on advertising and thin on news. In retaliation, *The*

Oklahoman published classified advertising for free. This was only the beginning of what turned out to be a bitter and costly fight for *The Oklahoman* at a time when drought was causing economic problems across most of Oklahoma. *The Oklahoman's* battle against *The Pointer* and *Examiner* lasted until 1911 when the *Oklahoma City Times* purchased the printing equipment used by *The Pointer* and *Examiner*. *The Oklahoman* immediately ceased to publish the *Evening Free Press,* its free paper, and resumed charging for classified advertising. *The Oklahoman* lost at least $65,000 in revenue during the battle.

✳

Late in 1908, *The Oklahoman* undertook an editorial campaign to improve fire protection in the city, a campaign that resulted in a better system of fire alarm boxes. At about the same time the paper hired a young woman named Edith C. Johnson to cover Oklahoma City's social activities. She had been on the job a little more than a month when on the morning of January 29, 1909, as she later recalled, "I smelled smoke in my office. Wrapping my cloak around me I ran down the stairs to the street to see where the fire could be. To my amazement I found that the Oklahoman building was afire, and in the distance I could hear the clanging of engines approaching from several directions." Fire had broken out in the basement of *The Oklahoman* located on the northeast corner of California and Robinson. Ray Dickinson and other employees tried to put it out, but were forced to retreat as it spread. Within minutes the whole brick building was a mass of flames. The fire department arrived, but firemen were hampered by low water pressure. In those days it was necessary to notify the city waterworks when a fire occurred so pressure could be increased in the area where

the fire was being fought. The waterworks was late in getting the word. When the fire was out, *The Oklahoman's* press, only a few years old, and the typesetting machines were a tangled mess in the basement which was filled with three feet of water. The typesetting machines had also crashed through the first floor into the basement as flames destroyed the wooden floor and its supports. The cause of the fire was never determined. *The Oklahoman,* however, did not miss a single edition. Editorial offices were set up temporarily in the offices of the Chamber of Commerce, and the paper was printed on the press owned by the *Oklahoma News,* an evening paper started October 1, 1906, by Scripps-McRae, later to become the Scripps-Howard newspaper chain.

The offices and printing plant of *The Oklahoman* on the northeast corner of California and Robinson just after a fire gutted the building on January 29, 1909. Notice the horse-drawn fire wagon parked by the building.

After *The Oklahoman* fire in January 1909, the Oklahoma City Chamber of Commerce provided space for the staff to put out the paper. Pictured here are W. F. Kerr, managing editor; Jerome K. Farber, telegraph editor; Burns Hegler, state editor; George Saunders, police reporter; Evans A. Nash, courthouse reporter; Samuel J. Bowles and J. T. Land, advertising salesmen; P. K. Parks, Associated Press operator; and a visitor from the Miller Brothers 101 Ranch.

E. K. Gaylord's outlook and attitude toward *The Oklahoman* was expressed on the front page of his paper the day after the fire. He wrote:

> The Oklahoman's *building practically was gutted by fire. Most of the printing plant was destroyed. Of the eight typesetting machines, only one was saved. The big press costing $25,000—it was our pride—was scorched, blistered and burned in many places. Some thousands of dollars worth of type, paper, motors and other material was lost.*
>
> *But* The Oklahoman *did not burn. A newspaper does not consist of presses and machinery. That trained organization of men and boys known as* The Oklahoman *"force" is what makes* The Oklahoman. *It is they who* ARE *The Oklahoman and they are unharmed and undaunted.*
>
> *Their courage, brains and skill created* The Oklahoman *and will re-create it. From the newsboy who gets out at 4 A.M. to the captains of the many departments, each of the more than one hundred men is a living unit of a great human machine, and each earned his place by his own peculiar ability and faithfulness.*
>
> *To a man, their strength and loyalty has been stimulated by this calamity. Their tools have been burned from their hands, but new and more cunning tools will replace them.*
>
> The Oklahoman *is needed by the state. Its responsibility, always realized, is now more than ever impressed upon us by the hosts of public spirited citizens who have come forward offering assistance and sympathy.*
>
> *We are deeply grateful—we can't tell you, but we will* SHOW *you. There will be a greater* Oklahoman *in the future.*

Even before the fire, Gaylord had made plans to build a new and larger newspaper plant at Northwest Fourth and Broadway. As the building was burning, he contacted the St. Louis construction company that was to build the new building and told them to begin construction as soon as possible. Almost before the firemen had left the scene, Gaylord ordered five new Linotype machines from Chicago and new rollers and other parts for the waterlogged and damaged press. As the firemen departed, workmen started cleaning up the debris and pumping water from the basement while carpenters began repairing the damaged interior of the brick building. By February 6 the building had been repaired, new equipment installed, and the paper's press was operating. About seven months later on October 10, 1909, *The Oklahoman* moved into its new building located at Northwest Fourth and Broadway.

About two months after the fire, *The Oklahoman* in April 1909, published a special 100-page edition to mark the 20th anniversary of "The Run." It was the most ambitious undertaking attempted up to that time by any newspaper in the new state. Designed to promote the progress that had been made in Oklahoma, *The Oklahoman* printed a coupon with space for 10 names and addresses of friends outside of Oklahoma. Readers were encouraged to complete the coupon and return it to the paper which sent a free copy of the special edition to each name listed.

✳

In July 1909, about three months before *The Oklahoman* moved into its new building, the newspaper started a campaign to move the east-west Frisco and Rock Island railroad tracks that the city's founders had worked so hard to obtain. The tracks traversed the business district between Northwest First and Northwest Second and were hampering orderly growth of the business

section. It was many years, however, before the tracks were moved south of the business district.

Oklahoma City was rapidly growing. *The Oklahoman* ran an unceasing campaign to promote various bond issues to improve the city, but the paper opposed a bond issue for a new city hall, saying the city needed many things more than a new city hall. The paper disclosed that a city councilman held an option on the proposed building site and would sell it to the city if the bond issue passed. The bond issue did not pass.

By this time Gaylord had moved from Miss Waynick's boardinghouse on Northwest Fourth, just west of Robinson, to a house in the 300 block of Northeast Fifth. Gaylord and nine other bachelors engaged a cook and housekeeper. The young men formed what they called the Pickwick Club. They were all active in civic work ranging from helping police break a street-railway strike to staging the governor's inaugural ball. Their new home became the social center of Oklahoma City. They furnished the high-ceilinged house and put up lace curtains and made it something of a showcase. The

The 21-member Oklahoma City police force in 1907.

Carriers of *The Oklahoman* posed for the camera at a Labor Day picnic in 1909.

Sunday dinners of the club were the high points of the social week. Each member would invite his favorite girl, and invitations were regarded as a signal honor by Oklahoma City's young women. But each time one of the young bachelors married, the remaining members of the Pickwick Club would hang a photograph in the house depicting a neat, well-kept grave adorned with a headstone and wreath. Each headstone bore the name and date when one of its members left to enter into holy matrimony. Within a few years nearly every member of the Pickwick Club would marry including Edward K. Gaylord.

✳

During the summer of 1909 a young man named Charles J. Brill, who had just graduated from Logan County High School, was hired as a reporter. He became what many consider the first true sports editor on any Oklahoma newspaper. He served *The Oklahoman* from 1909 to 1916 when he was hired away by the *Tulsa World*. But four years later Brill was hired back by *The Oklahoman* as sports editor, a position he held until 1929 when he turned his attention to game conservation and

outdoors writing, things he pursued for the next 27 years.

By late 1909, *The Oklahoman* was waging a crusade to move the capital from Guthrie to Oklahoma City. The enabling act passed by a Republican Congress called for the capital to remain at Guthrie, a GOP stronghold, until 1913. But now Oklahoma was a sovereign state and not bound by federal provisions in locating any of its institutions. Leading lawyers in Oklahoma agreed that the people could move the capital anywhere they wanted at any time. Oklahoma City, Guthrie and Shawnee each wanted to be the capital. In Oklahoma City, E. K. Gaylord was named chairman of the campaign committee, and *The Oklahoman* had petitions printed and distributed over the state by the circulation people. Oklahoma then had a population of 1,657,155. Four special trains carried people in all directions to gain support for Oklahoma City as the capital. Some citizens in Oklahoma City even pledged free land for the site of the capitol building.

Oklahoma voters went to the polls on June 11, 1910, to vote on the location of the capital, but the proposition made no mention as to when the move would occur. Governor Charles Haskell was in Tulsa on election day. That evening, on the basis of unofficial and incomplete returns, Oklahoma City was winning by a large margin. Even before the final vote was tallied, Oklahoma City was winning by 50,000 votes. Haskell called his secretary, W. B. Anthony, and instructed him to move the state seal from Guthrie to Oklahoma City. The seal, only two-and-one-half inches in size, was taken to Oklahoma City, where Haskell returned the following day by special train and met Anthony and Bill Cross, secretary of state, at the Lee-Huckins

E. K. Gaylord may have been in the crowd watching this July 4 parade in downtown Oklahoma City about 1910. This view looks north on Broadway. (Courtesy Oklahoma Historical Society)

Hotel. Haskell wrote a proclamation declaring Oklahoma City the legal capital. Haskell then set up his own office in the hotel, an office he used until his term ended a few months later.

When news of what the governor had done was made public, the residents of Guthrie were up in arms. *The Oklahoman* was in an awkward position. If Oklahoma City won, the paper had said, there was no reason for moving the capital there until 1913. That would give time to select a site and to build a capitol building. But now the capital had already been moved. Civic leaders in Guthrie brought suit for recovery of the capitol. Eventually the state legislature got involved and established the capital in Oklahoma City on its present Northeast 23rd site.

In the meantime, candidates were campaigning to replace Haskell as governor. *The Oklahoman* supported Lee Cruce, a 47-year-old Ardmore resident. As the campaign heated up,

the *Times* in Oklahoma City and the *State Capital* in Guthrie claimed *The Oklahoman,* the *Guthrie Leader,* and the *Daily Ardmoreite* were dividing a $10,000 jackpot in return for supporting Lee Cruce in the governor's race. *The Oklahoman* immediately replied to the *State Capital* with these words:

> *Its pages constitute a political criminal record, devoid of a single virtue of a decent fight and rotten to the core with putrid, contemptible falsehoods that reek in their own puddle of filth and send out a sickening stench that stagnates in the nostrils of its readers.*

Such language was typical of early journalism in Oklahoma and elsewhere in the West. Editors knew or concocted virile expressions and applied them when they thought it would do the most good. But in time the vigor and colorful words were replaced with language that was dull by comparison. A month later Cruce was swept into the governor's office by a 35,000 vote margin, but as he prepared to take office, dry weather, forecasts of poor crops, and a national stagnation in business caused money to be tight. In Oklahoma City, a strike by street car workers in March 1911 added to Oklahoma City's problems.

Because Oklahoma City's population had dropped, many Oklahoma newspapers were writing that the real estate boom in the capital city had busted, but editorials in *The Oklahoman* maintained an optimistic tone. The paper's optimism was rewarded in July 1911 when rain fell over many areas of the state. Oklahoma City, with a population of more than 64,000, began to rebound economically. *The Oklahoman* sponsored a successful campaign to raise $75,000 to get the Missouri-Kansas-Oklahoma and Fort Smith and Western railroads to extend their lines into Oklahoma City. The paper

also began a campaign in 1911 for more adequate water supplies for Oklahoma City. But many residents accused *The Oklahoman* of frightening away new citizens by giving the impression Oklahoma City was arid.

One real estate man contended there was "plenty of water in the river" to serve the needs of Oklahoma City. *The Oklahoman* pointed out the critic had not looked at the almost dry river for some time. "A very ordinary yellow dog could jump across the stream at most any point," related one editorial in *The Oklahoman,* which continued its crusade for an adequate water supply in Oklahoma City for decades following. That year, 1911, an editorial in *The Oklahoman* told readers, "A high-class, fair-minded newspaper which gives all the news and maintains an intelligent and progressive editorial policy exerts an influence on the community second only to the public schools."

✳

When E. K. Gaylord purchased an interest in *The Oklahoman* in 1903, he also received an interest in the *Weekly Oklahoman.* From its start the weekly had been oriented toward rural readers across the state. In September 1911, the *Weekly Oklahoman* became the monthly *Oklahoma Farmer-Stockman,* a real agricultural publication dedicated to serve rural readers. In 1912, E. K. Gaylord became general manager of *The Oklahoman* and Ray M. Dickinson, who had come to Oklahoma with Gaylord, was named business manager. Dickinson was lean, wiry, and quiet spoken.

On April 16, 1912, *The Oklahoman* printed a full headline across the front page telling readers that 1,245 people had died when the British luxury liner *Titanic* sank in the Atlantic. The paper reported all of the details available. The largest ship of its kind and the fastest afloat, the *Titanic* was on its

This photo was made during a streetcar workers' strike March 16, 1911. The crowd is listening to a speech by Kate Barnard, state commissioner of charities and corrections. Barnard was the first woman in the nation to hold a statewide office and the only one to do so before women were allowed to vote in federal elections in 1920. (Courtesy Oklahoma Historical Society)

maiden north Atlantic crossing from Southampton to New York. The ship had been considered unsinkable because of its double-bottomed, watertight hull, but 95 miles south of Newfoundland it struck a submerged iceberg that ripped the ship open and sent it to the bottom. Among the Americans lost in the disaster were millionaires John Jacob Astor IV and Benjamin Guggenheim. Six hundred and seventy-five survivors were rescued and taken to New York.

By the end of 1912, the future looked bright for Oklahoma City. Businessmen who arrived in Oklahoma City before E. K. Gaylord had done much to start building the town. E. K. Gaylord recalled that "Henry Overholser was the outstanding town builder. He was the one responsible for getting the Frisco Railroad to build into Oklahoma City instead of Guthrie. Henry insisted that we should have a state fair and he bought 160 acre of school land on Eastern Avenue and built some buildings as a start for a state fair. He wanted [Anton H.] Classen, who owned the street railway to

build a car line out to the fairgrounds. Classen said he would not build it unless they would pave Eighth street so they could put the car tracks on a paved street. Overholser tried to sign up property owners along 8th street, but many refused. There were a good many vacant lots on the street and Overholser bought them all up, got a majority of lots along the street and signed the papers to have the paving charged to the lot owners and the paving and the street car line were built."

In 1912, Theodore Roosevelt came to Oklahoma City to speak. A few months earlier President William Howard Taft was nominated at the Republican National Convention in Chicago even though Roosevelt had won all but one primary and caucus. Roosevelt and his supporters bolted the convention and formed the National Progressive party better known as the "Bull Moose" party. His Oklahoma City speech was part of his campaign for the presidency. Roy Stafford sent Edith Johnson to interview Roosevelt. A friend of hers at the new Skirvin Hotel agreed to lock her in the hotel's

These pre-fabricated buildings were shipped to Oklahoma City by train soon after the town was settled. They were erected in what was called the Overholser Block on the north side of Grand Avenue west of Robinson. The Colcord Building stands on the site today. (Courtesy Oklahoma City Chamber of Commerce)

Fifteen special trainloads of cattle from big ranches in Texas will be delivered to the grazing pastures of Oklahoma today and tomorrow

40,937 Week Day Average for March.

THE DAILY OKLAHOMAN

47,363 Sunday Average for March.

VOL 23. NO. 306. OKLAHOMA CITY, OKLAHOMA, TUESDAY, APRIL 16, 1912—TWELVE PAGES. PRICE FIVE CENTS.

OCEAN STEAMER TITANIC SINKS; 1525 ABOARD

MOST APPALLING MARINE DISASTER IN HISTORY OF MANKIND BRINGS GRIEF TO MANY HOMES

Monster Ice Floe Rends the Largest Steamship in World

SHIP CARRIED 2,200 SOULS 866 ARE REPORTED SAVED

Many Notables Were Aboard Ill Starred Vessel Which Also Carried Vast Treasure in Diamonds and Other Valuables—Property Loss Amounts to Millions of Dollars.

FLOATING PALACE AND ITS VALUABLE CARGO.

London, April 15.—The Titanic was insured at Lloyds for $5,000,000. No definite confirmation is obtainable as to the amount of valuables on board, but it is generally understood that the vessel took diamonds of the estimated value of $500,000, consigned to dealers. She also took a large amount of bonds.

The vessel cost $10,000,000 to build. Her hull was valued for insurance purposes at $5,000,000. There are all sorts of miscellaneous matters to be taken in account for disbursements and for passage money and for freights paid in advance, as well as for stores, baggage and other things.

The Titanic was the largest steamer ever built. She was 882 feet long and had 46,328 tons displacement. She was launched last May. This was her maiden trip.

BULLETIN.

[illegible], April 15.—A wireless message picked up late tonight relayed from the Olympic says that the Carpathia is on her way to New York with 866 passengers from the steamer Titanic aboard. They are mostly women and children, the message said, and it concluded: "Grave fears are felt for the safety of the balance of the passengers and crew."

More than 1,500 persons, it is feared, sank to death early yesterday when, within less than four hours after she crashed into an iceberg, the mammoth White Star line steamer Titanic, bound from Liverpool to New York on her maiden voyage, went to the bottom off the New Foundland banks. Of the approximately 2,200 persons on board the giant liner, some of them of world wide prominence, only 675 are known to have been saved. The White Star line offices in New York, while keeping up hope to the last, were free to admit that there had been "a horrible loss of life."

Accepting the early estimates of the fatality list as accurate, the disaster is the greatest in the marine history of the world. Nearest approaching it in magnitude were the disasters to the steamer Atlantic in 1873, when 574 lives were lost and La Bourgogne in 1898 with a fatality list of 571.

Should it prove that other liners, notably the Allan liners, Parisian and Virginian, known to have been in the vicinity of the Titanic early yesterday had picked up other of her passengers, the extent of the calamity would be greatly reduced. This hope still remains.

News of the sinking of the liner and the terrible loss of life in consequence came early last evening with all the greater shock because hope has been buoyed up all day by reports that the steamship, although badly damaged, was not in a sinking condition and that all of her passengers had been safely taken off. The messages were mostly unofficial, however, and none came directly from the liner, so a lurking fear remained of possible bad news to come.

HORRIBLE LIFE LOSS.

New York April 15.—Vice President Franklin at 8:40 o'clock conceded that there had been "a horrible loss of life" in the Titanic disaster. He said he had no information to disprove the Associated Press report from Cape Race to the effect that only 675 of passengers and crew had been rescued. He said that the monetary loss could not be estimated tonight, although the intimated that it would run into millions. "We can replace the money," he added, "but not the lives."

"As far as we know it has been rumored from Halifax that three steamers have passengers on board, namely the Virginian, the Carpathia and Parisian. Now we heard from Captain Haddock that the Titanic sank at 2:20 this morning. We have also learned from him that the Carpathia had 675 survivors on board. It is very difficult to learn if the other two have any survivors on board. We have asked Captain Haddock and our agent at Halifax to ascertain if there are any passengers aboard the two steamships.

"We very much fear, however, that there has been a great loss of life, but it is impossible for us to give further particulars until we have heard from the Parisian and Virginian. We have no information that there are any passengers aboard these two steamships."

Mr. Franklin said there was a sufficient number of life boats to take all the passengers from the Titanic. He said he had been confident Monday when he made the statement that "the Titanic was unsinkable" that the steamship was safe and that there would be no loss of life. The news came in the message from Captain Haddock, he said, and was given to the Associated Press at once.

COLLIDED WITH ICEBERG.

New York, April 15.—A wireless message from the Titanic received soon after midnight today announced that the giant new liner had struck an iceberg off the banks of New Foundland and was in a sinking condition.

Transfer of the passengers to the lifeboats began at once. The accident occurred at 10:25 o'clock Sunday night. Two hours later the ship's wireless apparatus, which had been working so badly as to permit of only intermittent and fragmentary messages, failed completely.

The last words sent by the operator told that the vessel was apparently doomed, "sinking by the head," and that the women passengers were being rushed into the life boats. A reassuring feature was that the weather was calm and clear and help only a few hours away.

The Titanic's first "S. O. S." message was received by the Allan liner Virginian, which, according to the position given by the Titanic's operator, was not more than 170 miles away. The captain of the Virginian at once started his boat at full speed for the scene of the disaster, wiring his brother officer on the bridge of the Titanic that the Virginian should reach him by 10 o'clock this morning.

The Titanic's accident happened in latitude 41.6 north, longitude 50.14 west. This point is about 1,150 miles due east of New York city and 450 miles south of

FABULOUS WEALTH REPRESENTED BY TITANIC'S PASSENGER LIST

New York, April 15.—Untold wealth was represented among the passengers of the Titanic, there being on board at least six men each of whose fortunes might be reckoned in tens of millions of dollars. A rough estimate of the total wealth represented in the first-class passenger list would reach over half a billion dollars.

The wealthiest of the list is Col. John J. Astor, who is reputed to be worth $150,000,000. Mr. Astor was returning from a tour of Egypt with his bride, who was Miss Madeline Force, to whom he was married in Providence on September 9 1911.

Benjamin Guggenheim, probably next in financial importance, is the fifth of the seven sons of Meyer Guggenheim, who founded the American Smelting and Refining company, and is a director of many corporations. His fortune is estimated at $97,000,000. G. D. Widener is the son of P. A. B. Widener, the Philadelphia "traction king," whose fortune is estimated at $50,000,000.

Isador Straus, one of New York's most prominent dry goods merchants, and notable for his philanthropies, has a fortune also estimated to be worth $50,000,000.

J. Bruce Ismay, president and one of the founders of the International Mercantile Marine company, who has always made it a custom to be a passenger on the maiden trip of every new ship built by the company, is said to be worth $40,000,000. It was Mr. Ismay who, with J. P. Morgan, consolidated American and British steamship lines under the International Mercantile Marine's control.

Col. Washington Roebling, builder of the Brooklyn bridge, president and director of John A. Roebling Sons company, is credited with a fortune of $25,000,000.

Among others of reputed wealth who were on board are J. P. Thayer, vice president of the Pennsylvania railroad; Clarence Moore, a well-known sportsman, whose wife was Miss Mabel Swift, daughter of the Chicago meat packer, and Charles M. Hays, president of the Grand Trunk Pacific and vice president and general manager of the Grand Trunk railway of Canada.

Other passengers of note in the first cabin list are W. T. Stead, writer, journalist and war correspondent; Jacques Futrelle, the short story writer; Frederick M. Hoyt, a well-known New York yacht man; Henry Sleeper Harper, grandson of John Wesley Harper, one of the founders of Harper Brothers' Publishing company; William E. Carter of Philadelphia and Newport, and Thomas Pears a Pittsburg steel manufacturer.

ANXIOUS THRONGS WAIT FOR NEWS

Wealth Rubs Shoulders With Poverty in Front of Steamship Office.

WOMEN HYSTERICAL

Told That Company Knows Little of Fate of Their Loved Ones.

New York, April 15.—News of the probable terrible loss of life in the sinking of the Titanic was limited in its circulation in the early evening, but by 9 o'clock it had brought a good crowd of persons to the White Star line offices. Women were in tears and men were frantic after their plea for assuring news was met with the frank admission that very little was known of the fate of passengers who were not in the first or second cabins.

By midnight Bowling Green, in front of the White Star line offices, was the parking place of many automobiles of prominent residents of the city awaiting first hand information. Wealth rubbed shoulders with poverty in the crowd that besieged the White Star officials.

There were many instances of fashionably gowned women going into hysterics when the hopeful reports of the afternoon were flashed with the news that probably only 675 persons had been saved.

Vincent Astor, only son of Col. John Jacob Astor, accompanied by A. J. Biddle of Philadelphia, were among the crowd at the offices and left with tears in their eyes after a fifteen minutes' conference with Vice President Franklin. Relatives of other prominent passengers had similar conferences with Mr. Franklin and came away dejected.

Police reserves had to be called to several sections of the city Monday night to control crowds gathered around newspaper bulletin boards for news of the Titanic. The disaster stunned the gay Broadway district as perhaps no disaster ever had so completely before. Many of those who poured out of the theaters had friends on the steamer. The newspaper district was crowded until after midnight.

Washington, April 15.—President Taft was in great anxiety Monday night for news of his aide, Captain Archibald Butt, who was on the Titanic. The president had frequent inquiries made of the newspaper offices and the steamship agency.

FOREIGNERS REGARD WARNING AS TIMELY

Mexico City, April 15.—President Taft's warning to the Mexican government that the United States "expects and must demand that American life and property within the republic of Mexico be justly and adequately protected," received at the United States embassy late last night, was transmitted to the Mexican foreign office this morning. The United States ambassador declined to make any comment upon the subject.

The warning is generally regarded by foreigners here as wise and timely, though it is recognized that the administration is disposed to respect American lives to its utmost capacity. It is believed that the warning will have the effect of causing sharp instructions to be issued to General Villa, whose "irregulars" constitute the danger point, if any, in the federal control.

The foreign minister was unwilling to make any comment.

CHINESE PRESIDENT FOR AMALGAMATION

Pekin, April 15.—A manifesto issued by the president of the republic urges the five races to amalgamate through intermarriage.

General Sheng Yun, ex-governor of the Province of Shen Si who, early last month, began a march on Pekin with a large number of troops, is irreconcilable, but is unable to continue the struggle, his Mohammedan allies having accepted Yuan Shi Kai's terms. It is reported that these include monetary compensations.

WILSON TO GEORGIA.

Trenton, N. J., April 15.—Governor Woodrow Wilson of New Jersey will leave tonight or early tomorrow for Georgia. He expects to be away several days and will possibly speak at Jacksonville, Fla., before he returns. The governor's plans are in the hands of his Georgia friends and he does not know his itinerary.

HARRISON-HEARST CROWD ROMPED ALL OVER R. SULLIVAN

Sullivan Men Held Convention Hall in Defiance of Court Order.

MILITIA STOOD GUARD

Police Broke Open Doors and Sullivan Crowd Went to Another Hall.

Chicago, April 15.—Conflict of court orders and the battering of sledges and axes on barred doors preceded the Cook county democratic convention, Monday, which chose two sets of delegates to the state convention in Peoria, April 19.

For more than three hours twenty-five militiamen, unarmed and under the command of a captain of the Seventh regiment Illinois National Guard, had possession of the Seventh regiment armory while two rival forces, the Heart-Harrison faction and the followers of Roger C. Sullivan, national democratic committeeman, disputed the right of each other to enter the armory.

The Sullivan men insisted that the county judge had no right to order an election commissioner to open the convention. The Hearst-Harrison men declared that his order alone would insure fairness.

Batallions of police, reinforced by more than a hundred deputy sheriffs, acting under the orders of County Judge John E. Owens, controlled the crowd outside the armory.

Coroner Hoffman, with twenty-five deputies, was busy throughout the morning serving police officials and the sheriff's men with an injunction issued in the county superior court restraining them from interfering.

The injunction was waved aside and the coroner himself was summoned before County Judge Owens to answer a charge of contempt of court for conflicting with the orders of Judge Owens.

The sheriff and police and Election Commissioner Czarnecki also are under contempt charges.

Demands were made by the commissioner, republican, delegated by Judge Owens to open the convention, that the door be unbarred.

The militia defiantly refused and Judge Owens, in person, went to the armory and demanded admittance. He too, was refused.

Then the police were ordered by Judge Owens to break in the doors. No shots came from the guardsmen. The outer door fell and then an inner door barricaded with trunks and furniture gave way. County Judge Owen and the commissioner entered.

Captain Octigan who commanded the guardsmen was arrested but was released on habeas corpus proceedings. The Hearst-Harrison precinct committeemen, who had been standing in line wearing badges inscribed "harmony," entered the building.

Commissioner Czarnecki called the roll and the machinery of the convention was turned over to the delegates. Not a man of the Sullivan forces was present. Instead, they and those known as Dunne men remained outside and, after a long delay, left the vicinity of the armory and held a convention at another hall.

As a result the state convention will be called on to decide between the two sets of delegates.

WRITING EXPERTS' VIEWS AID NORRIS

Fort Worth, Texas, April 15.—Practically the entire court session Monday in the case of Rev. J. Frank Norris, charged with perjury in connection with his testimony before a grand jury regarding certain anonymous letters the pastor received, was devoted to the opinion of witnesses who had had experience in studying hand writing.

Others who testified were J. O. East, son of a member of the grand jury which indicted Rev. Norris on the perjury charge, and W. W. Wilson, a member of the Norris grand jury.

The witnesses who testified regarding a comparison of the character of handwriting appearing in anonymous threats written Rev. Norris and G. H. Connell, and a manuscript written by the pastor, were of the opinion that the same person did not write the Norris manuscript and the anonymous letters.

Those witnesses were J. D. Watkins, who was on the stand Saturday; F. C. Read, an instructor in a business college, and J. A. Wright, a postal employee. Each stated that, in their opinion, the author of the Norris manuscript was not the writer of the anonymous letters.

FOUNDATION IS STILL ON SAND

Washington, April 15.—Upon protests of a number of members that the creation of a great corporation of $100,000,000 might compete with private interests and end in controlling the government, the house today refused to pass a bill incorporating the Rockefeller foundation and struck it from the calendar. The bill has been before congress two years.

NEWS SUMMARY

WEATHER REPORT.

FORECAST—Generally fair weather.

Yesterday's Temperature.

7 a. m.	49	1 p. m.	65
8 a. m.	49	2 p. m.	66
9 a. m.	52	3 p. m.	67
10 a. m.	54	4 p. m.	68
11 a. m.	58	5 p. m.	67
12 noon	62	6 p. m.	66
		7 p. m.	64

Maximum at 4 p. m.	68
Minimum at 7 a. m.	49
Mean temperature	58
Highest actual barometer	28.72
Lowest actual barometer	28.45
Average wind velocity	15
Highest wind velocity N.	28
Relative humidity at 7 a. m.	62
Relative humidity at 7 p. m.	28
Dew point at 7 a. m.	37
Dew point at 7 p. m.	37
Precipitation	.00

Comparative Figures.

Maximum this date last year	66
Minimum this date last year	41
Highest in past 21 years (1896)	87
Minimum in past 21 years (1907)	34

Washington Forecast.

Oklahoma—Fair and cooler Tuesday; Wednesday fair.

East Texas—Showers in south; fair and cooler in north portion Tuesday; Wednesday fair except showers on the coast.

West Texas—Probably fair Tuesday and Wednesday.

Arkansas—Fair and cooler Tuesday; Wednesday fair.

Louisiana—Showers Tuesday; Wednesday fair and cooler.

Kansas—Fair Tuesday and probably Wednesday; rising temperature Wednesday.

CONGRESS.

SENATE—Met at noon.

Senator Cummins resumed his speech advocating tobacco decree intervention bill.

Reached agreement to vote April 22 on Cummins' bill authorizing appeal by independents in American tobacco reorganization decree.

President Taft in special message urged immediate appropriating aggregating $778,000 for Mississippi river floods.

Adjourned at 5:35 p. m. until noon Tuesday.

HOUSE—Met at noon.

Considered bills on unanimous consent calendar.

Erdman act mediators advocated before interstate commerce commission on acts extensions to all branches of industry.

Rivers and harbors committee voted to report favorably bill appropriating additional $300,000 for Mississippi river and tributaries flood work.

Adjourned at 5:44 p. m. until noon Tuesday.

DOMESTIC.

Monster steamship Titanic sinks, carrying 1,525 persons to watery graves, it is believed.—Page 1.

Experts in handwriting at Fort Worth give testimony favoring Rev. Norris.—Page 1.

Supreme court of United States renders decision making allotted Choctaw Indian lands salable.—Page 1.

Thirteen parishes in northeast Louisiana overrun by Mississippi flood.—Page 1.

Hearst-Harrison forces have lively tilt with Roger Sullivan crowd in democratic convention in Chicago.—Page 1.

FOREIGN.

President of Chinese Republic urges amalgamation of five races through intermarriage.—Page 1.

Foreigners in Mexico regard as timely warning issued by United States government.—Page 1.

STATE.

Two victims added to list in Porum feud cases, Jack Davis shooting down Jesse Maxwell and Leonard McCullough on streets of Muskogee.—Page 4.

Central Fuel Oil company of Muskogee placed in hands of receivers on application of Bankers Trust company of New York.—Page 3.

Tulsa city election Tuesday, race is close.—Page 3.

Leon Fries, murderer of Artie Rose, Oklahoma City chauffeur, stabbed by negro in penitentiary at McAlester, may die.—Page 3.

Meeting of Oklahoma Segregated Land association called at McAlester for Saturday, April 27.—Page 3.

Boy steals horse near Shawnee, is arrested, confesses and sentenced to Granite reformatory, all in one day.—Page 3.

SPORT.

Baseball results, National, American and Texas leagues and American and Southern associations.—Page 8.

Pitcher Billings of Aggie school wins own game with Southwestern college of Texas by stealing home in thirteenth inning; score is 8 to 7.—Page 4.

Sooners meet Southwestern college on Boyd field at Norman Tuesday and Wednesday.—Page 4.

University of Oklahoma agrees to meet Nebraska on gridiron on November 27, at Lincoln.—Page 4.

New York ring bouts feature boxing calendar for this week.—Page 8.

President Meyer of state baseball league suspends for 10 days player limit; local club to incorporate.—Page 8.

MARKETS—(Page 9.)

Cotton shows decided weakness.

Reports of damaged crops in the west may send May and June wheat prices skyward. Trading reached a magnitude seldom equaled except in war times.

CITY.

Fifteen train loads of cattle on way to Oklahoma pastures to graze this summer.—Page 12.

Governor Cruce commutes death sentence of James Holmes (negro) and Frank Edwards to life imprisonment.—Page 12.

Will H. Clark declares Oklahoma wastes $250,000 a year in method of caring for paupers and insane.—Page 6.

Dr. A. C. Scott and the Rev. T. H. Harper to debate "evolution" at First Methodist church evening of April 29.—Page 12.

Packed house greets first night's performance of Shriners' minstrels at Overholser theater.—Page 7.

LOUISIANA NOW FLOOD CENTER

Thirteen Counties in Northeast Part Experience Deluge.

New Orleans, April 15.—Parts of the thirteen parishes in northeastern Louisiana are today feeling a deluge unparalleled in the history of disastrous floods of the lower Mississippi valley. Numerous small towns in East Carroll and Madison parishes already are wiped out, vast stretches of valley lands are covered by from six to twenty feet of water and a wall of the devastating flood waters twenty feet high and more than a mile in width is rushing through the great Dog Tail crevasse near Alsatia, La.

Already thousands are homeless and destitute. What will be the toll when the waters from the Panthers Forest and Redfork crevasses in Arkansas join their forces with the sea of water pouring through the Dog Tail breach no one can say. Parts of thirteen Louisiana parishes and two Arkansas counties will be under water and a conservative estimate is that the homeless in that territory will total at least 50,000, maybe 75,000.

No human agency can check the rushing waters before they have reached the Red river, which means that a large percent of a territory 160 miles in length and from eight to sixty-five miles in breadth will be inundated.

No further breaks occurred in the levees of the Mississippi Monday but at many points the flood waters already have exceeded the previous record stage and the United States engineers and state levee boards from Vicksburg south are working desperately against great odds.

To add to the alarming situation a vertible cloudburst in the Tensas basin Monday gave forth from four to six inches of rainfall in the brief space of ten hours. High winds accompanied the rain and made more difficult the work of rescue in the overflowed district and the almost hopeless efforts of some to save their few remaining chattels.

Relief work is centered at Vicksburg, where already hundreds of homeless and destitute people from the flooded Louisiana territory are quartered. Governor Brewer of Mississippi has sent tents and supplies there for the unfortunates and yesterday Governor Sanders of Louisiana ordered tents and bedding sent to the Mississippi city.

BREAK AT MORGANSEA.

Baton Rouge, La., April 15.—A telephone message received here early Monday night from Morgansea, 35 miles north of Baton Rouge, on the west side of the Mississippi river, stated that the levee there is cracking and caving badly and that water was coming through on the side.

Every effort is being made to hold the levee, which is on the lower side of a sharp bend. If a crevasse should occur there it would flood the richest farming territory along the river in south Louisiana.

New Orleans, April 15.—The reported threatened condition of the levee at Morgansea was confirmed in a report received at the office of Captain Sherill, of the U. S. engineering corps in charge of the work of the fourth levee district.

COURT DECISION CLEARS TITLES

First Case Wherein Allotted Indian Lands are Held Subject to Sale.

Washington, April 15.—Investors in the rich Indian lands of Oklahoma Monday won a victory in the supreme court.

The court held that no restrictions upon the sale by Choctaw fullblood Indians of inherited lands allotted in the names of fullblood Choctaws, but who died before the land was set aside under the allotment.

This is the first case wherein land allotted to the Indian has been held subject to sale.

The court considered the Chickasaw fullbloods had the same rights as the Choctaws. On April 1 the court held that land allotted to fullblood Cherokees was not subject to sale.

The court still has under consideration restrictions in the sale of Seminole lands.

NEW ORLEANS BANK CLOSES ITS DOORS

New Orleans, April 15.—Following closely upon the arrest last night of two o fits officers, Eugene F. Buhler, president of the institution, and Joseph H. Gomila, chairman of the finance committee, charged with swearing falsely to the bank's condition, the Teutonia Bank and Trust company, was ordered closed by State Bank Examiner Young. Frank J. Braud, a former assistant cashier of the bank, was also arrested, charged with the embezzlement of $60,000 of the institution's funds. Buhler and Gomila were released on a bond of $10,000 each, while Brand failing to secure bond is being held.

Owing to the disappearance of certain records and papers no definite statement as to the total loss to the bank has been obtained. Some estimates, however, place the amount between $300,000 and $400,000.

Mr. Gomila admitted to the authorities today that his indebtedness to the bank is $150,000.

The Teutonia Bank and Trust company had a capital of $200,000. According to its last statement on March 7 last, it had resources of $2,039,676.37, with deposits of $1,413,569.71.

The New Orleans Clearing House association of which the Teutonia was a member, held a meeting last night.

Police have been stationed in front of the bank's building to keep back the crowds, composed principally of small depositors, who began to gather during the early hours of the morning after the suspension of the bank had become generally known.

TROLLEY WRECK; ONE KILLED.

Lima Center, Mich., April 15.—One person was killed and about a dozen injured, several probably fatally, late today when two interurban cars on the Michigan United railway collided about two miles east of here Monday. One or more of the injured may die before medical aid reaches them.

This August 13, 1912, view looks west on California Avenue, the city's market street, where farmers sold fresh vegetables, fowls and other produce. Housewives shopped here on weekdays. (Courtesy Western History Collections, University of Oklahoma Libraries)

presidential suite on the mezzanine floor before Roosevelt arrived. Johnson later wrote that the "suite consisted of a drawing room, dining room and bedroom. Shortly after Mr. Roosevelt's arrival, I was listening with fast-beating heart to the shouting and tumult which hailed the Colonel's arrival. Presently the door was unlocked and flung open and Mr. Roosevelt strode in, pressed close on both sides by secret service men. Imagine their astonishment when they saw a 95-pound woman waiting in the dining room. Accompanied by his doctor, Colonel Roosevelt passed quickly into the bedroom. George Roosevelt, his secretary, promptly informed me that his cousin Theodore never gave interviews. Without arguing the question I quietly waited until Colonel Roosevelt came out. Although

he refused to answer questions of a political nature I got my story. It appeared on the first page of the next morning's *Oklahoman* with headlines of red ink."

✳

When E. K. Gaylord arrived in Oklahoma City, he strongly supported efforts to build the growing city. Late in his life, he recalled that "I. M. Putnam was a real estate developer and a great town booster. When Thomas E. Wilson came to town and had a secret meeting with leaders of the Chamber of Commerce, he offered to build a $3,000,000 packing plant provided a large tract of ground was made available and the citizens would pay a bonus of $300,000. John Shartel, who ran the street railway for Mr. Classen,

OPPOSITE
The front page of the April 16, 1912, issue of *The Oklahoman*.

The Oklahoman, Oklahoma City

The Oklahoman building at Northwest Fourth and Broadway as seen in a 1913 hand-colored postcard.

Sidney Brock, president of the Chamber of Commerce, and I were the committee to make a deal with Mr. Wilson. At one o'clock in the morning, after hours of negotiation, we each signed a contract with Mr. Wilson that the citizens would pay a $300,000 bonus and the land for the packing house site would be optioned. The deal was kept secret for several weeks until all the farm land needed was purchased or contracted for. The Chamber of Commerce called a meeting of citizens to raise the $300,000. I. M. Putnam was master of ceremonies. One citizen after another volunteered a pledge until finally $265,000 had been raised. When that point was reached, Putnam waved his hands in a grand manner and said, 'I will take the rest.' It had taken less than two hours to raise that money."

Gaylord added, "A year later another packing company offered to build a plant costing $3,000,000 and demanded a $300,000 bonus. It took about two weeks to obtain pledges in that amount. Many individuals gave small sums, $100 or even less, but every one wanted to participate. Such was the spirit of loyalty to Oklahoma City."

While crops were good, the state's oil and gas production were leading the nation, and the livestock business was flourishing, *The Oklahoman* was also growing, but at the start of 1913, 30 of Oklahoma City's leading merchants organized what they called the Oklahoma Advertisers Association. They announced they would not advertise in *The Oklahoman* because advertising rates were too high. The announced boycott came as merchants were being asked to renew advertising contracts at the previous year's rates. *The Oklahoman* could not understand why there had been no previous protests. The paper fought back with page one editorials charging merchants with wanting to "dictate" the paper's advertising rates. *The Oklahoman* challenged the advertisers to find another paper in North America with an equal circulation having lower advertising rates. The paper obtained figures to show that the *Dallas Morning News,* with approximately the same circulation as *The Oklahoman,* charged $1.12 an inch for advertising space while *The Oklahoman's* rate was only 60 cents on weekdays and 67 cents for the Sunday edition. *The Oklahoman* prepared to drop its policy of refusing advertising from mail order concerns, and prepared to publish wholesale prices local merchants paid for merchandise and then point to the markup on each item.

The boycott suddenly ended 10 days after it started. *The Oklahoman* announced that "through the kindly offices of the president of the Chamber of Commerce," the newspaper and the rebellious merchants had reconciled their differences. Ironically, as a result of their agreement, *The Oklahoman* gained a 10 percent average increase in its advertising rates in their agreement. *The Oklahoman* continued to grow slowly in terms of advertising revenue and circulation while the *Times* and the *Oklahoma News* slipped.

✳

The Oklahoman gave front-page coverage in 1914 to Lee Cruce, Oklahoma's second governor, when he broke ground with a silver pick for the new capitol building in Oklahoma City. More than 5,000 citizens attended the ceremony. The project had been delayed by the state's economic slowdown.

In May 1914, *The Oklahoman* announced a new editorial policy. For years its editorial columns had been filled with plugs for Democratic candidates several weeks before elections. *The Oklahoman* said in future it would not be interested in the personal political fortunes of candidates. The paper declared it would only print announcements for political office and not be used by candidates to test the public pulse before running for office.

The same month *The Oklahoman* announced its new editorial policy, the U.S. refused to recognize a new government in Mexico headed by Victoriano Huerta, who was trying to build his army. President Woodrow Wilson ordered the U.S. Navy to seize the port of Vera Cruz to prevent the delivery of weapons to Huerta's army. *The Oklahoma City Times* accused President Wilson of provoking the situation as a "cure for hard times" at home. *The Oklahoman* replied and called the *Times* "asinine" and pointed out that U.S. forces landed in Mexico "because our flag was insulted and the uniform of our navy spat upon." *The Oklahoman* lauded Wilson for his "coolness" and predicted he would go down in history as a "man of peace."

As the Mexican situation cooled, *The Oklahoman* began reporting on the war in Europe. What began as war between Austria-Hungary and Serbia in July 1914, quickly was transformed into a general European conflict. After Great Britain declared war on Germany and her allies, the U.S. entered the war in January 1917. *The Oklahoman* devoted much space to war news but did not neglect local, state and other national news.

During 1914 Al Jennings, a reformed train robber, announced that he was a Democratic candidate for governor, *The Oklahoman* said it had nothing against Jennings, but pointed to the national publicity Oklahoma would get if the former convict was elected governor. *The Oklahoman* supported another Democrat, Robert L. Williams, who came to Oklahoma from Alabama. He won the nomination and was elected Oklahoma's third governor in 1914.

That same year Oklahoma was plagued with bank robberies and was gaining a notorious national reputation. *The Oklahoman* demanded that the legislature do something to stop the robberies. The paper suggested that the state pay a reward for the arrest or capture of a bank robber. The legislature took the suggestion and created such a reward fund. Soon Henry Starr, then the state's most notorious outlaw, was shot and captured by 17-year-old Paul Curry when Starr and his gang tried to escape after robbing a bank in Stroud. *The Oklahoman* cheered Starr's capture as an example of what could be accomplished in ridding the state of its outlaws through the cooperation of its citizens spurred by a reward.

The year also saw *The Oklahoman* promote a milk and ice fund to provide pure milk and ice for babies in destitute homes. The program existed from 1914 through 1953, promoting sports competitions, cultural events and live shows. Also during 1914 *The Oklahoman* begin advocating the city manager form of government for Oklahoma City.

✷

In the fall of 1914, *The Oklahoman* reported: "A source of much surprise to the friends of Mr. Edward K. Gaylord is the announcement of his engagement to Miss Inez Kinney of New York City, the wedding to be an event of December. Miss Kinney is the daughter of Mr. and Mrs. James Kinney, Jr. of Bellaire, Ohio, and is a woman of unusual charm and intellectuality. She has been engaged for the past seven years in YWCA work and is one of the assistant national secretaries. . . . Miss Kinney visited here a little more than two years ago, but only for a short time. Mr. Gaylord, the general manager of *The Oklahoman,* and a well-known business man, has been one of the most incorrigible bachelors of the Pickwick Club for a number of years, and the announce-

ment of his approaching wedding comes as a complete surprise."

Gaylord had met Inez Kinney while she was visiting in Oklahoma City. A few days before the wedding, the Pickwick Club gave a luncheon at the Savoy in Oklahoma City to honor Gaylord who left that afternoon by train for Ohio. On December 29, 1914, Gaylord, 41, married Inez Kinney in her family home at Bellaire, Ohio. Following the wedding, the newlyweds went to Philadelphia and New York and returned to Oklahoma City by way of New Orleans and the Gulf coast. Just before the wedding a small item appeared in *The Oklahoman* which read: "E. K. Gaylord is having the plans drawn for a $3,000 residence to be erected on property recently purchased in Highland Park. The Pickwick Club has called a special meeting to investigate the matter of sedition within its ranks and to establish quarantine against Cupid." When the couple returned to Oklahoma City, Mr. and Mrs. Roy Stafford held a reception and ball in the couple's honor in the ball room of the Lee-Huckins Hotel. There were 300 guests. Among the gifts was a silver coffee service presented by members of the Pickwick Club.

The union of E. K. Gaylord and Inez Kinney would be blessed with three children—Edith, Edward and Virginia —and many grandchildren. When they married, Inez Gaylord became a member of the board of directors of The Oklahoma Publishing Co. E. K. Gaylord and his wife worked hard to help Oklahoma City grow and to build *The Oklahoman*. E. K. hired the best possible people and provided them the best equipment money could buy to enable them to do their jobs. Gaylord was especially fascinated with science and technology and constantly kept up with new advancements, especially in printing, communications and autos.

E.K. Gaylord in 1915 soon after his marriage to Inez Kinney.

At Gaylord's suggestion, the paper began promoting endurance tests over Oklahoma roads and tours of the state in various types of autos. This promotion led to a crusade for better roads.

Gaylord's interest in aero planes, as the airplane was first called, paralleled that of the automobile. Orville and Wilbur Wright's first successful flight at Kitty Hawk, North Carolina, came only days before Gaylord came to Oklahoma City late in 1902. As the development of the airplane accelerated dramatically during World War I, *The Oklahoman* gave such news prominent play. The paper did the same when the first farm tractor appeared in Oklahoma. Demonstrations of the tractor's use in agriculture so impressed the farm-minded newspaper that the tractor received much promotion from *The Oklahoman*. In one editorial, the paper noted: "The use of the tractor is growing so rapidly that perhaps in a

few years there will be nothing left for the horse to do."

During 1915, doctors told Ray Dickinson, the paper's business manager, that he had tuberculosis. They advised him to quit work and go to California. Dickinson left *The Oklahoman*. Later, after his health improved, Dickinson became advertising manager and later business manager of the *Long Beach Telegram*. Dickinson retained his financial interest in The Oklahoma Publishing Co. After his death his interest passed to his son Donald C. Dickinson, who served on the OPUBCO board until his death in 1991 at age 83. His son Martin C. Dickinson was then already on the board of directors.

Chapter Five

POLITICAL
INDEPENDENCE

By 1916, *The Oklahoman* was continuing to grow in circulation and advertising revenue and in its coverage of news and community service. The competing *Times,* however, was faltering. It began a downhill slide about 1909 after Omer Benedict purchased the paper and made arrangements to have it printed each afternoon on *The Oklahoman*'s press. At the time its editorial and business offices were located in a building adjoining *The Oklahoman.*

Soon after the 1909 fire that damaged *The Oklahoman*'s press, the *Times* changed hands. John Fields, Frank D. Northrup and Thomas A. Latta took over the paper and operated it until November 25, 1915. On that day the paper was turned over to trustees. On January 1, 1916, the *Times* was sold at public auction. *The Oklahoman* was the only bidder and purchased the paper for $35,000. The next day the *Times* rated only a two paragraph story on page 20 of *The Oklahoman,* but that day the *Times* told its readers the paper was now owned by *The Oklahoman* and a new political policy had been established for both the *Times* and *The Oklahoman.* An editorial began: "The vicissitudes of the *Times* for the past 10 years are well known. Its pillar-to-post existence, we trust, is ended." Then the editorial, for the first time, crystallized the new political policy for both papers. The editorial continued:

> The policies of the *Times* under its new management will necessarily be the
> same as The Oklahoman's. That means, of course, that it will be conducted as
> an independent Democrat journal.
>
> But it will not be the organ for any party at any time and never offensively parti-
> san. Its columns will be open to Republicans and Democrats alike on every public
> question, in campaign and out. We shall strive, in short, to be a people's paper in the
> best sense of the term and indulge the hope that we will have the public's co-operation
> to this end.

The "independent" attitude of *The Oklahoman* had grown slowly during the years just before The Oklahoma Publishing Co. purchased the *Times,* but now its policy was firmly stated in writing. The editorial in the *Times* admitted that the change in policy left Oklahoma City without a Republican mouthpiece among newspapers, but it added: "there is no more valid reason for having a Republican newspaper in Oklahoma City than for having a Republican dry goods store, a Republican telephone system, a Republican preacher, a Republican lawyer or a Republican bank. . . . We don't mix politics with business in anything else and the day is rapidly passing when it is successfully mixed with newspaper making. . . . A party organ serves a limited clientele; an independent newspaper serves every reader except the office seeker."

With the editorial both the *Times* and *The Oklahoman* established its independent attitude toward politics that to this day remains the policy of The Oklahoma Publishing Co. But many Oklahoma politicians took a dim view of the Company's new policy. A reporter from *The Oklahoman* was soon banned from attending sessions of the state senate because a story he had written incurred the wrath of some influential senators. After a number of senators moved to lift the ban, a heated debate followed on the senate floor with several senators referring to *The Oklahoman* as a "newspaper of questionable politics." The Oklahoma Publishing Co. held firmly to its new policy.

The Company's acquisition of a second paper meant that a managing editor was needed to oversee both *The Oklahoman* and the *Times.* Gaylord hired Walter M. Harrison for the job. Harrison had worked as a reporter on newspapers in Sioux

City, Iowa, Des Moines, and San Francisco before serving as managing editor of the *Winnipeg Tribune* in Canada and as news editor of the *Minneapolis Tribune.* Lean, wiry and quick, Harrison was to develop a reputation for snap intuitive decisions that made him something of a legendary figure in Oklahoma journalism. He became known as the "Skipper."

On the evening of November 8, 1916, Harrison and others in the papers' newsroom were following the presidential election results from the 48 states as they came in on two wires. The race pitted Republican nominee, Charles Evans Hughes, against Woodrow Wilson, the Democrat incumbent. The race appeared close, but at 10 P.M. Harrison learned the St. Louis *Post-Dispatch* had conceded the election to Hughes. At 10:30 P.M. the *New York World* did the same.

Gaylord looked over the returns and the information that had been received and then said he was going home. He told Harrison to wait and to make a decision for the morning paper. About midnight it appeared obvious that Hughes had won. Harrison wrote a banner headline that read "HUGHES NAMED PRESIDENT," laid out the front page accordingly, sent the material to the composing room and soon the presses rolled. But Harrison was wrong. When he returned to the paper early the next morning he learned that California, after seesawing from Hughes to Wilson, and from Wilson to Hughes, finally fell in the Wilson column early in the morning and returned President Wilson to a second term. Gaylord told Harrison it was a logical mistake but did not rebuke the managing editor. Harrison later recalled, "I was several years in living that one down, but under the leadership of a less considerate publisher, I might have walked the plank."

The fact that *The Oklahoman* and the *Times* were locally owned and had more at stake in Oklahoma and Oklahoma City than did the *News,* which was owned by a national newspaper chain, gave Gaylord an advantage. It is not surprising that his influence continued to grow because of his avid interest in and work for Oklahoma City, Oklahoma and the nation.

When work on getting a state capitol built continued to lag, *The Oklahoman* urged the commission charged with building a capitol to get on with its business. Governor Robert I. Williams asked the legislature to authorize an advisory committee of citizens to assist in its construction. The legislature did and the governor appointed Gaylord as one of seven members of the advisory committee. The committee quickly concluded that the building methods adopted by the official commission were inefficient, costly and much too slow. The committee set out to build the finest capitol possible and to do the job without any graft whatever.

"The advisory commission actually took over the direction of the building of the capitol and let a contract for the construction," Gaylord later recalled. "We were able to build a state capitol for $1,600,000 on that contract and it contained more space than the New York Capitol at Albany which cost more than $40 million and the Pennsylvania Capitol which cost $70 million," Gaylord added in a 1953 interview. Gaylord also remembered that the legislature had a provision that the capitol be a three-story building. "Well, when you figure all of the departments that had to go into a capitol, we couldn't possibly get them into three stories on the amount of ground we had. So the architect solved the problem. The plan had a basement, a sub-basement, a mezzanine plus three other floors.

It's a three-story building with six floors," Gaylord recalled in 1970.

In the spring of 1916, *The Oklahoman*'s crusade for an adequate water supply for Oklahoma City, started in 1911, paid off. Voters approved a $1,500,000 bond issue to build a storage reservoir at Lake Overholser.

On E. K. Gaylord's 43rd birthday, March 5, 1916, Inez Gaylord presented her husband with their first child, Edith. As she later recalled, "When I was graduated from college, Dad told me I'd have some vacation time and then go to work in what was then called the society department at *The Oklahoman* and *Times*. Now understand I had never had a single day of instruction about how to write a news story. I'd never had a journalism class." She learned on the job and then moved to news reporting and the copy and layout desks, becoming a fine journalist. "I learned a great deal about what goes on and what is needed in a newsroom. I was fortunate enough to be working under the guidance of some of the best veterans of the newsroom," she said. In 1942, after World War II began,

she wanted to find out if she could get and hold a job someplace other than on her father's paper. She went to work for the Associated Press, first in New York City, and later in Washington D.C. There, in 1944, she was elected president of the Women's National Press Club. President Franklin D. Roosevelt's wife Eleanor was the featured speaker at the meeting where Edith Gaylord took over as president of the Women's National Press Club. "I had asked her to be the principal speaker that evening and she graciously agreed. Now you know she was a tall woman, and I wasn't. She sent me an orchid from the White House conservatory and I wound up putting it on my head instead of putting it on my shoulder. I thought it would give me a little more height," recalled Edith in 1998, adding she regretted doing so and soon removed it.

✳

At a meeting in 1918, the directors of The Oklahoma Publishing Co. proposed reelecting officers and making

In 1944 Edith Gaylord (left) was elected president of the Women's National Press Club in Washington D.C. Eleanor Roosevelt (right), wife of President Franklin D. Roosevelt, was the principal speaker at the dinner where Edith became president. At the time Edith Gaylord was a reporter with the Associated Press in Washington.

42,516 Week Day Average for March

THE DAILY OKLAHOMAN

49,718 Sunday Average for March

VOL. 28. NO. 190. SIXTEEN PAGES—OKLAHOMA CITY, TUESDAY, APRIL 3, 1917. WEATHER FORECAST—Tuesday, fair. Maximum temperature yesterday, 61; Minimum 33. PRICE FIVE CENTS

WILSON ASKS STATE OF WAR

"I AM not now think ing of the loss of the property involved, immense and serious as it is, but only of the wanton and wholesale destruction of the lives of non-combatants, men, women, and children engaged in pursuits which have always been, even in the darkest periods of modern history, deemed innocent and legitimate. Property can be paid for; the lives of peaceful and innocent peaple cannot be. . . Our motive will not be revenge or the victorious assertion of the physical might of the nation, butonly the vindication of right, of human right of which we are only a single champion. . . We will not choose the path of submission and suffer the most sacred rights of our nation and our people to be ignored or violated. The wrongs against which we now array ourselves are not common wrongs; they cut to the very root of human life.——" From President Wilson's address.

Armed American Steamer Aztec Sunk By Submarine

500,000 Volunteers on First Call And Universal Military Service President Demands of Congress

Sixteen Americans Missing From U. S. Vessel Torpedoed Off Brest, France —Wilson Declares We Should Co-operate With Entente Allies To Fullest Extent of Navy, Financial Credits and Ability To Produce Munitions and Supplies.

WASHINGTON, April 2.–President Wilson tonight asked congress to declare a state of war existing between the United States and Germany.

While the news of the submarining of the steamer Azetc, the first American armed ship to sail into the war zone, was being told from mouth to mouth in the capital, the president, appearing before house and senate in joint session, asked congress to recognize and deal with Germany's warfare on America.

The president said war with Germany would involve practical co-operation with the governments now at war with Germany, including liberal, financial credits. He urged the raising of 500,000 men and universal military service.

The president made it clear that no action was being taken against the Austrian government and the other nations allied with Germany.

President's Message To Special Session

The president spoke as follows:

"I have called the congress into extraordinary session because there are serious, very serious choices of policy to be made, and made immediately, which it was neither right nor constitutionally permissible that I should assume the responsibility of making.

"On the 3rd of February last I officially laid before you the extraordinary announcement of the imperial German government that on and after the first day of February it was its purpose to put aside all restraints of law or of humanity and use its submarines to sink every vessel that sought to approach either the ports of Great Britain and Ireland or the western coasts of France or any of the ports controlled by the enemies of Germany within the Mediterranean.

Boat Restrictions Ignored by Germany

"That had seemed to be the object of the German submarine warfare earlier in the war, but since April of last year the imperial government had somewhat restrained the commanders of its undersea craft in conformity with its promise then given to us that passenger boats should not be sunk and that due warning would be given to all other vessels which its submarines might seek to destroy when no resistance was offered or escape attempted and care taken that their crews were given at least a fair chance to save their lives in the open boats. The precautions taken were meager and haphazzard enough, as was proved in distressing instance after instance in the progress of the cruel and unmanly business, but a certain degree of restraint was observed.

Vessels Ruthlessly Destroyed at Sea

The new policy has swept every restriction aside. Vessels of every kind, whatever their flag, their character, their cargo, their destination, their errand, have been ruthlessly sent to the bottom without warning and without thought of help or mercy for those on board, the vessels of friendly neutrals along with those of belligerents. Even hospital ships and ships carrying relief to the sorely bereaved and stricken people of Belgium though the latter were provided with safe conduct through the proscribed areas by the German government itself and were distinguished by unmistakable marks of identity, have been sunk with the same reckless lack of compassion or principle.

Minimum of Right Ignored by Germans

"I was for a little while unable to believe that such things would in fact be done by any government that had hitherto subscribed to the humane practices of civilized nations. International law had its origin in the attempt to set up some law which would be respected an dobserved upon the seas, where no nation had right of dominion and where lay the free highways of the world. By painful stage after stage, has that law been built up with meager enough results, indeed, after all was accomplished that could be accomplished but always with a clear view at least what the heart and conscience of mankind demanded.

"This minimum of right the German government has swept aside under the plea of retaliation and necessity and because it had no weapons which it could use at sea except these which it is impossible to employ as it is employing them without throwing to the winds all scruples of humanity or of respect for the understandings that were supposed to underlie the intercourse of the world.

Money Will Not Pay For Innocent Lives

"I am not now thinking of the loss of the property involved, immense and serious as that is, but only of the wanton and wholesale destruction of the lives of non-combatants, men, women and children engaged in pursuits who have always, even in the darkest periods of modern history, been deemed innocent and legitimate. Property can be paid for; the lives of peaceful and innocent people cannot be.

"The present German submarine warfare against commerce is a warfare against mankind. It is a war against all nations. American ships have been sunk; American lives taken in ways which has stirred us very deeply to learn of, but the ships and people of other neutral and friendly nations have been sunk and overwhelmed in the waters in the same way. There has been no discrimination. The challenge is to all mankind. Each nation must decide for itself how it will meet it. The choice we make for ourselves must be made with a moderation of counsel and a temperateness of judgment besetting our character and our motives as a nation. We must put excited feeling away. Our motive will not be revenge or the victorious assertion of the physical might of the nation, but only the vindication of right, of human right of which we are only a single champion.

Armed Neutrality Is Proved Impracticable

"When I addressed the congress on the 26th of February, last, I thought that it would suffice to assert our neutral rights with arms, our right to use the seas against unlawful interference, our right to keep our people safe against unlawful violence. But armed neutrality it now appears, is impracticable.

"Because submarines are in effect outlaws when used as the German submarines have been used against merchant shipping, it is impossible to defend ships against their attacks as the law of nations has assumed that merchantmen would defend themselves against privateers or cruisers, visible craft giving chase upon the open sea. It is common prudence in such circumstances, grim necessity indeed, to endeavor to destroy them before they have shown their own intention. They must be dealt with upon sight if dealt with at all.

Neutrals Are Denied Right to Use Arms

"The German government denies the right of neutrals to use arms at all within the areas of the sea which it has prescribed, even in the defense of rights which no modern publicist has ever before questioned their right to defend. The intimation is conveyed that the armed guards which we have placed on our merchant ships will be treated as beyond the pale of law and subject to be dealt with as pirates would be. Armed neutrality is ineffectual enough at best; in such circumstances and in the face of such pretensions it is worse than ineffectual; it is likely to produce what it was meant to prevent; it is practically certain to draw us into the war without either the rights or the effectiveness of belligerents.

State of War With Germany Is Asked

"There is one choice we cannot make—we are incapable of making: We will not choose the path of submission and suffer the most sacred rights of our nation and our people to be ignored or violated. The wrongs against which we now array ourselves are not common wrongs; they cut to the very roots of human life.

"With a profound sense of the solemn and even tragical character of the step I am taking and of the grave responsibilities which it involves, but unhesitating obedience to what I deem my constitutional duty, I advise that the congress declare the recent course of the imperial German government to be in fact nothing less than war against the government and people of the United States; that it formally accept the status of belligerent which has been thrust upon it, and that it take immediate steps not only to put the country in a more thorough state of defense, but also to exert all its power and employ all its resources to bring the government of the German empire to terms and end the war.

Country's Resources Must Be Organized

"What this will involce is clear. It will involve the utmost practicable co-operation in counsel and action with the governments now at war with Germany and as incident to that extension to those governments of the most liberal financial credits in order that our resources may so far as possible be added to theirs. It will involve the organization and mobilization of all the material resources of the country to supply the materials of war and serve the incidental needs of the nation in the most abundant and yet the most economical and efficient way possible. It will involve the immediate full equipment of the navy in all respects, but particularly in supplying it with the best means of dealing with the enemy's submarines. It will involve the immediate addition to the armed forces of the United States already provided for by law in case of war at least 500,000 men who should, in my opinion, be chosen upon the principal of universal liability to service, and also the authorization of subsequent additional increments in equal force so

The Act of War

NEW YORK, April 2.—The American steamship Aztec, owned by the Oriental Navigation company, the first armed ship to sail from an American port, was sunk yesterday by a German submarine near the Island of Brest, according to advices received here tonight by the company from the United States consul at Brest, France.

The cable message gave no information as to the fate of the crew.. There were thirty-nine men aboard the vessel. Sixteen of them Americans.

The Aztec sailed from New York March 18 for Havre. She was commanded by Captain Walter O'Brien.. Sixteen members of the crew were native born Americans.

The Oriental Navigation company, owner of the Aztec also owns the Orleans, one of the first American vessels to run successfully Germany's submarine blockade. The Aztec carried a full cargo of food stuffs and general supplies valued at more than $500,000.

Some of the crew were rescued and are being brought into Brest. A number of the men are missing. The steamer was torpedoed at night while a heavy sea was running..

William Graves Sharp, the American ambassador at Paris, was informed by the French government of the torpedoing and immediately cabled the state department.

The Azetc was armed with two five inch guns, one forward and one aft. The crew of naval gunners on board was in command of a warrant officer.

The Aztec, formerly owned by the Pacific Mail Steamship company, was a ship of 3,727 tons gross. and 2,345 tons net. She was built in New Castle, England, 1894. She was 350 feet long with a beam of 43 feet.

WAITING FOR THE ANSWER

E. K. Gaylord president rather than Roy Stafford, who owned a majority of the Company's stock. Gaylord largely had been responsible for the Company's financial success. On the other hand Stafford had shown he could not manage money. Gaylord later recalled that Stafford liked to gamble. Angered by the apparent vote of no confidence, Stafford offered to sell his share in the Company or buy out the other stockholders. He admitted, however, that he doubted if he could get a bank loan to raise the money. In response, Gaylord and the other stockholders offered to buy Stafford's interest for $300,000. Stafford agreed, and when the transaction was completed, Gaylord was elected president. Stafford took his proceeds and entered the oil business.

By the time E. K. Gaylord became president of The Oklahoma Publishing Co., his close associates recognized his ability to pick good employees, and trust them. Then too, he cared about his employees and their welfare. One associate said Gaylord's "steel spring constitution" was amazing, and he had a wide range of interests including a fascination with Washington D.C. That year, 1918, Gaylord decided his papers needed a news bureau in the nation's capital. The bureau, which continues today, is responsible for assembling rosters listing how members of the Oklahoma congressional delegation votes on important bills, compiling lists of federal grants to Oklahoma, and covering Washington stories that affect the lives, welfare and interests of Oklahomans. E. K. Gaylord's intense interest in and curiosity about Washington was even greater than that of most of his papers' editors when it was started.

Since 1918 various journalists from Oklahoma have headed the bureau, beginning with Otis Sullivant and later Ray Parr. Both spent January to the end of the Congressional session in Washington and then returned to Oklahoma City. By the time Cullen Johnson became bureau chief during the 1930s, the demands of the job had increased, and he made his home in Washington during the four years he spent as bureau chief. Johnson was followed by Roy Stewart, and next came Al Cromley, who served as bureau chief from 1953 to 1987. Cromley recalled that E. K. Gaylord occasionally brought him back to Oklahoma to "purge me of 'Potomac Fever.'" He remembered that on one occasion he ran across E. K. Gaylord in the elevator of *The Oklahoman* building. Gaylord introduced Cromley to two or three other persons there. "This is our man in Washington, Allan Cromley. He keeps track of what's going on and writes up our congressional delegation." Cromley added, "Mr. Gaylord paused, chuckled, and amended his statement. 'No, he writes them DOWN.'" When Cromley retired, Ed Kelley headed the bureau until 1990 when he returned to *The Oklahoman* as managing editor. Kelley was followed by Chris Casteel.

✳

As World War I ended in 1918, the circulation of *The Oklahoman* topped 61,000, and on November 7 of that year the *Oklahoma City News,* owned by the Scripps-Howard chain, hit the streets with an Extra announcing that World War I was over, that an Armistice had been signed. The story was credited to United Press, a news service to which The Oklahoma Publishing Co. did not subscribe. Editors at *The Oklahoman* checked the Associated Press wire and there was no word about an armistice. Gaylord came into the newsroom with a copy of the competition's Extra and asked, "Has the AP anything on this?" He was told no. But an editor at *The*

OPPOSITE
The front page of the April 3, 1917, issue of
The Daily Oklahoman.

The United War Work campaign starts this morning, and every community, city and county in Oklahoma is expected to go over its quota

THE United War Work campaign is the nation's big brother movement for the soldiers. Your subscription next week will help make some fighter happy. Be ready to give your utmost.

THE DAILY OKLAHOMAN

63,339 Net Paid Daily in October
69,695 Net Paid Sunday in October

Entered at the Oklahoma, Oklahoma, postoffice as second class mail under the Act of March 3, 1879.

VOL. 30. NO. 47. TWELVE PAGES—OKLAHOMA CITY, MONDAY, NOVEMBER 11, 1918. WEATHER FORECAST—Monday fair and warmer. Maximum temperature yesterday, 64; minimum, 38. PRICE FIVE CENTS Price $7.50 a Year. Published Daily.

WHOLE OF GERMANY SWEPT BY REVOLUTION AS HOUR OF DECISION ON ARMISTICE NEARS

Former Kaiser And Crown Prince Flee Over Dutch Border

William Hohenzollern and Eldest Son Cross Frontier as Fugitives while German Nation Is in Throes of Revolution and Famine and Anarchy Stalk Through Land.

LONDON, Nov. 10.—(Midnight.)—Both the former German emperor and his eldest son, Frederick William, crossed the Dutch frontier Sunday morning, according to advices from The Hague.

WASHINGTON, Nov. 10.—William Hohenzollern has arrived in Holland and is proceeding to the town of Desteeg, near Utrecht, according to a dispatch received by the American army general staff today from The Hague.

The message said: "Press reports state that the kaiser arrived this morning in Maastright, Holland, and is proceeding to Middachtan Castle in the town of Desteeg, near Utrecht."

BASEL, Switz., Nov. 10.—(Havas.)—Wilhelm II, the reigning king of the monarchy of Wurttemberg, abdicated on Friday night.

By the Associated Press.

BERLIN, Saturday, Nov. 9.—(German wireless to London, Nov. 10, 12:56 p. m.)—The German people's government has been instituted in the greater part of Berlin. The garrison has gone over to the government

The workmen's and soldiers' council has declared a general strike. Troops and machine guns have been placed at the disposal of the council.

COPENHAGEN, Nov. 10.—(8:15 a. m.)—Berlin was occupied by forces of the soldiers' and workmen's council on Saturday afternoon, according to a Wolff Bureau report received here.

LONDON, Nov. 10.—(8:57 a. m.)—Severe fighting took place in Berlin between 6 and 8 o'clock last night and a violent cannonade was heard from the heart of the city. The revolution is in full swing in Berlin and the Red forces occupy the greater part of the German capital, according to a Copenhagen dispatch to The Exchange Telegraph company quoting Berlin advices sent from there at 3 o'clock this morning.

Guards Patrol City.

Many persons were killed and wounded before the officers surrendered. The Red forces are in control and have restored order. Strong guards are marching through the streets.

The crown prince's palace has been seized by the revolutionists. The people are shouting "Long live the republic," and are singing the "Marseillias."

When revolutionary soldiers attempted to enter a building in which they supposed a number of officers were concealed shots were fired from the windows. The Reds then began shelling the building.

Other Buildings Under Fire.

When the cannonade began the people thought the Reichsbank was being bombarded and thousands rushed to the square in front of the crown prince's palace. It was later determined that other buildings were under fire.

By The Associated Press.

The German people, for a generation the obedient and submissive servants of their war lords, for more than four years his pliant instruments in ravaging the world, have spoken a new word and the old Germany is gone.

From the confused, sometimes conflicting and often delayed advices from Germany in the last two days, it has now become apparent that William, emperor and king, has been stripped of his power. He is now plain William Hohenzollern, a fugitive in Holland. With his fall topples into ruin William's mad design to rule the world.

Situation in Germany Obscure.

Little is known today of the situation in Germany, for that country is in the first days of its new adventure. It is not clear whether the old regime has been permanently dislodged or whether the new authorities, with the unscrupulous adroitness which has long marked German politics, are merely sacrificing the chief figureheads of kaiserism in the hope of obtaining an easier peace. It appears probable that no one in Germany knows and that it is still to be determined which of the contending elements will gain the upper hand.

Revolution is spreading rapidly and from the fact that a socialist is now chancellor, it may be gathered that the object of the revolution is not merely

(Continued on Page 6, Column 3.)

EBERT, LEADER OF SOCIALISTS, SUCCEEDS MAX

New Chancellor Says Revolutionary Government Is in Agreement With Various Parties.

MINISTRY OF WAR IN HANDS OF REDS

Whatever Happens in Germany in No Wise Can Alter Armistice Terms, Washington View.

COPENHAGEN, Nov. 10.—(8:30 a. m.)—Friedrich Ebert, the socialist leader, has been appointed imperial chancellor. He has issued a proclamation saying that he plans to form a people's government which will endeavor to bring about speedy peace.

Chancellor Ebert said he would endeavor to fortify the freedom which the people had won. He begged support in the hard work ahead and appealed for co-operation in the country and cities in the problem of provisioning.

Herr Ebert in his proclamation said that Prince Maximilian of Baden, had transferred the chancellorship to him, all the secretaries of state having given their consent. The new government, he added, would be in agreement with the various parties.

ZURICH, Switzerland, Nov. 10.—Because of the troubles in the interior of Germany, Prince Maximilian of Baden, and all the bourgeoisie ministers have resigned, says a dispatch from Berlin. Friedrich Ebert, the German socialist leader, has been definitely recognized as chancellor.

COPENHAGEN, Nov. 10.—8:43 a. m.)—It is officially announced from Berlin that the war ministry has placed itself at the disposal of Friedrich Ebert, the socialist leader, whose appointment as imperial chancellor was forecast yesterday by the decree of Prince Maximilian. The action was for the purpose of assuring the provisioning of the army and assisting in the solution of demobilization problems.

No Modification of Armistice Terms

WASHINGTON, Nov. 9.—The tremendous news from Germany that the kaiser had decided to abdicate was heard in Washington with scarcely more than a ripple of interest.

Everywhere the question was asked "has the armistice been signed?" So far as the American government knew late tonight it had not been signed, and the prevailing belief was that the German answer to Marshal Foch could not be expected before tomorrow.

Abdication Was Expected.

To members of the government and diplomats who a few short weeks ago would have been amazed and gratified beyond belief, the announcement that William II had bowed before the will of the world, was accepted as a thing to be expected. It was accepted as one

(Continued on Page 6, Column 7.)

UNITED WAR WORK DRIVE FOR FUNDS TO START TODAY

State Thoroughly Covered By Efficient Staff of Earnest Workers.

OKLAHOMA'S QUOTA FIXED AT $1,700,000

Seven Big Organizations Combine Efforts to Raise Huge Sum.

Intensive work will start this morning when the highly organized machinery of the United War Work campaign committee is set into motion to raise Oklahoma's quota, assessed by the national committee, of approximately $1,700,000 for the relief of our fighting men, both at home and abroad, through the seven organizations comprising the United War Workers.

Teams will start in every section of the state for their goals. The school district has been selected as the basis of assessment. The organization is complete in every county. The three or four counties that had not reported Friday and Saturday wired E. W. Marland, state chairman, yesterday that their quotas had been accepted.

Put on Cash Basis.

Many counties, wishing to avoid the after work of making collections, have gone on a cash basis. The plan of the national committee is to make the subscription due in three payments. No cash will be required with the subscription in Oklahoma City. City Chairman Leon Levy urges, however, that as many cash payments as possible be secured by the workers.

Apparently the county chairmen are forgetting their actual quotas. All who have reported have accepted their quotas with a 50 percent addition. E. W. Marland, state chairman, insists that nothing short of $2,000,000 or $2,500,000 will be acceptable to him as a final report.

Tulsa Quota Raised.

Mr. Marland returned yesterday from Tulsa and Pawhuska. He declared that he had personally asked that some quotas made by the Tulsa committee be raised. Mr. Marland reported that he had secured five subscriptions for $10,000 and ten for $5,000 while in Tulsa.

"The people in some sections of Oklahoma have never learned what it means to give," Mr. Marland said yesterday. "Now they are going to have a chance to learn to pay. This is not a matter of giving, but one of paying. I want it pounded home to every man in the state that he owes a debt, a debt incurred by the spilling of blood—the blood of our heroes who have died.

"I have been drafted for the work I am doing. I shall accept no excuse from any man able to pay. I shall consider myself slack in my duty if I per-

(Continue don Page 10, Column 5.)

President Chosen By Polish State

AMSTERDAM, Saturday, Nov. 9.—A message from Cracow announces the formation of a Polish republic under the presidency of Deputy Daszynski.

AMSTERDAM, Nov. 10.—Professor Lammasch, the Austrian premier, has received official notification, says a dispatch from Vienna, that Poland has assumed sovereignty over Galicia.

Galicia is a crown land of Austria-Hungary north of the Carpathians. It has an area of 30,307 square miles and in normal times had a population of some 7,000,000.

TWO AMERICAN ARMIES ATTACK ON WIDE FRONT

Pershing's Troops Advance On Seventy-one Mile Line From Moselle to the Meuse.

YANKS TAKE STENAY AFTER BITTER FIGHT

British Cross Belgian Frontier South of Sambre to Within Gunfire of Brussels.

WITH THE AMERICAN FORCES ON THE MEUSE FRONT, Nov. 10.—(7:30 p. m.)—The First and second American armies, in their attacks today, extending along the Moselle and the Meuse, advanced on a front of approximately 115 kilometers, (seventy-one and a half miles.

By The Associated Press.

WITH THE AMERICAN FORCES ON THE LORRAINE FRONT, Nov. 10.—(5:40 p. m.)—The Second American army this morning launched its initial attack in Lorraine. Its objectives were limited. The villages of St. Hilaire and Marcheville were captured as also were a number of woods.

Stenay Falls To Americans

By The Associated Press.

WITH THE AMERICAN FORCES ON THE MEUSE FRONT, Nov. 10.—(6 p. m.)—General Pershing's troops this afternoon captured Stenay, on the east bank of the Meuse, notwithstanding terrific opposition.

Stenay, which was strongly fortified was taken in an attack from the south. The Americans swept forward against streams of machine gun bullets and artillery fire fro mthe hills northeast of Stenay.

The entire district in the region of Stenay was flooded by the Germans who dammed the canal and rivers. The Americans crossing the river Meuse from below took tSenay in a great northward push.

LONDON, Nov. 10.—The British have crossed the Franco-Belgian frontier south of the Sambre river, Field Marshal Haig reports from headquarters tonight. They have advanced four miles east of Renaix, bringing them within gunfire of Brussels.

Gouraud Enters Sedan.

By The Associated Press.

WITH THE FRENCH ARMY IN FRANCE, Nov. 10.—The French General Gouraud made his official entry into Sedan at 2 o'clock this afternoon.

Allies in Hot Pursuit of Foe

LONDON, Nov. 10.—Field Marshal Haig's forces are closely following up the retreating Germans along the entire front in Flanders. The official statement issued today by the war office announces that the British troops have occupied Faubourg de Bertaimont, on the southern outskirts of Mons, Belgium.

PARIS, Nov. 10.—French troops this morning renewed their pursuit of the Germans. The French official statement issued today says the retreat of the enemy is becoming more and more precipitate. Everywhere

(Continued o.) Pag 10, Column 7.)

Extension of Time Is Possible if Delay Seems Unavoidable

Paris Paper Says That 72 Hours of Grace Might Be Prolonged Owing to Courier's Necessary Slowness in Reaching Headquarters; Revolt Not Expected to Prevent Acceptance.

The acceptance of the armistice terms prepared by the allies and submitted by Marshal Foch must be made by Germany before 11 o'clock this morning, or 5 o'clock a. m., Oklahoma City time.

PARIS, Nov. 10.—(Havas.)—The German courier from the meeting place of the armistice negotiations arrived at the German grand headquarters at 10 o'clock this morning, according to an official statement issued here.

PARIS, Nov. 10.—(5:05 p. m.)—"It is possible," says the Temps, after recording the arrival of the German courier at Spa with the armistice conditions at 10 o'clock this morning, "that owing to this delay, owing to material circumstances, the seventy-two hours' grace may be prolonged. Such prolongation may be necessary through the events which are occupying Germany."

LONDON, Nov. 9.—(Saturday.)—The German armistice terms, the Daily Express says it understands, are even more stringent than those forecast October 31. Germany will be absolutely deprived, the newspaper adds, from further military power or action on land and sea and in the air.

Revolt Not Expected To Prevent Acceptance

WASHINGTON, Nov. 10.—Unless a revolutionary government in Germany definitely repudiates the authority of the German armistice commissioners now within the allied lines, the belief here is that the revolt spreading through the enemy country will not prevent General Foch from accepting the signatures of the envoys and proceeding to put the armistice conditions into effect.

Revolution for Peace.

According to official information, the armistiee delegation came with full powers and is authorized to sign terms, although it elected to send a courier back to grand headquarters before acting. Moreover, the object of the revolution is assumed to be peace, and since signing of the armistice is the shortest road to immediate peace it is thought the revolutionaries will not seek to interfere.

If there should be a repudiation of the envoys, or if what is happening in Berlin should delay an answer beyond the time allowed by Marshal Foch, 11 o'clock tomorrow morning, the American and allied armies would continue their advance and hostilities probably would end only through the surrender of individual military units on the field.

Capital Without Official News.

Washington had no official information early today of the events transpiring in Europe. President Wilson read the press dispatches and then went to church as usual. He was there when the news came from Paris that the courier of the German armistice envoys had been so delayed that he did not arrive at German great headquarters until 10 o'clock this morning.

German Wireless Explains Delay.

A wireless dispatch from the German Nauen station picked up by the American naval towers says it has been officially explained in Berlin that the courier bearing the armistice terms was delayed in crossing the lines by an explosion on the German side, but that the terms could be expected at any hour. The message follows:

"It has been officially reported concerning the delay in transmission of the armistice terms:

"The courier commissioned to bring armistice conditions sent in the night of the ninth of November by wireless from Eiffel tower made (?) statement that he could not pass the lines since Germans had not ceased firing. He was probably led to this statement by circumstances that on German side an ammunition depot had caught on fire and was blown up with continuous detonations. Courier had the circumstances explained to him by wireless and received directions immediately to cross the line. Arrival of armistice terms in Berlin can be expected at any hour."

Fire Destroys Machine Shops.

GULFPORT, Miss., Nov. 10.—Fire today destroyed the saw mill and machine shops of the Ingram-Day Lumber company at Lyman, Miss. The estimated loss is $200,000.

Bill Shivered And Said "It May Be For the Good Of Germany," Then Signed

LONDON, Nov. 10.—(2:04 p. m.)—Emperor William signed a letter of abdication Saturday morning at the German grand headquarters in the presence of Crown Prince Frederick William and Field Marshal Hindenburg, according to a dispatch from Amsterdam to the Exchange Telegraph company.

The German crown prince signed his renunciation to the throne shortly afterward.

It is believed that King Ludwig of Bavaria, and King Frederick August of Saxony, also have abdicated.

The former kaiser and the former crown prince were expected to take leave of their troops on Saturday, but nothing has been settled regarding their future movements.

Before placing his signature to the document an urgent message from Philipp Scheidemann, who was a socialist member without portfolio in the imperial cabinet, was handed to the emperor. He read it with a shiver. Then he signed the paper saying:

"It may be for the good of Germany."

The emperor was deeply moved. He consented to sign the document only when he received the news of the latest events in the empire.

Serious food difficulties are expected in Germany owing to the stoppage of trains. The council of the regency will take the most drastic steps to re-establish order

Seven Great Bodies Joined in United War Work Drive

Pay Your Debt

Pay Your Debt

These symbols are the emblems of the seven organizations whose campaigns for funds are joined in the United War Work campaign. Reading from left to right, the shields represent the Y. M. C. A., the American Library Association, the War Camp Community Service, the Salvation Army, the National Catholic War Council, the Jewish Welfare Board, and the Y. W. C. A. You can pay a portion of your debt to the American expeditionary force by supporting this campaign to the limit of your ability.

It was a clear day on January 19, 1919, when this photograph was made from an airplane flying out of Post Field at Fort Sill. The Oklahoma Publishing Co. building (bottom, right of center) was located at Northwest Fourth and Broadway. The view looks east-northeast.

OPPOSITE
The front page of the November 11, 1918, issue of *The Oklahoman.*

Oklahoman said he had asked the AP to verify the story.

By the time *The Oklahoman's* first edition hit the streets of Oklahoma City late that night, the Associated Press had explained the hoax. Roy Howard of the United Press had sent a cable reporting the Armistice even before German envoys had crossed the border into France to negotiate. The actual Armistice was signed four days later on November 11. *The Oklahoman* gained credibility for not borrowing the United Press story, while the *Oklahoma City News* suffered as it tried to justify and explain the fake Armistice story to its readers.

In late May 1919, E. K. Gaylord was with his wife Inez and daughter Edith

in Colorado, where the family was building a summer cottage at Estes Park, about 70 miles northwest of Denver. Although Mrs. Gaylord was expecting another child, the birth was not expected for several days. When this changed, her husband rushed her to Mercy Hospital in Denver. There, on May 28, 1919, Edward Lewis Gaylord was born. As he later recalled, "I arrived a little early and mother did not have time to return to Oklahoma." Soon after the family returned to Oklahoma City, Edward's older sister Edith, more than three years older, rushed up to a friend who came to visit her mother to tell the news. "The preacher is coming. We're going to advertise my baby brother," she recalled in 1994.

Chapter Six

THE ROARING '20S

As the 1920s began, Oklahoma City had a population of 91,295, and the state's was 2,028,283. The year 1920 saw the birth of a third child to Edward K. and Inez Gaylord. She was named Virginia. Now the mother of five grown children, she lives at Cashiers, N.C. The year she was born, women in Oklahoma gained the right to vote. Although Oklahoma had granted women full suffrage in 1918, the state's legislature did not ratify the 19th Amendment to the U.S. Constitution until 1920. *The Oklahoman* and *Times* gave it much coverage The papers provided extensive coverage of the visit by Gen. John Joseph Pershing, who had led American troops to triumph in World War I, when he visited Oklahoma City on February 10, 1920. Mayor Walter Dean declared a holiday and ordered every soldier in Oklahoma City to wear his uniform. The city was under martial law for the day.

During the decade of the '20s, *The Oklahoman* had its "first" in newspaper technology. It pioneered a mechanical process for transferring metal type to papier-mâché, an important step on the way to a curved press plate to speed up the production of newspapers. *The Oklahoman* was the city's only morning newspaper while the *Times,* its evening paper, was holding it own against the *Oklahoma City News,* owned by the Scripps-McRae chain. Owning and operating both a morning and evening paper gave The Oklahoma Publishing Co. an advantage over the afternoon only *News.*

The Oklahoman and *Times* also devoted much space reporting on the Supreme Court's decision in the Red River cases, which gave Oklahoma title to the bed of the river. The decision was based upon the fact the Spanish had long considered the south bank of the stream as its border. This did not change when the Republic of Texas was formed in 1836. During 1920, *The Oklahoman* and *Times* also provided extensive coverage of the election of Republican Warren G. Harding as president, the beginning of a period of unusual prosperity for U.S. industry, and then Harding's sudden death from a stroke in San Francisco. The papers also reported on the shocking political scandals of Harding's administration including Teapot Dome that surfaced following his death. Albert B. Fall, Harding's Secretary of Interior, secretly leased federal oil reserves in Wyoming and California to private oil companies.

During the early years of the decade, the papers reported the elections of the state's first two Republican U.S. senators, John W. Harreld in 1920, and William B. Pine in 1924. The Republican landslide in Oklahoma pushed Jake Hamon, an Ardmore oil millionaire and GOP national committeeman, into the news. Before Hamon could enjoy his new power, however, he was shot and killed in an Ardmore hotel, supposedly by a former secretary who then disappeared. The story caused a sensation across the state and *The Oklahoman* gave it much coverage. The former secretary, Clara Smith, was finally located in Mexico and returned to Ardmore to face trial in Hamon's death. *The Oklahoman's* Edith Johnson wrote daily page one stories based on interviews with the accused woman. When the case went to the jury, Smith was freed after 30 minutes of deliberation.

Jack C. Walton was elected the fifth governor of Oklahoma in 1922 over the opposition of *The Oklahoman* and *Times*. Walton had served as Commissioner of Public Works and then as Mayor of Oklahoma City before running for governor. As Mayor, Walton had declared Oklahoma City police records to be "secret" after *The Oklahoman* criticized police for refusing to take action against a patrolman who, in firing at a fleeing traffic offender, killed an innocent pedestrian. *The Oklahoman* brought legal action and forced police to open what are public records.

When Walton ran for governor, the papers opposed him, pointing out that he had been given a mansion by an oilman. They also labeled Walton as an opportunist who had embraced the Farm-Labor Reconstruction League, a socialist inspired and backed organization. During the campaign Walton threatened to have his bodyguards plant dynamite under the building housing The Oklahoma Publishing Co. The newspapers kept printing the facts. *"The Oklahoman* still believes Walton's leadership is not the best leadership," was the only comment made by the paper just before the election.

But Walton was elected, and as he had promised Oklahomans, he held a great barbecue which he labeled "the greatest celebration ever." It started with a parade that was 16 miles long and included workers, farmers, nearly 20 bands, and the entire student body of the University of Oklahoma. The parade ended at the Oklahoma City fair grounds where country music entertainers, half a hundred jazz bands and ten dance orchestras provided entertainment. As many as 300,000 people attended, and at the barbecue they reportedly consumed 289 cows, 30 sheep, 70 hogs, 3,540 rabbits, 4,000 chickens, 34 ducks, 110 turkeys, 25 squirrels, 15 deer, 135 possums, and 3 bears. Walton had arranged for 42 cases of whiskey for the celebrants, but they were seized by federal agents before the bottles were distributed. As governor, Walton looked at the office as a patronage distribution center and began tampering with the University of Oklahoma and the A & M College (now Oklahoma State University) at Stillwater making them places where he could give jobs as rewards to his friends.

When a grand jury in Oklahoma City prepared to investigate the governor's office, Walton placed the entire state under martial law on September 15, 1923. To prevent the grand jury from meeting, the Oklahoma National Guard set up a battery of 30-caliber machine guns that were trained on the old Oklahoma County courthouse. Other newspapers across the state joined *The Oklahoman* and *Times* in demanding the legislature impeach Governor Walton, but on orders from the governor, the Oklahoma National Guard, with bayonets fixed, stood guard at the doors of the House and Senate chambers at the capitol causing the lawmakers to disperse.

Trying to divert attention, Walton called a special session of the legislature on October 11 to consider his request to "unmask the Klan and destroy its power." The Klan, which had been revived in southern states, had moved into Oklahoma and burned crosses in Oklahoma City, Tulsa and Enid. The legislature refused to consider Walton's request and recessed. But it met again on October 17. The House formulated 21 charges against the governor and voted for impeachment. Six days later Walton was removed from office and Lt. Governor Martin E. Trapp became governor. In the aftermath, Victor Harlow, who published a political paper called *Harlow's Weekly,* wrote early in 1925 that "breaking the power of Walton would have been impossible had it not been for the persistent and consistent opposition of E. K. Gaylord."

In 1923, The Oklahoma Publishing Co. helped to organize the first community chest, which began with a first-year budget of $216,990. Since then it has been known under many names including United Fund, the Red Feather Campaign, the United Appeal, and the United Way of Greater Oklahoma. Now called the United Way of Metro Oklahoma City, the organization benefits 60 separate agencies in the city and receives millions in contributions.

The year 1924 saw The Oklahoma Publishing Co. battle for circulation among readers in rural areas. Thirteen years earlier, Gaylord had changed the name of the *Weekly Oklahoman* to the *Oklahoma Farmer-Stockman* and made it a monthly farm paper. By 1924, it was competing head-on against *The Oklahoma Farmer* published by Arthur Capper, the well-known Kansas publisher and politician. Determined to achieve primacy in the agricultural field, Gaylord bought Capper's paper and merged it with the *Oklahoma Farmer-Stockman*. Within a decade the monthly became a regional publication and gained so much circulation in Oklahoma, Texas and Kansas that it was simply renamed the *Farmer-Stockman*.

Late in 1924, with the approval of the Governor and the County Attorney at McAlester, *The Oklahoman* sent reporter Dorothy Dayton Jones to the state penitentiary to see what life was like for a woman behind bars. Even the warden did not know she was a reporter. *The Oklahoman* had heard that conditions in the women's ward located in the basement of the main prison were wretched. Privacy was beyond price and the ward was described as the "Black Hole of Calcutta." When the reporter left the prison on January 17, 1925, she wrote her story which ran serially in the papers for several weeks while the legislature was in session. Lawmakers acted and a new women's ward was established at the state penitentiary.

The Oklahoman and *Times* crusaded successfully in 1926 for the city manager form of government in Oklahoma City. Voters approved the change by a 3 to 1 margin. In April 1927, E. M. Fry became Oklahoma City's first city manager and served until April 1931.

In 1926 E. K. Gaylord's doctor told him he needed to get out-of-doors more for his health. Gaylord loved to work and maintained a strenuous schedule. He would arrive at the office at 8 A.M., sometimes after a breakfast meeting, preside over an editorial conference at 9 A.M., then meet with department heads before dictating correspondence and meeting with anyone who wanted to see him. He would then rush out for a community meeting or luncheon, where he would keep up on city, county and state affairs. He would then return to the office and complete the day's business.

After his doctor told Gaylord to spend more time outside, he established the Gaylord Golden Guernsey Dairy in 1930 on 514 acres of land he purchased in 1928 north of where Lake Hefner stands today. His afternoon

E. K. Gaylord established the Gaylord Golden Guernsey Dairy in 1930 after his doctor told him to spend more time outdoors.

schedule then changed. After completing the day's business at the paper, Gaylord would often drive to his dairy farm in mid-afternoon and walk around checking on his cattle and the dairy which provided regular milk delivery in Oklahoma City. Being out-of-doors improved his health. In time, he helped to develop methods and procedures in animal health and milk production that gained him national recognition.

Many years later Guernsey milk deliveries ceased when other local non-Guernsey dairies persuaded the city council to pass an ordinance forbidding dairies located outside Oklahoma City from delivering milk inside the city limits. Promptly, Gaylord wrote his regular Guernsey milk customers that if they would bring their empty milk bottles to the dairy to be sterilized, the dairy would sell them milk on the spot. Many customers did just that. E. K. Gaylord operated the farm until December 1971. He sold the land to developers in 1972, a few years before his death.

In 1927, *The Oklahoman* and *Times* strongly supported a $10 million bond issue in Oklahoma City to remove the Rock Island railroad tracks in the center of downtown. Voters approved the measure which also financed new bridges across the North Canadian River at Robinson Ave. and at Exchange Ave.

In 1928, E. K. Gaylord invested in the infant business of radio broadcasting. Radio had been used for point-to-point communication before World War I. The practice of broadcasting to wide audiences began in earnest in the early 1920s. Two Oklahoma City radio buffs, H. S. "Dick" Richards and Earl C. Hull, built a radio transmitter in 1921 in a garage behind Hull's home in the Westwood addition south of Exchange Avenue. At the time there were less than 30 radio receivers in Oklahoma City. Using the call-letters 5XT, assigned by the Department of Commerce, their little station broadcast rather crude programs a few hours each week. Richards and Hull hoped

This is the radio transmission room in 1921 at 5XT radio established by H.S. "Dick" Richards and Earl C. Hull in a garage behind Hull's home in the Westwood addition not far from old Rotary Park in Oklahoma City. On March 16, 1922, the station was licensed by the Department of Commerce and given the call-letters WKY. The station was purchased by The Oklahoma Publishing Co. in 1928.

The entire Oklahoma City fire department is reportedly shown in this photo dated 1923. (Courtesy Oklahoma City Chamber of Commerce)

to make money, not from broadcasting but from manufacturing and selling radio receivers.

E. K. Gaylord, fascinated throughout his life with new inventions and scientific developments, helped the little station remain on the air. At the time, however, Gaylord was not yet convinced that radio could be a profitable business. Radio was still a novelty. As such he recognized that the new medium was capturing the hearts and minds of Americans, but would it last? *The Oklahoman* described the station as "The Oklahoman's Radio Service" and reported almost daily on what programs were to be broadcast over 5XT. The newspaper had an informal arrangement whereby it provided publicity and helped to arrange talent for the broadcasts.

The growth of radio soon resulted in new government licensing requirements. On March 16, 1922, Richards and Hull obtained a commercial license from the Department of Commerce "to transmit entertainment, police, crop and weather reports" using a homemade 100 watt transmitter. The station was assigned the call letters WKY and broadcast on weekdays from noon to 1 P.M., and from 7:30 to 9:30 P.M. On Sundays it was on the air from 3 to 4 P.M. and from 7:30 to 9:30 P.M. But there were few commercials on WKY. Richards and Hull were not salesmen. The station was able to remain on the air because of the profit they made selling radio receivers, the help it received from *The Oklahoman,* and funds from other firms who manufactured radio receivers. One strong supporter was Harrison Smith, who represented Atwater Kent, a company that produced low-cost radio receivers that were easy to operate.

In 1925, E. K. Gaylord decided that *The Oklahoman* should sponsor an "Oklahoman Radio Fair" featuring various dealers of radio receivers and other businesses that purchased booth space in the auditorium of the Baptist Tabernacle. Perhaps because of WKY's shaky financial situation, Gaylord hired Dudley Shaw, owner and operator of KFJF (now KOMA), to construct a 500-watt radio station at the fair site. The station broadcast nightly programs during the week-long event which included national and local entertainers and frequent mention of the sponsors, those persons who had purchased booth space. The fair was a great success and provided E. K. Gaylord with the opportunity to explore the business of broadcasting.

Meantime Richards and Hull struggled to keep WKY on the air, but their business of manufacturing radio receivers was suffering because major manufacturers began turning out sets faster and cheaper. Finally, late in 1925, they were bankrupt. Richards left the radio business, but Hull continued to keep WKY on-the-air by selling shares of the station to radio dealers in Oklahoma City. The dealers paid Hull a small salary to keep the station broadcasting, but the financial drain became too much. The radio dealers decided to get out. Led by Harrison Smith, they approached E. K. Gaylord and offered to sell him WKY for $5,000. Even though Gaylord knew WDAF in Kansas City, Missouri, was owned and operated by the *Kansas City Star*, and that a few other radio stations across the nation were owned by newspapers, he refused. By 1928, however, radio

was becoming a profitable business nationally. In July, while Gaylord was vacationing in Europe, Harrison Smith called an official of The Oklahoma Publishing Co. and reportedly said, "If you're not going to buy the station for $5,000, we're going to give it to Scripps-Howard," the newspaper group that owned the *Oklahoma News*. That day officials at The Oklahoma Publishing Co. sent a cablegram to Gaylord in Paris advising him what Smith had said and added, "INDIAN TERRITORY ILLUMINATING OIL CO. NUMBER ONE WENT THROUGH THIRD SAND YESTERDAY. BURDETTE BLUE SAYS BIG WELL CERTAIN AND OIL FIELD IN OKLAHOMA CITY IS DEFINITE." The next day Gaylord cabled his office to buy WKY radio.

The Oklahoman and *Times* then told their readers that The Oklahoma Publishing Co. had purchased WKY radio and would acquire new broadcasting equipment, ask the Federal Radio Commission for a new broadcast frequency, and boost the station's power with a new 1,000-watt transmitter purchased from RCA. The transmitter would be located on the southern edge of Oklahoma City, and new studios would be set up in Plaza Court by the fall 1928. The formal opening of the new WKY was set for November 11, 1928, but the station went on the air five days earlier to carry the presidential election returns as Herbert Hoover swept Al Smith aside in a Republican landslide. The election put Oklahoma in the GOP column for the second time since territorial days. When WKY had its formal opening on November 11, The Oklahoma Publishing Co. made the following pledge:

> *The ambition of the management of the new station is to be the best in the country. No claptrap or shoddy will be on WKY's programs.*

The Illinois legislature has voted against state enforcement of prohibition, but it is not believed residents of Chicago will notice an appreciable difference

The Weather

SUNDAY: Cloudy, local rains

THE DAILY OKLAHOMAN

Daily April Paid Circulation
152,263
Morning 79,866 Evening 72,397
Sunday 93,628

Entered at the Oklahoma City, Oklahoma, postoffice as second class mail matter under the act of March 3, 1879.

VOL. 35. NO. 131. (AP) MEANS ASSOCIATED PRESS SIXTY-FOUR PAGES—OKLAHOMA CITY, SUNDAY, MAY 22, 1927. (AP) MEANS ASSOCIATED PRESS

Price: City and Suburban, Daily, 5c; Sunday, 10c; Month, 65c; Year, $7.10. Outside, Month, 85c; Year, $10.

NEW YORK, PARIS LINKED BY AIR

★ ★

Lindbergh Lands Safely After Spanning Atlantic

Index

U. S. CAPITOL IN NOISY JUBILEE FOR LINDBERGH

Officials, Led by President Coolidge, Send Cables Of Congratulation.

SORROW FOR FRANCE

Note of Sadness Sounded Over Loss of Nungesser And Coli.

WASHINGTON, May 21.—(AP)—Charles Lindbergh's history-making flight to France, Saturday, thrilled Washington out of its traditional stolidity.

The thought of this young airman, winging his way alone through the darkness of the night, over deserted ocean waters, and depending for his life on his own skill and courage, aroused the interest and touched the imagination of the capital as few things have done in the past.

Loneliness Captures Fancy

There had been the army's world-circling flight, the hop of the NC-4 across the Atlantic, the trans-Atlantic voyage of the Los Angeles, and other feats of aviation which had brought admiration and praise from Washington, but the adventuresome solitary attempt of Lindbergh forced the young flyer's personality into the picture and made his flight a test wherein a young sportsman staked everything in the face of the forebodings of experts. That appealed to the popular fancy.

Everybody in Washington "pulled" for Lindbergh steadily and hopefully, and as the day wore along, confidently. When the news of his arrival at Paris was flashed over the city, there was a spontaneous, city-wide expression of gratification. Officials, led by President Coolidge sent their congratulations and praise speeding over the cables to the daring aviator.

Friday, when Lindbergh made his sensational hop-off, the word high and low was "I hope he makes it." Saturday, as his progress was charted, the admiration and amazement of the city grew in direct ratio to his approach of Paris and exploded as he landed with the jubilant cry: "He made it."

Plane Makes Announcement

An airplane winged up from Bolling field, bearing streamers which told the people that Lindbergh had made a safe passage. Cheers went up from crowds on the streets, automobile horns were honked, and the city's workers went home glowing with pride.

All through the messages of congratulations sent to France there ran, however, a note of sorrow over the failure of the Nungesser-Coli flight and President Coolidge, as well as others, made sympathetic reference to the French fliers in their cablegrams.

To Washington the day was one of suspense which recalled the pre-Armistice days. Thousands called newspaper offices for information of Lindbergh's progress. Government departments were abuzz with excitement, army and navy officers threw their whole souls into the job of furnishing the flier with moral support. Not much else was talked about at the capital, and from the attitude of the people on the street, little would have been needed to send the city into one of its infrequent impromptu celebrations.

No Thought For Future

Not a great deal of consideration was given to the practical value of Lindbergh's feat in furthering commercial aviation. That will be figured out later. The thing Saturday was that this young man had flown alone from New York to Paris without a stop, and that was a feat never before performed and one which had been accomplished almost as casually as though the aviator had been flying over his old mail route.

Expressions of admiration for the flight were phrased in superlative terms and came from all branches of the government and from private citizens. The feminine population of Washington seemed particularly thrilled as they sought every word of news touching upon the flight.

New York Begins Noisy Celebration

NEW YORK, May 21—(AP)—Broadway's celebration began with receipt

(Continued on Page 2, Column [illegible])

Next Stop—Paris, France

—By Pacific & Atlantic.

A curtain of fog was wrapped at times around "The Spirit of St. Louis," Capt. Charles Lindbergh's monoplane, as he took off from New York on his special flight to Paris. The photo, transmitted by telephone over the wires of the American Telegraph and Telephone company, shows Lindbergh's plane about an hour after the hop-off, as it was winging its way over Massachusetts.

STATE JUDGES ORGANIZE UNIT

Temporary Body Is Formed Pending Meeting At Oklahoma City.

ARDMORE, May 21.—(Special)—Twenty-five district judges from all sections of Oklahoma attended the organization meeting here Saturday to form a state district and superior judges' conference.

John B. Ogden, Ardmore, on whose suggestion the meeting was called, was elected temporary chairman, and John L. Norman, Okemah, temporary secretary. The temporary officers will hold over until the first regular meeting, called for Oct. 24, 1927, in Oklahoma City, when regular officers will be elected to hold office for one year.

A program committee for the October meeting was named to work out plans for the first regular meeting. Tom Chambers, Lucius Babcock and Wiley Jones, all of Oklahoma City, compose this committee.

A business session was held Saturday morning at 10 o'clock devoted largely to discussion of the purposes and need of an organization for district and superior judges in this state.

A barbecued chicken dinner was served at Chickasaw Club lake, under the direction of Sheriff Ewing C. London at noon. Fishing tackle and golfing equipment were supplied. A banquet was served Saturday night at Hotel Ardmore.

NEW POLICE CHIEF ORDERS BLACKWELL SUNDAY CLOSING

BLACKWELL, May 21.—(Special)—Grocery stores will be closed all day here Sunday. This was the order issued Saturday by W. C. Harlan, new chief of police, appointed by O. J. Neal, recently decided as winner in the election for mayor. Recently several stores had remained open all day Sunday, with others being open until 9 o'clock in the morning.

Burke at Concho School

EL RENO, May 21.—(Special)—Charles H. Burke, commissioner of Indian affairs, from Washington, Saturday visited the Concho Indian school near here. He was accompanied by Inspector Roberts of the interior department. John A. Buntin of Anadarko, district superintendent, and a number of El Reno business men

Bellanca Plane Hop For Paris Postponed

Friends Persuade Pilot To Delay Attempt In View Of Unfavorable Weather Conditions.

ROOSEVELT FIELD, N. Y., May 21.—(AP)—Gasoline spilled from the Bellanca plane as it was being towed across the field, caught fire Saturday night and for a time threatened the plane with destruction.

ROOSEVELT FIELD, N. Y., May 21.—(AP)—The Paris flight of Clarence Chamberlin was "indefinitely postponed" Saturday night when friends persuaded him not to make an immediate attempt.

Chamberlin had announced that he would take the hop off Saturday night less than two hours after Charles Lindbergh landed in Paris. He had his plane hauled to the runway and was telephoning officials for permission to use the runway, when friends gathered about him to dissuade him.

They showed him that while weather was good Saturday night unfavorable conditions were predicted for Sunday. Also Carl Schory, secretary of the contest committee of the National Aeronautical society, was discovered to have gone to Washington, and it was said that the flight would not be official unless Schory sealed the barograph.

"All right, it's all off," Chamberlin said at length. "It's off indefinitely, and when we do take off it won't be for Paris in all probability. That has been done. We'll probably fly west instead of east. Perhaps Honolulu."

Electrician's Life Saved By Workers

SARNIA, Ont., May 21.—(AP)—Ten fellow employes, working in relays for forty-eight hours, have saved the life of Harold Hedges, 21 years old, by artificial respiration. Hedges was shocked by 26,000 volts of electricity while working on a pole here. A safety belt kept him from falling. He was lowered to the ground by a block and tackle and rushed to a hospital, where the ten fellow workers began their long effort to give him life. Late Saturday night Hedges's breathing became normal and Saturday he was resting easily.

Mexico May Retain Claims Commission

MEXICO CITY, May 21.—(AP)—Senor Estrada, under-secretary in charge of the foreign office in the absence of Foreign Minister Saenz, declared Saturday that negotiations were being carried on to prolong the life of the general claims commission beyond August 30, this year. He believed an agreement was likely. The foreign office, Senor Estrada stated, has not considered the possibility of a fusion of the special and general commissions appointed to settle claims growing out of revolutionary activities in Mexico.

Portuguese Flier To Return By Air

RIO DE JANEIRO, Brazil, May 21.—(AP)—Maj. Sarmento Beires, Portuguese aviator, who, in March, flew from the West African coast to the island of Fernando De Noronha, off the Brazilian coast, and then to the South American mainland, is completing plans to return to Lisbon by air. He expects to leave May 28, going by way of Natal and Belem, Brazil; Georgetown and Martinique, West Indies; Chicago, New York, Boston, Newfoundland and the Azores.

Fanatic Attacks Greek Church Head

ATHENS, Greece, May 21.—(AP)—A fanatic Saturday attempted to stab Archbishop Chrysostomos, primate of the Greek orthodox church, while the latter was officiating at a service in St. Constantine's church, Piraeus.

The archbishop fended off the blow and received only slight cuts.

RULES TO BE FORMED FOR STOCK CAR RACES

WASHINGTON, May 21.—(AP)—The contest board of the American Automobile association has invited representatives of the motor car industry to French Lick, Ind., May 26, to formulate rules for stock car tests. A general public interest in stock car racing was given as one of the reasons for the call.

OCEAN HOPPER QUIT FARM FOR CAREER IN AIR

Boy Aviator 'Flunked' In Engineering School; Not Studious.

HE LIKES SOLITUDE

Left University Upon Seeing His First Airplane; Was 'Chute' Jumper.

NEW YORK, May 21.—(AP)—The life story of Charles Lindbergh is a record of the attainment of a high ideal followed with unswerving determination.

At heart, the gangling aviator "is "just the boy he looks" say his friends, and his ideal, though not always the same, is one not unsimilar to that held by virtually every American boy. He had a "bent" and he hoped to achieve greatness in his chosen field.

Born in the middle west in 1902, the son of Charles A. Lindbergh, who later became a congressman, Charlie Lindbergh seemed at first destined for the life of a farmer. Up until six years ago he was plodding industriously behind plow and harrow, but every spare minute he spent on his old motorcycle or in any car that he could lay his hands on.

Used to Solitude

Besides that—and this had a bearing on the attitude of those who feared the flier would be lonesome on the New York-Paris hop—he almost always drove alone. He liked solitude, and he likes it yet.

On leaving farm work, Lindbergh went to college, to study mechanical engineering, but, according to fellow students, he was not an academic success.

He did more experimenting than most, they have said, but as soon as the results were plain to him he would go on to other work, not even bothering to turn in a report. So most of the marks he received were below passing.

Then one day an airplane landed on the college campus and a new fire was lit in this aloof boy's heart.

Plane Was Inspiration

"I'm going to be an aviator," he told his mother without preamble, and forthwith signed up for instruction at an aviation school.

Lindbergh became a student at the army school at Kelly Field in Texas. For two years he studied there and it was during that time that he had his first accident and first acquired the name of "Lucky" Lindbergh.

While stunting in the air he crashed with another plane and both he and the other aviator had to "go over the side." They had parachutes, but at that time it was a new idea that aviators might be saved by parachutes. But when the wrecked planes landed after the collision, the pilots were already on earth, congratulating each other on their escape.

Became Mail Flier

After two years at the army school and another in army service Lindbergh went back to the middle west and became an employe of the Robertson Aircraft corporation. It was in the capacity that he became an air mail flier and was able to pile up a total of 1,800 hours in the air in the six years after he first left the ground. It has been estimated that this is equal to the average aviator's fifteen years' experience.

As an air mail flier, Lindbergh was three times more forced to place his life in the effectiveness of his parachute. He escaped without injury each time, though once he stayed with his plane so long that he was badly jarred in landing and another time was in danger of being mangled by the wild circlings of the unmanned plane from which he had leaped as he drifted down to earth.

It was a year ago that he first conceived the idea of making the New York-Paris hop. He went to Maj. William Robertson, head of the company for which he worked, and confided his ambition. Major Robertson became enthusiastic and was instrumental in influencing leading citizens of St. Louis to back the project.

There was no fanfare of publicity, no beating of drums for the young flier who hoped to beat all the vet-

(Continued on Page 2, Column 1.)

French Crowds Give Daring Flier Ovation As Long Flight Ends

"Well, Here We Are; I Am Very Happy," Is His Comment While 25,000 Surge Forward To Greet Him; Monoplane Is Brought to Perfect Landing; Pilot Tired But Contented.

LE BOURGET, May 21.—(AP)—From New York to Paris by air is accomplished. The greatest feat in the history of aviation ended on Le Bourget flying field at 10:21 o'clock Saturday night (5:21 p. m., New York time) when Capt. Charles A. Lindbergh, lone American aviator, taxied to earth in the flare of red beacons and huge searchlights.

The youthful Lindbergh, who piloted a "blind" plane with a periscope, navigated his way across the Atlantic with a precision a veteran navigator of great ocean vessels might well envy. He landed in the midst of a mighty crowd that gave him the tremendous welcome his achievement deserved.

Lindbergh came over Le Bourget flying high, slightly to the east of the field. He circled twice slowly, then settled down 200 yards west of the main building.

He made a beautiful landing, headed due west with the ground lights flashed on him. The crowd of 25,000 gave a great roar and rushed forward. Dozens of persons were swept off their feet in the wild excitement to reach the wonderful American.

Crowd Swamps Plane

The crowd surged around Lindbergh's plane before he could get out of the cockpit. A few minutes before the lone aviator reached the ground, the American ambassador, Myron T. Herrick, arrived, witnessing his descent from the administration building.

The plane was hauled in front of the building. The daring youth was lifted out and carried shoulder high into the open, where he was enthusiastically acclaimed and cheered for twenty minutes.

"Well, here we are," was what he had to say. "I am very happy."

Then a vast flood of spectators broke over the field and surged around the plane. Hundreds tried to get the boy on their shoulders.

High in the air they carried him to the administration buildings on Le Bourget field, where Myron T. Herrick, an ambassador of the airman's own country, and high officials of France, together with French and American notables with tears in their eyes, stammered their congratulations.

Airmen Very Tired

Terribly drawn and tired, Lindbergh, yet had the grit to smile and wave his arms in acknowledgement of the tributes of the crowd.

They bore him into the building, where an unofficial reception committee awaited, but the people wanted more of him and cheered wildly until ambassador Herrick brought his helmet to the window and exhibited a great bunch of flowers that had been presented to the flier.

The reception was as short as decently could be, and within a few minutes after landing, Lindbergh, in the ambassador's car was threading his way toward Paris and a bit of sleep. Before he started he had a thorough massage for his tired and cramped arms and legs, and some coffee to brace him until he could get to bed.

ESTIMATE IS EXCEEDED BY ITALIAN BUDGET SURPLUS

ROME, May 21.—(AP)—A treasury statement, just issued, shows a budget surplus of 255,000,000 lire on April 30, or 97,000,000 more than estimated for the first ten months of the fiscal year. (The lire at the present rate of exchange is worth about 5½c.)

New McAlester Bank Opens

M'ALESTER, May 21.—(Special)—The Bank of Commerce of McAlester, recently chartered by the state banking department, opened for business Saturday. The new bank has a capital stock of $50,000, with a $10,000 surplus. Ned Holman is chairman of the board; James McClenahan, president; M. L. Stockton, vice president and cashier; J. G. Puterbaugh and A. U. Thomas, vice presidents.

Bank Suspect Taken to Texas

DURANT, May 21.—(Special)—Teza Ray, 21 years old, alleged to have confessed to participation in the robbery of the Ovalo, Texas, state bank in March, left here Saturday in custody of Sheriff Ohar from Taylor county, Texas, to be returned to Abilene. Ray was arrested here by Sheriff Conn. Loot of $2,850 was taken in the robbery.

New York To Paris In One Long Jump

Capt. Charles Lindbergh

Lindbergh Notes

NEW YORK, May 21.—(AP)—Newspaper offices have received numerous telephone calls from persons who complained that it was not proper to call Capt. Charles A. Lindbergh the "flying fool."

Meantime, however, the nickname has preceded Lindbergh to France, and in Paris he will be greeted, cable dispatches said, by the phrase "fou volant."

* * *

Took Short Route

WASHINGTON, May 21.—(AP)—To the question "Why did Lindbergh go so far out of the way?" the National Geographic society answers, "He did not." Even casual examination of a globe would show that the young aviator made a bee line for Paris, the society said, but the landsmen are accustomed to looking at maps, with their inevitable "distortions," always necessary if a spherical surface is projected upon a flat surface.

* * *

An Aerial Anniversary

PARIS, May 21.—(AP)—Seventeen years ago Saturday Count Jacques de Lesseps of France negotiated the English channel from Calais to Winston Court Farms, in a fifty horsepower monoplane in fifty minutes. He was the second aviator to perform this feat, Louis Bleriot having flown virtually the same course the previous year.

* * *

Lindbergh Not Wealthy

PARIS, May 21.—Immediately Capt. Charles Lindbergh landed in Paris Saturday night he became a potentially wealthy young man. In addition to the $25,000 Orteig prize, his feat opened the magic doors of stage, screen, and advertising, which mean fat contracts for public appearances and use of his name on trade goods.

* * *

Another $25,000 Offer

NEW YORK, May 21.—S. L. Rotpafel (Roxy) announced Saturday afternoon that he had cabled his Paris representative authorizing him to offer Captain Lindbergh $25,000 for a week's appearance at the Roxy theater.

In December 1928, WKY became an affiliate of the National Broadcasting Co. and began broadcasting the network's programs. By the following year WKY was attempting to operate like the large radio stations in the East. Aside from NBC programs, everything broadcast by WKY originated locally. The typical weekday programming began at 6:30 A.M. with the "Early Risers Club," a morning exercise show from the Oklahoma City YMCA. Next came news and weather plus market reports and farm oriented programs sponsored by OPUBCO's Farmer-Stockman. Other morning programs included the "Aunt Susan Show" which featured beauty, household and cooking tips for women. The afternoon programs included organ music from the Christian Church, musical programs performed by WKY staff musicians including a call-in request program and some children's programs like the "Gloomy Gus Show." Afternoon programs included live broadcasts by the Whalin Brothers' Band. Evening broadcasts included programs from NBC plus broadcasts of local dance orchestras from the Silver Glade Room of the Skirvin Tower Hotel and folk shows such as "Martha, Pete and Babe" and "Slim and Jim." It did not take WKY long to become a profitable business.

During the late 1920s, *The Oklahoman* and *Times* reported on the creation of Braniff airlines founded by Oklahoma City residents Paul and Tom Braniff. Paul Braniff was a World War I pilot and barnstormer. Tom Braniff was a prominent insurance man. In September 1927, Oklahoma City prepared to welcome Charles Lindbergh, who, earlier in the year, had flown solo non-stop New York City to Paris in a Ryan monoplane named *The Spirit of St. Louis,* winning a prize of $25,000 offered by New York restaurateur Raymond Orteig. *The Oklahoman* told readers, in a front-page story on September 28, of preparations to welcome the man who had gained sudden fame.

The oil boom of the 1920s brought optimism to many poor people in the state. Oil companies began paying their roustabouts, the semiskilled men who worked the drilling rigs, an average of $130 a month. This was more money than a sharecropper might earn in three years on a farm. Thousands of men put down their plows and headed for the nearest oil field. One of the largest was the Greater Seminole field centered in Seminole County to the east of Oklahoma City. *The Oklahoman* and *Times* soon received letters from readers in Seminole alarmed by conditions in their oil-boom community. The papers sent a reporter to Seminole, who found gambling, prostitution and every other form of vice flourishing in the Bishop's Alley, a four square block area along the town's

A WKY radio favorite during the station's early years was "Aunt Susan," a native of Missouri who grew up in Oklahoma City and was a home economics major at Oklahoma A&M College, now Oklahoma State University. She pioneered the radio cooking show. This photo was made in the 1930s.

The Silver Glade Room of the Skirvin Tower Hotel was specifically designed as an auxiliary studio for WKY radio. The room could accommodate 1,200 people. The dance orchestra in the 1938 photo is not identified.

main street that took its name from the man who owned a barn that became the first dance hall. *The Okla-homan* and *Times* published many reports describing conditions and how Bishop's Alley operated. Their civic pride smarting, many Seminole residents met the train delivering *The Okla-homan* and publicly burned the copies on the city's streets. The paper's circulation people and reporters were also threatened.

A few weeks after the papers exposed conditions in Seminole, the Indian Territory Illuminating Oil Co.'s discovery well, 6½ miles south of the city, blew a gusher and Oklahoma City had an oil field. A four-column photograph of the gusher was spread across page one of *The Oklahoman*. News stories relating to the discovery pushed all other news off the front page except for a story about the illness of King George V.

The Oklahoman then conducted a moderately successful campaign to keep oil drilling from spreading all over Oklahoma City. The paper said in an editorial, "There are certain sections within the city limits which might be drilled without any resultant danger at all. There are other sections which cannot be drilled without the gravest possibility of disaster." The paper compared the wells to "stored dynamite, creating the gravest possibility of disaster."

By then readers of *The Oklahoman* and *Times* were following the difficulties of Governor Henry S. Johnston that started in 1927. The legislature began to attack Johnston after he proposed to enlarge the State Highway Commission from three to five members. Patronage became a lively issue. Lawmakers began to criticize the

During the 1930s the Whalin Brothers' Band performed on WKY each weekday afternoon at 2 P.M. Pictured left to right are: Whalin, Clifford Wells, Kermit Whalin, Laudon Beaver, J. Owen Howell, Perry Ward (announcer), Pat Trotter, Rae DiGier and Willie Wells. This photo was made in April 1936.

This view looks north on Broadway in downtown Oklahoma City during the 1920s. The boxy building at the center is the Huckins Hotel. (Courtesy Oklahoma Historical Society)

E. K. Gaylord at his desk in the 1930s.

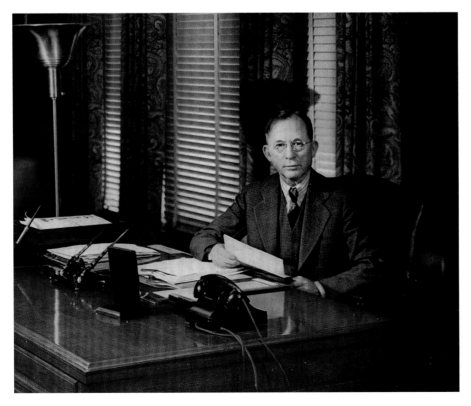

governor at every opportunity and accused him of neglect of duty. Although the State Supreme Court had ruled that the legislature could meet only in regular session or at the call of the governor, the lawmakers announced they would call their own special session. Oklahoma National Guard troops, on Governor Johnston's orders, turned lawmakers away from the capitol. The lawmakers soon convened in the Huckins Hotel in downtown Oklahoma City and proposed impeachment charges against Johnston and others. Realizing the courts were on the governor's side, the lawmakers adjourned without taking any action.

The Oklahoman, in an editorial labeled "Once More Bayonets," noted: "There is no warrant for his action. There is no excuse for his arbitrary order. This makes it impossible for his friends to defend him. If it were an impeachable offense in 1923 to call out the National Guard to prevent a meeting of the legislature, it is an impeachable offense in 1929." *The Oklahoman* went on to predict the legislature would eventually impeach Johnston.

When state lawmakers gathered for their regular session in January 1929, 13 charges against Johnston were presented to the senate. Eleven were accepted. Johnston was suspended from office and Lt. Governor William J. Holloway became acting governor. Johnston's impeachment trial began on February 6 and lasted for more than six weeks. On March 20, the senate voted to remove him from office on the charge of general incompetence. *The Oklahoman* and *Times* reported these stories.

The papers also reported the return to Oklahoma in 1929 of William H. "Alfalfa Bill" Murray from Bolivia, where he had tried, but failed, to established a cotton-growing colony. Murray borrowed $20,000 from a bank and announced he was running for governor. Earlier Murray had been president of the Oklahoma constitutional convention, where he left his views in many of the constitution's more innovative provisions. When Oklahoma became a state, Murray served as speaker of the first legislature and in 1912 won one of Oklahoma's two at-large seats in the United States House of Representatives, and two years later was elected as the Congressman representing the state's fourth district. Now he was running for governor. He did not try to conceal his opinions. For instance, Murray proposed to cut costs by pardoning any Oklahoma convict who promised to leave the state.

E. K. Gaylord did not believe Murray was the best man for the job. Gaylord thought Murray was personally dirty, never took a bath, didn't shave more than twice a month, forced his wife to live in a house with a dirt floor, and probably never changed his underwear all winter. *The Oklahoman's* editorials opposed Murray as governor, and Edith Johnson, the paper's society editor, wrote a story belittling Murray's

"dirty drawers." In his campaign speeches Murray would frequently attack in his bull voice what he called the "capitalistic press" and then bring Edith Johnson into his attack. On one occasion he said: "I see where Sister Edith is complaining that I wear dirty drawers! What the hell does she know about my underwear? And what the hell difference does it make to her?" In spite of the paper's opposition to Murray as governor, he won the 1930 gubernatorial general election. The hard times in Oklahoma were right for "Alfalfa Bill."

Murray did keep his promise to pardon convicts and exported more than two thousand criminals, which was not appreciated by neighboring states. In another instance he ordered the state militia to close bridges across the Red River in a dispute with Texas. He also ordered national guardsmen to shut down more than three thousand producing oil wells in Oklahoma calling an end to hopeless competition and over production.

Before 1929 ended, E. K. Gaylord announced plans to build two additions to The Oklahoma Publishing Co. building constructed in 1909 at Northwest Fourth and Broadway. One new building costing $1,500,000 would house printing facilities. Another structure costing $350,000 would be used for storing newsprint. It would be built farther east on Northwest Fourth next to Santa Fe railroad tracks for fast unloading of the giant rolls of newsprint. The 1920s had been a period of growth and prosperity for Oklahoma, Oklahoma City, and *The Oklahoman* and *Times,* and its newly acquired WKY Radio. But all of this changed following the stock market crash in New York City on October 29, 1929. Oklahoma and the nation entered the worst economic depression in the nation's history.

This aerial view of downtown Oklahoma City was made in April 1928. The state capitol is in the upper left of the photo. (Courtesy Western History Collections, University of Oklahoma Libraries)

Chapter Seven

THE DEPRESSION '30S

As 1930 began, the economic depression was being felt throughout Oklahoma, a state whose population had reached 2,396,040. Oklahoma City's population had grown to 185,389, but during the next 20 years the city's population and that of the state would decrease. By April 1930, the new building for the mechanical plant of The Oklahoma Publishing Co. was completed, but the hard times stopped the construction of the newspapers' newsprint warehouse. The discovery of oil in Oklahoma City, however, provided some cushion for the state's economic problems. Still, many factories and mines closed. The oil market became depressed, and unemployment in Oklahoma was soon the highest in history. Poverty-stricken citizens formed long lines at public soup kitchens, and *The Oklahoman,* the *Times* and WKY radio reported what was happening.

In 1930, *The Oklahoman* finally succeeded in its campaign to remove railroad tracks from downtown Oklahoma City. More than four decades later, E. K. Gaylord remembered, "For more than 20 years the city had tried to get the Rock Island and the Frisco railroads to take their tracks out of the business district. Finally, a committee of three tentatively agreed with the railroads that freight trains would be routed around the city but passenger trains would remain. Trains frequently blocked traffic on Broadway, Robinson and other streets. I was greatly disturbed and it occurred to me that both railroads were bankrupt and in the hands of a receiver and the Metropolitan Life Insurance Co. owned most of their bonds. Mr. Ecker, the president, was a friend of Frank Buttram, and they were partners in some oil wells. I asked Mr. Buttram to see if Mr. Ecker would order both companies to remove the tracks. He immediately took the matter up and Mr. Ecker said, 'Of course, Oklahoma City ought to have the tracks moved,' and he ordered the officials of the roads to make the best deal they could, but remove the tracks."

The removal of the tracks gave a boost to civic pride, but when an eight million dollar bond issue was put before Oklahoma City voters a little later to provide more parks, sewers, and a new city hall and convention center, the measure was defeated 4 to 1. In response, an editorial in *The Oklahoman* observed:

> *It is perhaps unfortunate that the people of Oklahoma City haven't as much courage and faith in their city as the people of Tulsa. The latter city, although burdened with a much heavier bonded indebtedness than Oklahoma City, recently voted an additional $16 millions in bonds because it had the courage to vision its need of continuous progress.*

On November 19, 1930, WKY radio had its first major opportunity in public service. Its reporters provided on-the-scene coverage of the destruction caused by a tornado at Bethany, then located on the western outskirts of Oklahoma City. The station stayed on the air continuously for two days broadcasting information and appealing for funds to help the victims. WKY raised $34,368.51 in less than 48 hours. This was an accomplishment considering the depression.

By 1931, *The Oklahoman*'s circulation topped 104,000 and the paper continued to grow even though Oklahoma and the nation were in the grip of depression. When several fast trains that carried *The Oklahoman* statewide were eliminated because they had few passengers, the newspaper suddenly had a delivery problem. The Mistletoe Express, started by The Oklahoma Publishing Co., was born of necessity. As E. K. Gaylord later recalled, "We'll just have our own trucks deliver the papers and quit depending on the railroads." The Oklahoma Publishing Co. purchased its own trucks to deliver *The Oklahoman* statewide. The truck line soon grew into a

After a tornado struck Bethany on the western outskirts of Oklahoma City at 10 A.M. on November 19, 1930, more than 650 persons were left homeless and 23 persons were either killed instantly or died later from their injuries. Red Cross officials and the Governor appealed for relief funds. Here Edgar T. Bell, OPUBCO business manager (left) is appealing to WKY radio listeners for funds. The other man is WKY station manager Gayle Grubb. With the station's help $34,368.51 was raised.

By 1938 The Oklahoma Publishing Co.'s Mistletoe Express Service fleet consisted of 76 trucks which traveled 11,000 miles a day over Oklahoma highways. That year Mistletoe Express carried 40,000,000 pounds of freight. OPUBCO's newspapers accounted for only 26 percent of the freight load.

major service for Oklahoma merchants, manufacturers, wholesalers and distributors, and by 1971 Mistletoe Express had terminals in 50 or more cities in Oklahoma and in cities in four neighboring states including Dallas and Fort Smith. Before the arrival of television, Mistletoe Express transported movie reels to small-town theaters throughout Oklahoma.

It was during the early 1930s that E. K. Gaylord hired a full-time cartoonist for the papers. He was Charles Werner, and before he left during the late 1930s, he won a Pulitzer Prize for an editorial cartoon published on October 6, 1938.

The Oklahoman gave extensive coverage in 1932 to Amelia Earhart when she became the first woman to fly solo across the Atlantic. She appeared in Oklahoma several times and even adopted a 15-year-old Oklahoma City girl as a protegée and taught her to fly. Earhart and 98 of her friends formed the Ninety-Nines, a group of women pilots, and chose Oklahoma City as their headquarters.

In July 1933, aviator Wiley Post, a close friend of Oklahoman Will Rogers, set out to make the first solo flight around the world in the Winnie Mae, a Lockheed Vega monoplane. The plane was named for the daughter of Oklahoma oil man F. C. Hall of Chickasha, who backed Post. *The Oklahoman* sent its aviation editor and the managing editor to New York City to cover the end of the flight, but the story was almost knocked off the front page by an Oklahoma City kidnapping story the morning after Post returned.

Tennessee-born George Kelly Barnes, better known as bank robber

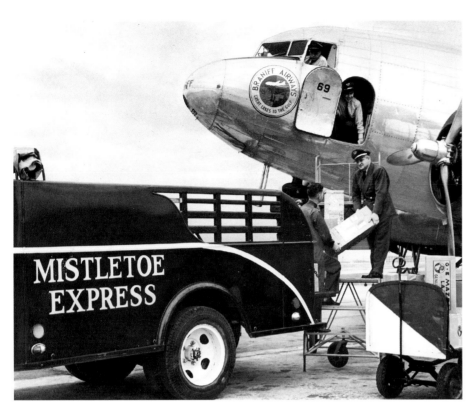

During the late 1940s Mistletoe Express Service joined with Braniff Airways to provide shippers with faster delivery. Mistletoe's air freight service had the slogan "Shipments at three miles a minute." Here Mistletoe's Leo Porter and Braniff's Young Dogget are loading freight at the Oklahoma City airport.

Carriers for the Oklahoma City *Times* collect their papers from a Mistletoe Express Co. driver. By starting the trucking company, The Oklahoma Publishing Co. was able to deliver its papers across Oklahoma without depending on the railroads.

This aerial photo of the Oklahoma City airport, now Will Rogers World Airport, was made on May 20, 1933, during a "Milk and Ice Fund Benefit Show." The fund had first been promoted by *The Oklahoman* in 1914 and continued until 1953. Amelia Earhart was the guest of honor and demonstrated the autogiro seen in the lower left hand corner. Earhart acquired an autogiro and set a women's autogiro altitude record of 18,415 feet two years before coming to Oklahoma City. (Courtesy Oklahoma City Chamber of Commerce)

"Machine Gun Kelly," and two other men entered the Oklahoma City home of Charles F. Urschel, wealthy oilman, on July 22, 1933. Urschel, his wife and another couple were playing bridge when Kelly, carrying his trademark machine gun, and the two men armed with pistols stormed in and threatened to "blow everyone's head off." When Kelly could not learn which man was Urschel, he forced both men into his auto and fled. Once Kelly found Urschel's identification in his clothes, he dumped Walter Jarret on the side of a deserted road, but not before robbing him of $51.

When news of the kidnapping spread, the story probably had the greatest national coverage of any event that had occurred in Oklahoma. Although the FBI took over the Urschel home and sealed it off, *The Oklahoman* and *Times* were getting exclusive information from inside. As it turned out, the son of the managing editor was a high school friend of the kidnapped man's daughter, Betty, and with her school friends would visit the Urschel home daily. He would then report to the papers what he had

learned. After Urschel's family friend, E. E. Kirkpatrick, delivered $200,000 in ransom to a drop in Kansas City, Missouri, on July 30, Urschel was released the next evening near Norman. Urschel walked to a café, called for a cab and returned home. Later he met with the press. *The Oklahoman* and *Times* gave it front page coverage.

Although Urschel had been blindfolded while a prisoner, he made sure his fingerprints were spread everywhere in the room where he was kept. He counted his footsteps to various places and mentally catalogued all of the sounds he could hear including the times when an airplane would fly over. Federal agents located a ranch near Paradise, Texas, where Urschel had been held and arrested one kidnapper. A little more than a month later "Machine Gun" Kelly and his girl friend were found hiding in a friend's house in Memphis, Tenn. Kelly was flown back to Oklahoma for trial. Eventually all of the accomplices were arrested. Kelly and five others were given life sentences. *The Oklahoman* and *Times* provided extensive coverage.

The papers also provided much coverage on many bank robberies that occurred during the depression thirties across Oklahoma. Charles Arthur "Pretty Boy" Floyd, who grew up in Sequoyah County, bragged that he had robbed 32 banks, many in Oklahoma. In one robbery at Sallisaw, it appeared that just about everyone in town except the police and banker knew Floyd was going to rob the local bank on November 1, 1932. It was reported that his 75-year-old grandfather even came to town to watch as "Pretty Boy" Floyd escaped with $2,530. But less than two years later on October 22, 1934, Floyd was killed by federal agents near East Liverpool, Ohio. Friends and family and even the Sallisaw bank contributed money to return Floyd's body to Oklahoma for burial. Nearly 40,000 people attended the funeral which the papers covered.

In 1933, *The Oklahoman* and *Times* opposed a proposal to drop the city manager form of government which had proved worthwhile in Oklahoma City. When voters went to the polls, the proposal was defeated by a 4 to 1 margin.

In 1934, E. K. Gaylord was elected president of the Southern Newspaper Publishers Association. One of his first tasks was to appoint a committee to study the possibility of manufacturing newsprint from southern pine trees. Northern paper producers said southern pine was not suitable for making paper. Gaylord's efforts culminated with Southern publishers establishing Southland Paper Mills, Inc. in 1937. Gaylord was one of its four directors. Its first mill at Lufkin in east Texas began production in 1940, ending

During the mid-1930s this bank of 22 Linotype machines and operators composed the type for *The Oklahoman* and *Times*. The long pipe along the ceiling was a pneumatic tube system that delivered copy from the editorial and advertising departments.

This is The Oklahoma Publishing Co. building at Northwest Fourth and Broadway decked out in holiday lighting during the 1930s. Such holiday lighting ceased at the beginning of World War II.

E. K. Gaylord in 1934.

Switchboard operators at *The Oklahoman* and *Times* were deluged with calls about the deaths of Will Rogers and Wiley Post in a 1935 plane crash. Operators like Ruth McDonald (above) worked all day, answering between 8,000 and 10,000 calls that were received over 20 trunk lines.

OPPOSITE
The front page of the August 16, 1938, issue of the Oklahoma City *Times*.

WKY radio transmitted its signal from this complex during the 1930s.

northern domination of newsprint production.

From his arrival at *The Oklahoman,* E. K. Gaylord sought to provide readers with the best possible news coverage. During the early 1930s, he closely followed the development by the Associated Press of a process to transmit photos by wire. One day in 1934, E. K. Gaylord was in Dallas on business when he was paged in his hotel for a phone call. "The manager of the AP in New York told me that they could now give [Wirephoto] service to *The Oklahoman* and only 14 cities [across America] would be on the line to start with. We could get on the continental wire going through Kansas City to the west coast. I asked the cost. Roughly it was $39,000 [annually], plus the cost of the operator and the zinc metal for the pictures. I said, 'Well, roughly that will be $50,000 [annually], but we will take it.' *The Oklahoman* thus was a charter member among only 14 cities," recalled E. K. Gaylord in 1971.

Soon readers in Oklahoma City saw news photos that had been transmitted by wire across America. The first Wirephoto published showed an airplane crash in the Adirondack Mountains. As E. K. Gaylord later remembered, "Some months after this I met the publisher of the *Tulsa World* and he asked how in the world we could afford to spend $50,000 for Wirephotos. I said, 'That was not the question—the question was how we could afford to do without them.'"

The depression continued to cause hardships on Oklahoma City, the state, and nation. *The Oklahoman* and *Times* reported on the hard times but tried to be optimistic in their editorials. But all traces of optimism seemed to vanish when choking, paralyzing dust storms turned Oklahoma skies black. Another dark cloud appeared when the papers reported the deaths of Oklahoman

Will Rogers and Wiley Post. The *Times* put out an Extra on Friday, August 16, 1935, after learning they died in a plane crash off Point Barrow, Alaska. The headline read: CRASH KILLS POST, ROGERS. Rogers was the best-known satirist and highest-paid entertainer of his day.

Although *The Oklahoman* and *Times* lost much advertising revenue during the depression, WKY radio was beginning to make money. A modern broadcasting plant was erected on Northwest 39th. Then in 1936, eight years later, studios and offices were established on the fifth floor of the Skirvin Tower Hotel. In celebrating WKY's new facilities, The Oklahoma Publishing Co. held a banquet on April 13. E. K. Gaylord told those attending:

> When we acquired WKY few people had receivers and all receivers were battery sets. Most of them produced more static than music. Those were the days when you fished all over the dial, trying to bring in a station 500 miles away.
>
> If you were lucky enough to tune in Atlantic City or even Detroit, you called your neighbor on the telephone to brag about it. You didn't really listen to the radio for its messages or its music. You tuned in for the pleasure of logging a new station.
>
> All of this has changed. Whenever radio is discussed now it is the program or the artist, not the reception nor the distance from the transmitting station.

Within two years WKY received permission to operate with 5,000 watts during the daytime and 1,000 watts at night. A new transmitter was installed, expanding the station's coverage area throughout Oklahoma. In addition to news and entertainment programs,

The Wirephoto NEWSPAPER

OKLAHOMA CITY TIMES

Final Home

Paid Circulation Greater Than Any Other Evening Newspaper Published in Oklahoma
(Evening Edition of The Daily Oklahoman)

VOL. XLVI. NO. 79. | TWENTY-EIGHT PAGES—OKLAHOMA CITY, FRIDAY, AUGUST 16, 1935 | PRICE: THREE CENTS

Wilderness Crash Kills Rogers and Post; Plane Falls in Alaskan Take-off After Forced Landing in Fog; Bodies Recovered

The Tiny TIMES

FORT SILL, Aug. 16.—The news from Alaska is like a nightmare. The mind does not want to accept the ghastly word that Will Rogers, Oklahoma's most popular son, and Wiley Post, Oklahoma's greatest aviator, have been rubbed out in a moment, like ordinary mortals who sometimes fall from the clouds.

Two men who in life gave aviation its greatest stimulus, have by their sudden deaths cast a pall over the world's enthusiasm for air travel. Neither man knew what fear was. Both were as much at home sitting on a winged engine as they were in an arm chair on the ground. Each man did everything that he could to encourage aviation and each thought that death never could be aimed at him.

It is the air's greatest tragedy because the world characters that are lost will be impressed upon the millions who read. The world will forget the hazards taken in the most difficult flying country in the world. The world will forget that the tramp tour of Rogers and Post was the most dangerous sort of fun. The world will forget for a season the millions of safe hours of commercial flying and check off all of the progress against the loss of Oklahoma's most famous men.

* * *

PROBABLY Will Rogers is a shadow on a silver sheet to you, a droll humorist whose simple philosophy and fine character have given you an impersonal attachment. To me he was a friend. I have seen him on stage and off for 20 years. I knew him when a rope and a wad of gum constituted his stage business. I have seen him squatting on a corner in the streets of Claremore, which he advertised to the world. I have been with him at the 101 ranch and at the Mulhall farm near Guthrie with the folks he worked with before he was famous. I have barnstormed with him on charity tours. I have seen him pull aside old friends who were down at the heels and stuff their hands full of bills. I have seen him accept the plaudits of great crowds and again I have witnessed him quietly do some fine, generous act for an unfortunate individual. In everything he did he was a genuine gentleman, never posing for effect, always being human and decent and fine. His passion for aviation was amazing. He liked the mode of travel because it got him many crowds. He liked the feeling of new world that rushing through the air gives a man. He recognized the necessity for caution and he never was reckless and he always saw to it that he traveled in good equipment and with the best of pilots. Born to be much on the stage, he was altogether a home man. His center of happiness was Mrs. Rogers and their three children. His tastes were home tastes and the thing he liked best was to be at home alone with his own.

* * *

POST, the nerveless, taciturn all-steel farm boy, was an enigma to most of those with whom he came in contact. He came as near to being a mechanical flying machine as any human who ever held a stick. When he was working on the derrick floor of an oil rig as a tool dresser he said he would give his right eye to be able to fly. A steel splinter from a lathe pierced his eye. With the compensation that he received he paid for flying lessons and took to the air. He was a fatalist. He was in tight spots a dozen times during his two trips around the world in the Winnie Mae. More than once he was ready to abandon ship. He told me he approached these crises with utter calm, knowing that he would go when the time came and that nothing that he might do could change the result.

Post had the uncanny sense of direction of a homing pigeon. He had an amazing ability to orient his ship under the most trying of circumstances. He was greatly disappointed in his stratosphere experiments of the last year. He wanted to retire the Winnie Mae after he had flown the stratosphere from Glendale to New York. But he placed too much faith in the old Lockheed that had served him so faithfully twice around the globe. His final ambition for the Winnie Mae was to see the ship in Smithsonian Institution in Washington alongside of Lindbergh's Spirit of St. Louis. A bill for the purchase of the ship is before congress at the present time.

No one has ever learned the details of the Alaskan trip arrangement but my understanding is that Will Rogers suggested that he would be glad to go with Post and that Post's wife abandoned her plans for the trip in order to give way to the humorist. Post and Rogers were by no means cronies. They had met several times and Will thought Wiley was the best

PLEASE TURN TO PAGE [illegible] TINY TIMES

Oklahoma Will Bow Head For Famous Sons

Statewide Memorial Service Regarded as Likely.

City Stunned by News

Grief-Stricken Judge Leaves Bench at Word.

Bewildered Oklahoma bowed in mourning Friday before the single blow of an inscrutable fate that robbed her of her two foremost sons—Will Rogers and Wiley Post.

Gruff business men bowed their heads, while involuntary tears sprang to their eyes. "Maybe they're just hurt?" they asked hopefully—then hopelessly.

The flag on the capitol building slipped to half-mast.

Marland Suggests Memorial

In the United States district court a bailiff whispered to Judge Franklin E. Kennamer. His voice broke into proceedings.

"The court can't go on just now," he said, and walked from the chamber.

Governor Marland, booted and spurred commander of the national guard, sank back into his swivel chair. "The state will want to give them a memorial," he said, "but the state can't add anything to the honors already heaped upon them by the sovereigns and peoples of the world."

Thus did Oklahoma receive news of the last sky-ride of her cowboy humorist and oil-driller flying ace.

Garner Wires Mrs. Post

Highest officials in the nation tried to put their feelings into telegrams of condolence—and found no words.

"May God bless and keep you is my fervent prayer," wired Vice-President Garner to Mrs. Rogers at Beverly Hills, Calif., and his words were relayed as a similar wish for the home state of the two famous men.

"I was afraid for them," said Senator Gore in telegraphic messages to friends here. "I couldn't explain it."

Governor Marland, who prepared to leave for Fort Sill Friday morning.

PLEASE TURN TO PAGE 2, COLUMN 5 TWO SONS

Morro Castle Pictures Found on Dead Sailor

PORT ARTHUR, Texas, Aug. 16.—(AP)—Gabriel A. Larsen, 45-year-old unemployed ship officer, in whose clothing were found pictures of the ill-fated Morro Castle liner, hanged himself with a trunk strap in a park in the downtown section here Friday. A verdict of suicide was returned.

Pictures of the Morro Castle, burned off the New Jersey coast last December, a sea officer's cap bearing the Ward line house flag and the insignia, "second officer," were found.

The operator of the rooming house at which he stayed said the man had never told her where he worked but that he had been staying there since June 26.

Refund Checks Mailed To Disappointed Scouts

The executive board of the central Oklahoma Boy Scout area voted Friday afternoon to begin immediately the refunding of fees paid by city scouts for the national jamboree.

First checks were to be placed in the mail late Friday. Each payment will total $32.50, the portion of the fee retained by the local council. The remaining $25 will be refunded next week by national scout officials in New York, said Leroy Plumley, assistant scout executive.

Senate Votes Purchase Of Post's Winnie Mae

WASHINGTON, Aug. 16.—(AP)—The senate Friday passed and sent to the house the Thomas bill authorizing government purchase of the Post-Gatty round-the-world plane "Winnie Mae" for $25,000. The plane would be placed in the Smithsonian Institution.

Before the bill was passed Senators Gore and Thomas of Oklahoma paid tribute to Will Rogers and Wiley Post.

Gore said he saw Rogers "rise by his own talents from obscurity to the very summit of fame."

Post's Wife Longed For Quiet Years

'I Wish I Had Crashed With Him!' She Cries.

By GEORGE LIPE

Death Friday shattered a dream and an ambition that May Post has carried with her ever since she eloped in an airplane back in 1927 and married Wiley Post.

It was a dream of a cottage—a cozy home, a dream of a time when she wouldn't be sitting around waiting for word from her flying husband.

There Was No Break

"I wish to God I had been with him when he crashed," Mrs. Post cried Friday when informed of the death of her husband.

Mrs. Post was flown by L. E. Gray to Oklahoma City from Ponca City Friday afternoon. She was at Ponca City when informed of the death of her husband. They were accompanied here by Mrs. Gray. Gordon Post, brother of Wiley, Mrs. Gray, and Mrs. Post left by auto for Maysville immediately after landing here.

Her actions upon receiving the fatal word dispelled all talk of a break between her and Wiley, which started when she dropped plans to accompany her husband and Rogers on their fatal flight.

Mrs. Post has hoped for the last five years that each flight of her husband would be the last—not like this last tragic one—but last because he would voluntarily give up the flying business. She didn't object to it as a hobby.

They Were Children Together

Although the exploits and accomplishments of Wiley brought fame to him and his wife, May didn't realize any great happiness from it. She wished for a quieter life. She wanted children—and they had none.

May Laine and Wiley Post grew up together in Grand Saline, Texas, where both were born. They played together until she was 5 years old, when her family moved to Edgewood, Texas. Twelve years later she met Wiley in Maysville and they were married.

Soon after Wiley made his first world flight, Mrs. Post said, "Wiley has a philosophy that gives me comfort. He believes everything works out for the best."

Ohio Governor Agrees To Set 'Test' Election

NEW YORK, Aug. 16.—(AP)—Governor Martin L. Davey of Ohio said Friday he had telephoned his office to frame an order for a special election to name a successor to the late Representative Charles V. Truax, and also to arrange for a special session of the legislature.

The Weather

LOCAL—Probably showers and cooler Friday night and Saturday.

STATE—Cooler Saturday, and in western and central portions Friday night.

HOURLY TEMPERATURE

4 p. m.	95	4 a. m.	76
5 p. m.	93	5 a. m.	75
6 p. m.	91	6 a. m.	74
7 p. m.	89	7 a. m.	73
8 p. m.	86	8 a. m.	80
9 p. m.	85	9 a. m.	84
10 p. m.	83	10 a. m.	88
11 p. m.	81	11 a. m.	92
12 midnight	78	12 noon	95
1 a. m.	77	1 p. m.	95
2 a. m.	77	2 p. m.	98
3 a. m.	76		

Wiley Post   Will Rogers

Royalty Question Is Ruled Out Of Textbook Hearing

Murray Fades From Picture With Kennamer Decision.

William H. Murray, former governor, faded suddenly Friday from a federal court battle over state school book adoptions when Judge Franklin E. Kennamer ruled that authors' royalty payments to the William H. Murray educational foundation were not involved.

Testimony was completed and final arguments, begun Friday morning, were expected to be finished during the day. Fred Hansen, assistant attorney general, said the state will stand on its contentions covering illegal advertising of the 1934 text adoptions when the John C. Winston Co., plaintiff, was given a contract, and the allegation that the Winston contract was given seven months earlier than the law permits.

Holding the royalty fraud issue could not be raised because the Winston company paid no royalties, Judge Kennamer said:

"I disapprove of these royalty contracts, though, and I would not permit companies involved to come into a court of equity for relief."

Murray came from his farm near Broken Bow to defend his foundation and school book commission.

The End of an Ill-Fated Trail

PT. BARROW
CRASH 15 MILES SOUTH OF PT BARROW
ARCTIC OCEAN
AKLAVIK
ALASKA
CANADA
YUKON RIVER
FAIRBANKS
DAWSON
ANCHORAGE

Map of the flight that ended south of Point Barrow last night.

Will Rogers Last Dispatch

FAIRBANKS, Alaska, Aug. 15.—Visited our new emigrants. Now this is no time to discuss whether it will succeed or whether it won't, whether it's a farming country or whether it is not, nor to enumerate the hundreds of mistakes and confusions and rows and arguments and errors of management in the whole thing at home. Here, as I see it, there is not but one problem now that they are here, and that's to get 'em housed within six or eight weeks. Things have been a terrible mess. They are getting 'em straightened out, but even now not fast enough. There are about 700 or 800 of 'em. About 200 went back. Also about that many workmen sent from the transient camps down home. And just lately they are using about 150 Alaskan workmen paid regular wages. But it's just a few weeks to snow and they will have to be out of the tents. Both workmen and settlers have plenty of food. They can always get that, but it's houses they need right now, and Colonel Hunt, in charge, realizes it. You know after all there is a lot of difference in pioneering for gold and pioneering for spinach.

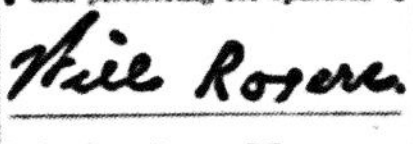

Methodist Merger Voted at Parley

Conferees Agree on Vast Three-Way Union.

CHICAGO, Aug. 16.—(AP)—Representatives of the three leading branches of Wesleyanism Friday voted approval of a plan to merge the Methodist Episcopal church, the Methodist Episcopal church, South, and the Methodist Protestant church into one body.

To be effective, the plan must next be ratified by the general conferences of the three churches. It will be presented to the northern and southern units of the Methodist Episcopal church next May and to the Methodist Protestant church conference in 1936.

The approved plan involves approximately 8,000,000 members and more than $1,000,000,000 in church property. The merged church would become the largest Protestant denomination in the United States.

Roosevelt Voices Sorrow of Nation Over Fatal Crash

Outstanding Americans Gone, Declares President.

HYDE PARK, N. Y., Aug. 16.—(AP)—President Roosevelt expressed the shock of the nation Friday upon learning of the death of Will Rogers and Wiley Post whom he said were "outstanding Americans and will be greatly missed."

Mr. Roosevelt was informed of the death of the two distinguished men by The Associated Press shortly after his arrival here from the White House for a brief visit home.

He made this statement:

"I was shocked to hear of the tragedy which has taken Will Rogers and Wiley Post from us. Will was an old friend of mine, a humorist and philosopher beloved by all. I had the pleasure of greeting Mr. Post on his return from his round-the-world flight. He leaves behind a splendid contribution to the science of aviation. Both were outstanding Americans and will be greatly missed."

Statuary Hall Niche Awaits Rogers's Image

WASHINGTON, Aug. 16.—(AP)—Patrick J. Hurley of Oklahoma, former secretary of war and friend of Will Rogers, said Friday his state's "quota of illustrious sons in statuary hall at the capitol will now be filled.

"Beside the statue of Sequoyah, in the very near future, will be that of Will Rogers. Oklahomans, I know, will want it so."

Each state is permitted statues of her two most illustrious sons in statuary hall. If Rogers's statue is placed there, Oklahoma will have as her representatives a Cherokee Indian chief and one with Cherokee blood.

Caskie on Commerce Board

WASHINGTON, Aug. 16.—(AP)—President Roosevelt Friday nominated Marion M. Caskie of Alabama as a member of the interstate commerce commission.

The Times Was First

The Oklahoma City Times and Radio Station WKY told Oklahoma about the Post-Rogers crash.

First on the air was WKY, with a flash of the tragic news from the first Associated Press dispatch, which came many minutes before the news was known to any other press association.

The Times extra, carrying the news of the crash, was on the streets in Oklahoma City 25 minutes ahead of any other newspaper.

Signal Corps Officer Takes Victims From Wreckage in River 15 Miles From Point Barrow in Far North Area; Mishap at 10 p. m. Thursday.

Related News, Pictures on Pages 4, 6, 12, 13, 16.

SEATTLE, Aug. 16.—(AP)—Death ended the aerial vacation of Will Rogers, famous humorist and actor and Wiley Post, noted around-the-world flier, when their plane crashed 15 miles south of Point Barrow in Arctic Alaska Thursday night. Word of the accident was received here Friday by the United States signal corps from Sgt. Stanley R. Morgan, operator at Barrow.

Sergeant Morgan said the accident occurred at 5 p. m. Alaska time (10 p. m. central time).

The first terse message said:

"Post and Rogers crashed 15 miles south of here (Point Barrow) at 5 o'clock (10 p. m., Oklahoma time) last night. Have recovered bodies and placed them in care of Dr. Greist (in charge of a small Point Barrow hospital). Standing by on Anchorage (Alaska) hourly."

The message was signed by Morgan, the only army man on duty at the small Point Barrow settlement.

Later, he wirelessed the plane crashed from only 50 feet in the air after taking off from a small river.

Sergeant Tears Plane Apart To Recover Body of Post.

His message continued:

"Navy runner reported plane crashed 15 miles south of Barrow.

"Immediately hired fast launch proceeded to scene found plane complete wreck, partially submerged two feet water.

"Recovered body of Rogers then necessary tear plane apart extract body of Post from water.

"Brought bodies to Barrow turned over to Dr. Greist, also salvaged personal effect which I am holding.

"Advise relatives and instruct this station fully as to procedure.

"Natives at Campaign, small river 15 miles south here, claim Post and Rogers landed, asked way to Barrow.

"Taking off engine misfired and plunged into the right bank of the river from an altitude of 50 feet.

"Plane out of control, crashed, tearing right wing off and topping over forcing engine back through body of plane.

"Both apparently killed instantly.

"Both bodies bruised.

"Post's wrist watch broken stopped at 8:18 p. m."

Henry W. Greist operates the Presbyterian hospital at Point Barrow, which is maintained primarily for the care of Eskimos.

Post and Rogers left Fairbanks, in the interior of Alaska, Thursday in their pontoon-equipped monoplane on their 500-mile flight to Point Barrow, but sat down on Harding lake, 50 miles away, to await better weather.

Dense fog, low clouds and rain were reported at Barrow at the time. No word had been received here Friday of weather conditions at Barrow, but fogs are frequent at this season when the warm sun has melted year around snow and ice to their lowest point.

Coast Guard Cutter to Bring Bodies Back to Seattle

The coast guard headquarters at Washington, D. C., ordered the Northland, which touched at Barrow Thursday in its annual visit, to return to bring the bodies back to Seattle and in Fairbanks a plane was available to fly to Barrow for the same purpose.

(A Washington dispatch said the Northland will transport the bodies to Nome. It said a doctor aboard will embalm the bodies and that probably a plane will be dispatched to contact the Northland and fly the bodies to the Pacific coast. It would take the cutter six or seven days to make the run).

Word of the tragic end of the jaunt which was to take Post and possibly Rogers to Siberia, where Post said he was going to hunt tigers, was telegraphed to the Post and Rogers families by the signal corps.

The tundra land south of Barrow is generally devoid of bodies of water large enough for a plane of this description to make a safe landing and while no details of the crash were received it was assumed the plane came down on the frozen ground.

Barrow, northernmost white settlement in America, has a population of several hundred natives and about a dozen whites, including the signal corps operator, his wife, and child, Doctor Greist, his family, and the nurses in the Presbyterian hospital.

Crash Was Post's Second Mishap While Flying Over Alaskan Area

The accident occurred at the height of the brief Arctic summer when it is daylight almost around the clock.

Post and Rogers had been entertained in Fairbanks for several days while their plane was being serviced. They flew in a regular transport plane to Anchorage Wednesday and visited the Matanuska colony near there.

Rogers said he wanted to go to Barrow to visit Charles Brower, known throughout Alaska as the "King of the Arctic" because of his 51 years of residence. Brower operates a trading post and whaling station at the settlement, which

This is the front page of *The Daily Oklahoman* on January 1, 1935. The issue contained the paper's first published Wirephoto, an aerial photo transmitted by the Associated Press showing the remains of an American Airlines transport plane that had crashed in the Adirondack Mountains of upstate New York the day before.

WKY radio broadcast the University of Oklahoma football games. For one season in the late '30s, Walter Cronkite did the play-by-play broadcasts. He previously had done simulated baseball broadcasts in Texas using Western Union ticker reports but, at the time, was working for Braniff Airlines in Oklahoma City. Gayle Grubb, manager of WKY, hired Cronkite, who recalled in his book *A Reporter's Life* (Knopf, 1996) that he moved to Norman about two months before the 1937 football season began to become familiar with the team. "The first game was the traditional opener against Tulsa. . . . The broadcast was a disaster. My spotters weren't worth a darn and the electric board was worthless. . . . I was hopelessly behind," Cronkite recalled. The following Monday morning WKY's Gayle Grubb told Cronkite that E. K. Gaylord wanted to see him. "I had never met him before. He could have stepped out of a New Yorker cartoon: the absolute epitome of the big boss." Cronkite remembered that Gaylord wore wire-framed glasses, was balding, and had a frown "that creased most of his extended forehead. He motioned us to chairs."

"Well, I thought you fellows did pretty good," Gaylord said. "The folks I've talked to thought it was good. I liked it. A few little things I know you're going to fix up, but I just wanted you to know that we liked it around here." Cronkite recalled, "We fixed up the 'little things.' I had learned a lesson that would prove highly valuable as the years went on. Never again would I be caught without having done whatever research was possible for whatever it was I was going to cover."

Years later Ralph Sewell, long-time OPUBCO employee, recalled sitting next to Cronkite at a dinner in the early 1970s and asking about his broadcasting days in Oklahoma. Cronkite told

Sewell that he first was confused trying to watch and describe a live game. Next time, Cronkite used spotters seated on either side to tell him what was going on, and Cronkite turned his back to the field. "It solved his problem, he said, and he finished the rest of the season. Then he moved on," Sewell said.

✳

In 1936, *The Oklahoman* and *Times* again supported the bond issue which had failed six years earlier to provide funds to build a new city hall and municipal auditorium. This time the bond issue passed. The following year both papers began a concentrated campaign for highway safety in Oklahoma after 85 persons had died in traffic accidents. With the papers' support, the Oklahoma Highway Patrol was born.

On July 2, 1937, readers learned that Amelia Earhart and her navigator, Fred Noonan, were lost in the Pacific as they tried to set a record flying around the world. Earhart was only 39. She and Noonan left New Guinea bound for Howland Island in the Pacific, 2,700 miles away. They never arrived.

In 1938, *The Oklahoman* engaged in a campaign that came to be known as "Pennies from Heaven." Ralph Sewell, who was then city editor, recalled: "The wife of a printer ran a cafe on the southwest corner of Broadway and 4th. She double-parked to take supplies into the cafe. When she came back, a cop was standing by her car, ticketing her. She mouthed off and the cop arrested her—apparently because she complained. Most of us at the paper ate at her cafe, and heard her story which we published. When E. K. Gaylord read it, he came to my desk, put a penny on it and said, 'Everyone has a right to sass a cop—let's run a campaign to pay her fine—acknowledge every penny.' I dug out my penny, of course. We ran the

When WKY radio established studios in 1936 in the Skirvin Tower Hotel in Oklahoma City, this sign was hung on the southeast corner. Each letter was nearly 6 feet tall.

This is WKY radio's mobile unit in late 1938. It was a converted Studebaker ambulance that carried a 200-watt radio transmitter with the licensed call KAXB. The mobile unit made its first broadcast on Christmas 1937. Although not visible in the photo, the vehicle's roof had an opening over the front seat to enable a reporter to stand and broadcast while the mobile unit was moving.

Charles Werner drew this Pulitzer Prize–winning political cartoon for *The Daily Oklahoman* on October 6, 1938. Werner depicted the uneasy situation in Europe where, without a shot, Czechoslovakia was sacrificed to Adolf Hitler's territorial demands.

OPPOSITE
The front page of the December 7, 1941, issue of *The Daily Oklahoman*.

story and pennies flowed in. As I recall, we ran about eight full pages listing the contributors."

The Oklahoman and *Times* were also instrumental in exposing a major scandal in 1938 by printing dozens of stories about illegal activities of the Oklahoma City school board. The treasurer of the board pleaded guilty to embezzlement and, following a grand jury probe, the entire nine-member board of education was ousted. Four members of the board were imprisoned for crimes including payoffs on contracts, accepting bribes, and misadministration. A woman board member was convicted but not imprisoned.

The year 1939 had hardly begun when the *Times'* evening rival, the *Oklahoma News,* without previous notice, suspended publication. On February 24, the *Oklahoma News* told its readers it had been published in Oklahoma City for more than 32 years.

> Most of that time it has been published at a loss. . . . The News would in time be able to stand on its own financial legs as a reasonably profitable institution. This continued effort and investment has been made in the face of constantly increasing production costs, due to mounting labor costs and rising newsprint prices. . . . The circumstances which made this action necessary rise from a trend in newspaper economics over which we have no control.

E. K. Gaylord was in Hawaii and learned by telegram that the *Oklahoma News* had folded. In reality, the suspension of the *Oklahoma News* was a tribute to The Oklahoma Publishing Co. and E. K. Gaylord's news sense and business acumen and the quality of his papers. The following afternoon the *Times* expressed its deep regret on page one, saying editorially:

> You may quarrel with a friend, you may compete vigorously with him, but when disaster overtakes a comrade, you fly to his defense. With the Oklahoma News gone, we feel an emptiness as real as if a human being with whom we labored for many years had died an untimely death.
>
> The trend of the times, with its increasing cost of newsprint, materials, labor costs, and taxes, made the burden of another publication too heavy to continue.
>
> Our Scripps-Howard contemporary was clean competition, a small unit in a vast chain operation, as fresh, fearless, alert and progressive as any lighthouse that flew the Scripps beam from its masthead. We are genuinely sorry to see it quit the field.

With the suspension of the *Oklahoma News,* as the 1930s ended, The Oklahoma Publishing Co. inherited a larger obligation and an increased responsibility in serving Oklahoma City and the state. The Oklahoma Publishing Co. recognized these things, and in an editorial told readers: "The *Oklahoman* and the *Oklahoma City Times* will try harder than ever to print the best newspapers circulated in any community of 250,000 in the United States. They will provide a forum for all shades of opinion. Both papers," the editorial noted, "will try to print all of the news and both sides of every story. They will persist in getting the best features and the best independent brains, editorially and mechanically, in the hope of always meriting the support of the readers by the policies, the technical excellence and the contents of its publications."

FIRST WAR EXTRA

THE DAILY OKLAHOMAN

Price 5 Cents

Entered at the Oklahoma City, Oklahoma, postoffice as second class mail matter under the act of March 3, 1879.

VOL. 50. NO. 334.   Morning and Sunday   OKLAHOMA CITY, SUNDAY, DECEMBER 7, 1941.

JAPANESE ATTACK HAWAII AND MANILA FROM AIR

Cannon Still Firing After Hour and Half

HONOLULU, Dec. 7.—(AP)—The sound of cannonading coming from the direction of Pearl Harbor, has been continuing for an hour and a half. So far, there are no reports of casualties. No bombs have fallen in Honolulu itself, so far as could be determined before this call was made.

There is a lot of commotion going on, with planes in the air and anti-aircraft firing.

The citizens of Honolulu have been cleared from the streets by military and naval units, assisted by civilian volunteers, all carrying arms.

But a lot of citizens have left the city for hills, to watch the planes and anti-aircraft, and get a general view of the excitement.

I heard one may say, as he passed me en route to the hills:

"I'll bet the mainland papers are going to exaggerate this."

Bombs Score At Honolulu

By EUGENE BURNS

HONOLUL, Dec. 7.—(AP)—At least two Japanese bombers, their wings bearing the insignia of the Rising Sun, appeared over Honolulu at about 7:35 a. m. (12:05 p. m. Oklahoma time) Sunday and dropped bombs.

Unverified reports said a foreign warship appeared off Pearl Harbor and began firing at the defenses in that highly fortified post.

The sound of cannons firing comes to me here in Honolulu, as I telephone this story to the San Francisco Associated Press office.

Reports say that the Japanese bombers scored two hits, one at Hickam field, air corps post on Oahu island, and another at Pearl Harbor, setting an oil tank afire.

Shortly before I started talking on the transPacific telephone, I saw a formation of five Japanese planes flying over Honolulu.

Some aerial dogfights are in progress in the skies over Honolulu.

At least two nine-plane formations of fourengined black bombers flew over Honolulu and Pearl Harbor. Each plane bore Japan's Rising Sun insignia.

There was a report from persons who came past Pearl Harbor that one ship there was lying on its side in the water and four others were on fire.

Bulletins

WASHINGTON, Dec. 7.—(AP)—The White House announced at 3:35 p. m. (EST) Sunday that the army had just received word that an American vessel, believed to be a cargo ship, had been sending out signals of distress approximately 700 miles west of San Francisco. Whether it had been torpedoed was not immediately learned.

LONG BEACH, Calif., Dec. 7.—(AP)—Rear Admiral Charles A. Blakely of the 11th naval district, Sunday issued orders shortly after announcement of the Japanese air attacks in the Pacific, requesting all officers and men attached to the district, or vessels of the district, to report to their stations or ships immediately.

The district embraces Southern California, from San Luis Obispo, south to the Mexican border, and all or Arizona and New Mexico.

Texas Air Cadet Is Killed in New York

NEW YORK, Dec. 6.—(UP)—Flying Cadet Charles L. Davenport, 24 years old, of Silsbee, Texas, was killed Saturday, less than a week before he was to be commissioned a second lieutenant, when his army P-40 pursuit plane exploded and crashed into the ocean. Coast guardsmen recovered the body. His half-opened parachute indicated he had made a futile attempt to jump.

HONOLULU, Dec. 7–(AP)–A naval engagement is in progress off Honolulu, with at least one black enemy aircraft carrier in action against Pearl Harbor defenses.

The sound of cannonading coming from the direction of Pearl Harbor, has been continuing for an hour and a half. So far, there are no reports of casualties. No bombs have fallen in Honolulu itself, so far as I could determine before making this call.

WASHINGTON, Dec. 7.—(AP)—Japanese air attacks on the American naval stronghold at Pearl Harbor, Hawaii, and on defense facilities at Manila were announced Sunday by the White House.

Only this terse announcement came from President Roosevelt immediately, but with it there could be no doubt that the far eastern situation had at last exploded, that the United States was at war, and that the conflict which began in Europe was spreading over the entire world.

A brief presidential statement disclosing the attacks was dictated to news agencies and press associations by Stephen Early, White House secretary. It said:

"The Japanese have attacked Pearl Harbor (in Hawaii) from the air and all naval and military activities on the island of Oahu, the principal base in the Hawaiian islands."

Then, a few minutes later, he dictated this:

"A second air attack has been reported. This one has been made on the army and navy bases in Manila."

This disclosure had been accepted generally as an

(Continued on Page 2, Column 1)

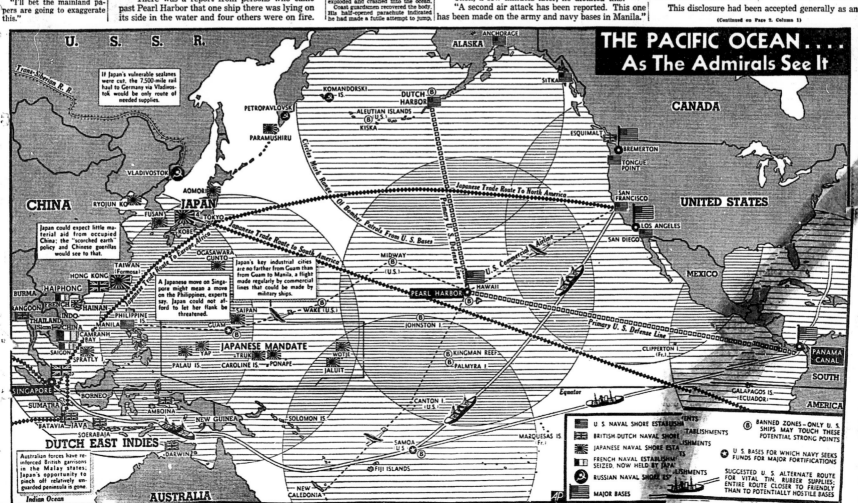

THE PACIFIC OCEAN.... As The Admirals See It

Chapter Eight

WORLD WAR AND CHANGE

As 1940 began, Oklahoma City had a population of 204,424 and the census showed the state with 2,336,434 people. The suspension of the *Oklahoma News* came as war clouds were rising over Europe and Oklahomans were seeing the depression fade. The year 1940 saw E. K. Gaylord elected a director of the Associated Press. He served for nine years but then declined to stand for re-election saying the AP board needed new blood. At home, the almost continuing campaign by *The Oklahoman* and *Times* for adequate water supplies finally saw a $6.9 million bond issue passed to complete another storage reservoir, Lake Hefner. In 1941, construction began on a new $250,000 transmitter facility for WKY radio on a 145-acre site on East Britton Road north of Oklahoma City.

Then came December 7, 1941. *The Oklahoman* published two Extras that day to give readers the news of the stunning Japanese air attacks on Pearl Harbor that opened World War II. Listeners to WKY radio heard NBC reports on the attacks and reaction from Oklahomans. E. K. Gaylord's daughter, Edith, was then in her twenties. In a 1998 interview, she recalled, "I was having Sunday dinner at my parents' home when they called Dad to tell him what happened." He left for the office at once to supervise the coverage of the bombing of Pearl Harbor. Edith Gaylord felt obligated to be there, too, even if it meant she took a dinner guest along. When they reached the office, Edith offered to fill in wherever needed and spent the evening pulling clippings from the newspapers' library known as "the morgue."

E. K. Gaylord's son Edward L. Gaylord was then attending Harvard Business School. He had gone there in the fall of 1941, but as he later recalled, "After Pearl Harbor I became disinterested and got out of there." Early in 1942, young E. L. Gaylord, 22, entered the U.S. Army as a private. He first spent time in Texas. "I got into the U.S. Army Air Corps, was an aviation cadet for a while, and then assigned to an anti-aircraft battery in California," he recalled. After he became an officer, he served for a time as a general's aide in Panama.

As the newspapers geared their operations to wartime coverage, *The Oklahoman* introduced to its readers an unknown cartoonist named Bill Mauldin, who would gain fame as the portrayer of the war's GI Joe, and later as a nationally syndicated artist.

Civic leaders realized that Oklahoma City was located midway between two army air corps bases: Langley Field in Virginia, and March Field in California. The leaders, including E. K. Gaylord, believed an aircraft depot installation at Oklahoma City could contribute to the defense effort. The Oklahoma City Chamber of Commerce organized the "Industries Foundation" and obtained $300,000 in cash from Gaylord and other local business leaders to handle any situation that might arise during efforts to obtain land for such an air base. The Chamber then compiled all the data needed to sell Oklahoma City as the site and sent it to Washington D.C. The civic officials soon learned that Fort Worth, Wichita, Chicago and Oklahoma City were all vying for the installation.

Without any warning a group of army officers arrived in Oklahoma City to inspect the site and met for two hours with Jack Hull, research expert of the Chamber of Commerce. The army officers gave Hull a list of what they wanted. They added, "We want it all today." Hull lost no time in meeting with civic leaders including Gaylord at the Chamber office. The army officers wanted iron-clad agreements for Oklahoma City to furnish the site for the aircraft depot and build a water line to it without cost to the government. They also wanted written assurance that public

Lt. Edward L. Gaylord during World War II.

This photo of Edward L. Gaylord was made in Boston in November 1941 while he was attending Harvard Business School. About one month later World War II began and he joined the military.

Midwest Air Depot in the early 1940s was to become Tinker Air Force Base in Oklahoma City.

utilities for gas, electric and telephone lines would be installed along with a railroad spur to the depot site plus hard surface roads all without cost to the government. The civic leaders went to work immediately. Gaylord arranged for the Oklahoma City, Ada & Atoka railway to furnish the spur track. The Oklahoma county commissioners readily agreed to build the necessary roads as did the state highway commission. After some discussion the city council finally agreed to ask voters to approve a bond issue to construct a water line to the depot site. Later the bond issue passed. That night Hull presented the written commitments for everything that had been demanded by Major P. J. McNaughton, who headed the group of visiting army officers. Hull later recalled that McNaughton replied, "Damned if you didn't do it. It's all here. I didn't think it could be done."

The day after the army officers returned to Washington D.C., the Chamber of Commerce was notified by telegram that Oklahoma City had been selected to be the site of Midwest Air Depot. It later became Tinker Air Force Base, named for Maj. Gen.

Clarence Tinker, an Oklahoma native, killed while leading a bombing raid on Japanese-held Wake Island in June 1942. E. K. Gaylord remembered, "Years later one of the men on that site board came back through Oklahoma City. He told me they had already decided the depot should be built in Wichita and had purchased tickets to that city, but after we wound the whole thing up in a day, the decision had to be changed." Within months the same civic leaders secured the $20-million Douglas Aircraft plant that would become part of Tinker's Oklahoma City Air Material Area installation at the end of World War II.

❋

As the war went badly for the Allies, *The Oklahoman* and *Times* launched full-scale campaigns to support the war effort. In 1942, *The Oklahoman* began a weekly GI newsletter for families to send to their servicemen. After the Korean war began in the 1950s, the paper resumed publication of the newsletter. When labor slow-downs caused production to lag during the early '40s, the paper editorially lashed out at the "slow downs" and "stretch outs" called for by some labor organizers. In one

editorial, *The Oklahoman* said, "The people of this country are fighting for the preservation of American liberty—not merely to make the world safe for labor racketeers." The papers urged their readers to flood their congressmen with telegrams and letters. H. V. Kaltenborn, a nationally known radio commentator, praised *The Oklahoman*'s "prairie fire" campaign and predicted it would "sweep the country" and force congress to pass anti-strike legislation for the duration of the war. But President Franklin Roosevelt opposed anti-strike legislation. FDR said the only thing necessary to improve the home front war effort was "more flag waving." To this *The Oklahoman* replied, "Let the president beware the wrath of fathers and mothers who lose their sons because he failed to give them fighting tools. Let Congress beware, also."

The papers urged Oklahomans to buy more war bonds to build the cruiser, U.S.S. *Oklahoma City.* They began reporting on the state's 45th division long before it spearheaded the invasion of Sicily and on into France and Belgium. The papers also reported on every phase of the war and provided readers with Bill Mauldin's cartoons and the columns of Ernie Pyle, whose simple, warm and human reports from the frontlines of the European battlefields were widely popular.

During World War II many people left Oklahoma to work in war plants in other localities. A further drop in the state's population occurred when production stabilized or even fell in some of the state's great oil fields. For example, the population in Seminole County, east of Oklahoma City, grew rapidly between 1920 and 1930, when its oil wells were being heavily exploited. But it began declining and by 1960 would fall to a level only a little higher than in 1920.

The papers provided readers with details of President Franklin D. Roosevelt's death at Warm Springs, Georgia, on April 12, and the swearing in of Vice President Harry Truman as President. When allied forces invaded Europe on June 6, 1944, *The Oklahoman* published an Extra, and when victory in Europe came on May 7, 1945, the *Times* published another Extra. E. K. Gaylord had special copies printed and sent them to employees with a note. It read: "You will perhaps want to file it away to be cherished in future years, when another Extra heralds victory over Japan and peace again comes to the world. In the meantime, there's work to be done, a war to be won. Let's all finish the job." V.E. day celebrations in Oklahoma City were modest and prayerful.

Oklahomans were startled in August when American planes dropped atomic bombs on Hiroshima and Nagasaki. Most Oklahomans tried to fathom the mystery of the new weapon. *The Oklahoman* told readers, "Let us remember that what the scientists of one nation can produce, the scientists of other countries can duplicate. Today the atomic bomb is an American weapon,

"Run it up th' mountain agin, Joe. It ain't hot enough." During World War II Bill Mauldin drew army life.

The Oklahoma City *Times* published this Extra when Germany surrendered unconditionally on May 7, 1945. E. K. Gaylord had special copies printed and sent them to employees with a note which read: "You will perhaps want to file it away to be cherished in future years, when another Extra heralds victory over Japan and peace again comes to the world. In the meantime, there's work to be done, a war to be won. Let's all finish the job."

OPPOSITE
The front page of the August 15, 1945, issue of *The Daily Oklahoman.*

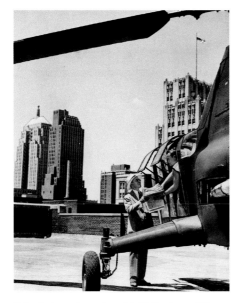

This photo made on June 14, 1946, shows E. K. Gaylord handing helicopter pilot Lt. James Bush a bundle of newspapers. The helicopter had landed on the roof of OPUBCO's mechanical building which had been designed and constructed to handle helicopter landings on the roof.

Although airplanes never landed atop the company's building to pick up newspapers, *The Oklahoman* did use airplanes for delivery. Here Muriel Overstreet, a Mistletoe driver, gives pilot C. R. Calloway of McAlester the first of many bundles for delivery in southeast Oklahoma.

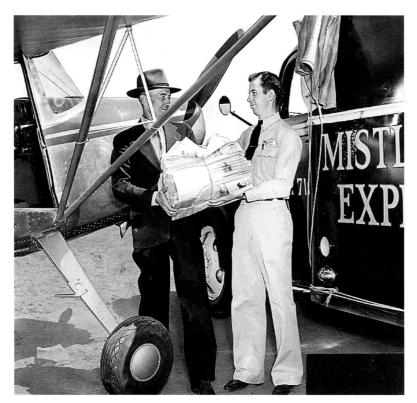

but tomorrow the United States may be the target." About a week later President Truman announced the end of World War II on August 15. *The Oklahoman* published another Extra as unrestrained and jubilant celebrations occurred across the state and nation. The headline on page one of the Extra read: PRESIDENT ANNOUNCES PEACE. Soon thousands of servicemen flocked home, many to enroll in Oklahoma colleges and universities. Their new roles as students and veterans were described by the papers.

When The Oklahoma Publishing Co. constructed its production building at Northwest Fourth and Broadway in 1929, plans called for the roof to accommodate aircraft. E. K. Gaylord believed that by 1934 newspapers would go from the presses to the roof of the production building for delivery by airplanes outside of Oklahoma City. But the 350-by-140-foot roof was not adequate for the planes of the day. It was not until June 14, 1946, that the roof was used as a landing spot by a helicopter. On that day a military helicopter participating in a Civil Air

Patrol–Army Air Force show at Will Rogers Field landed on the roof of The Oklahoma Publishing Company's mechanical building. E. K. Gaylord handed Lt. James Bush, the pilot, a bundle of newspapers to deliver to Will Rogers Field. The dream of delivering papers by air reflected the forward looking nature of E. K. Gaylord. In 1946, The Oklahoma Publishing Co. was taking papers to local airports and delivering them to distant locations in Oklahoma.

In the year 1946, the Gaylord family established Gaylord Philanthropies to help Oklahoma City and Oklahoma. Edward L. Gaylord left active military duty late that year and went to work full-time for The Oklahoma Publishing Co. He began in the circulation department and later moved into the advertising department. By 1948, Edward L. Gaylord was executive vice president, assistant general manager, a director, and treasurer of The Oklahoma Publishing Co.

"Building Oklahoma City and Oklahoma, that's what we're here for," Edward L. Gaylord later said, reflecting upon his father's contributions and his optimism for the future of the city and state. "He wanted to build this town fast, and he did. He was all wrapped up in building Oklahoma City. He was a strong Chamber of Commerce supporter," he said, recalling his father's dedication to civic affairs. "At the newspaper, he always wanted to have the newest and finest equipment, and that's what we have," Edward L. Gaylord said.

With the war over, *The Oklahoman* and *Times* turned to peace-time news coverage. Reporter Mike Gorman wrote a series of stories for *The Oklahoman* telling of appalling conditions in the state's mental hospitals. After more than 300 news stories and editorials were published by the paper, the legislature passed sweeping reforms for

5¢ PAY NO MORE

THE DAILY OKLAHOMAN EXTRA

Entered at the Oklahoma City, Oklahoma, postoffice as second class mail matter under the act of March 3, 1879

VOL. 54. NO. 220.   Morning and Sunday   EIGHT PAGES—500 N. BROADWAY, OKLAHOMA CITY, WEDNESDAY, AUGUST 15, 1945.

PRESIDENT ANNOUNCES

PEACE

War Over, Allies Win

WASHINGTON, Aug. 14.—(AP)—President Truman announced at 6:00 p. m. (Oklahoma wartime) Japanese acceptance of surrender terms.

They will be accepted by Gen. Douglas MacArthur when arrangements can be completed.

Mr. Truman read the formal message relayed from Emperor Hirohito through the Swiss government in which the Japanese ruler pledged the surrender on the terms laid down by th Big Three conference at Potsdam.

President Truman made this statement:

"I have received this afternoon a message from the Japanese government in reply to the message forwarded to that government by the secretary of state on August 11.

"I deem i.. s reply a full acceptance of the Potsdam declaration which specifies the unconditional surrender of Japan.

"In this reply there is no qualification.

"Arrangements are now being made for the formal signing of surrender terms at the earliest possible moment.

"General Douglas MacArthur has been appointed the supreme allied commander to receive the Japanese surrender.

"Great Britain, Russia and China will be represented by high ranking officers.

"Meantime, the allied armed forces have been ordered to suspend offensive action.

"The proclamation of V-J day must wait upon the formal signing of the surrender terms by Japan."

Simultaneously Mr. Truman disclosed that selective service is taking immediate steps to slash immediate inductions from 80,000 to 50,000 a month.

Henceforth, Mr. Truman said, only those men under 26 will be drafted for the reduced quotas.

The White House made public the Japanese government's message accepting that ended the war which started December 7, 1941.

Th text of their message which was delivered by the Swiss charge d'affaires follows:

"Communication of the Japanese government of August 14, 1945, addressed to the gov-

(Continued on Page 2, Column 1)

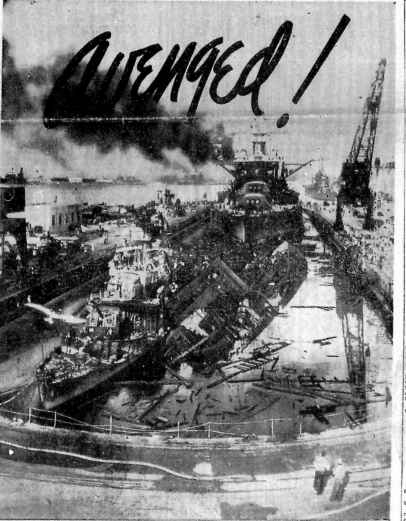

This is the scene at Pearl Harbor Dec. 7, 1941, when the Japanese sneak attack brought war to the Pacific. Shown here are the USS Cassin and USS Downes, victims of the treacherous bombing that came while Japanese diplomats were in Washington professing to seek peaceful solution of differences with the United States. The might of American industrial power soon began offsetting the vast destruction from Jap bombings and built the greatest naval fleet in the history of the world. This fleet, with American land and air forces, carried the fight straight to Tokyo for victory and vengeance.

U. S. Is Born Anew As Big Guns Cool

WASHINGTON, Aug. 14.—(AP)—The war clouds that now roll away reveal a tremendously changed United States—changed both in its relations to the world and in the problems it must face at home.

Seven nations were regarded as world powers when the guns began to roar in Europe six years ago: Great Britain, the United States, Russia, France, Germany, Italy, Japan.

Now that the guns are silent again, only two nations remain as undisputed major powers:

The United States and Russia. Great Britain, which has admitted it is bankrupt, follows closely. The other four will have to struggle to gain middle power positions.

This nation settled down with dogged determination to equal, and then to best, the collossal destruction which the axis launched on the world. In four years a young nation with little or no interest in the rest of the world turned into a mature nation determined to be heard in the council chambers of the world.

As proof of this, the senate ratified the world charter to secure the peace with only two negative votes. The same legislative body turned its back on the world 25 years ago when it refused to put the U. S. into the League of Nations.

The country had been moving toward world leadership since 1941. It had invited the United Nations, as they grew in number from 44 to 50, to its soil for the many conferences which it is now hoped will keep the war gods silent forever.

It had asked for the United Nations declaration in January, 1942, which bound the initial allies together.

And as the war years passed, the United States invited the nations here to write plans for relief, food, finance, aviation and, finally, for world security.

Many of the documents presented to these meetings grew from skeleton paragraphs turned out in the victorian, high-ceilinged offices of the American state department.

The fact now stands that world power rests on manpower and the industrial capacity to turn out the fantastic machines of war. In those two categories no single nation leads the United States and Russia.

A good many Americans feel that such power cannot exist without a re-

(Continued on Page 2, Column 1)

Army Cancels War Contracts

DAYTON, Ohio, Aug. 14.—(UP)— Maj. Gen. Lester T Miller, acting commanding general of the air technical service command, said Tuesday that the army air forces were working as fast as possible to terminate all outstanding war contracts.

Miller said all ATSC districts and areas had orders to begin contract terminations as soon as victory in the Pacific was announced officially at Washington.

"The air technical service command is faced with a tremendous work burden in the quickened defeat of Japan and the arrival of V-J day," he said.

"At this headquarters and at ATSC districts and areas throughout the United States, V-J day will see readjustment, procurement and supply divisions of the air technical service command working feverishly to shut off contracts and curtail all forms of air force manufacture as rapidly as possible—to effect the maximum saving to the taxpayers and facilitate conversion to civilian production.

Rations, Tax, Work Prospects Shown in Home Front Picture

WASHINGTON, Aug. 14.—(AP)—This is the home front picture in brief as the war is ended:

Cost of the War—Almost $300,000,000,000 so far.

Casualties—Over 1,068,216, with more than 250,000 of them killed.

Taxes—Heavy public debt likely to require continued high taxes although congress may insist on earlier cuts than treasury wants.

Government Spending—Taking care of army and navy, and relief costs to require considerable money, with gradual easing of expenditures.

Cutback—Navy already halted building 95 ships costing $1,500,000,000; army to trim purchases by $25,000,000,000 or more on an annual basis.

Price Controls—Due to be lifted soon from items the demand for which will exert no inflationary pressure.

Food Rationing—High military requirements likely to make it necessary for some additional time.

Shoe Rationing—Due to be ended soon.

Gasoline Rationing—Due to be ended within two or three weeks.

Tire Rationing—Not expected to last much longer with easing of military demands.

Manpower Controls—Revoked immediately with end of war.

Unemployment—Some 5,000,000 workers in munitions, shipbuilding, aircraft and ordnance plants expected to be jobless within 60 days. Some

due to leave labor market, with private industry likely to absorb much of balance.

Congress—To return to work September 4 to tackle such things as unemployment compensation, and legislation designed to take up any job slack in peacetime with public works.

Draft—Situation unchanged at present. Congress may pass law ending selective service at once.

Army Discharges—5,000,000 men may be released within a year, although no official statement yet.

Reconversion—Emergency program being rushed by war production board to expedite manufacture of civilian goods.

Travel—Tough travel conditions expected to last another 60 days before situation eases on railroads, buses and planes.

Food Prospects—Third largest general food and feed crop in nation's history, expected for 1945 on basis present crop outlook.

Consumer Goods—Accelerated production of vacuum cleaners, refrigerators, washing machines and toasters likely.

Automobiles—Flood of steel expected for production of 250,000 and allow big increases in other consumer goods.

Fuel Oil—Quick easing of rationing

A Stunned West Coast Laced for War When Enemy Subs Prowled the Pacific

SAN FRANCISCO, Aug. 14.—(AP)—The incredible impact of war as it exploded in the Pacific that Sunday morning—Dec. 7, 1941—shocked and stunned Americans from sea to sea.

But those on the west coast, imminently in danger of an attack as ferocious as that on Pearl Harbor, so they believed, became immediately responsive to the threat. From that day on, the west coast went to war. Cities became arsenals; dom-

inating headlands were fortresses. On that first day of war one of the Japanese long-range submarines prowling Pacific waters, claimed its first victim, the freighter Cynthia Olsen, with loss of 33 men.

Then came the night of radio stations hastily leaving the air as the

(Continued on Page 2, Column 4)

300,000 BY 1950

OKLAHOMA CITY TIMES

Steel Strike Threat Blamed on Congress —Story Page 1*

Paid Circulation Greater Than Any Other Evening Newspaper in Oklahoma

(Evening Edition of The Daily Oklahoman.) Entered at the Oklahoma City, Oklahoma, Postoffice as second class mail matter under the act of March 3, 1879.

VOL. LVIII. NO. 60. | EVENING EXCEPT SUNDAY | TWENTY-SIX PAGES—500 N. BROADWAY, OKLAHOMA CITY, THURSDAY, APRIL 10, 1947. | FINAL HOME EDITION | PRICE FIVE CENTS

152 KILLED, 85 IN WOODWARD, 1,000 INJURED BY TORNADO

This was the Main street of Woodward Thursday morning. Note the courthouse in the background.

Furious Storm Smashes Four State, Texas Towns

Woodward East Side Is Leveled

By MARK SARCHET

WOODWARD, April 10—(Special)—The tornado struck the southwest corner of Woodward.

Traveling northeast, it devastated the area west of the Katy tracks and south of Main street. Hitting the highschool building at the corner of Oak and Ninth, the storm angled east to Fifth street and north to the North Canadian river.

Included in the area was the west end of the business district which was destroyed. Every store on Main street was damaged as far east as Fourth.

* * *

THE entire industrial and wholesale area was heavily damaged and much of it was destroyed.

Streets in Woodward start at the east city limits and are numbered in rotation to the west city limits.

The twister hit at 8:42 p. m. By 9 o'clock rescue crews were searching the piles of broken lumber that had housed over a third of the city's population less than half an hour before.

At 11 p. m. the wind came back, its force spent, but carrying rain of cloudburst proportions, forcing the resue workers to halt their search for some thirty minutes.

THURSDAY morning Woodward was a stunned city. At noon residents were just beginning to see what had happened. The morgues were full and additional dead were being brought in as they were found in the debris.

Estimates of injured ran well over 1,000 but no definite check had been made. Many injured were rushed to hospitals at Mooreland, Shattuck, Fairview, Watonga and to Oklahoma City. Some were taken to Clinton and Elk City over mud-covered roads.

Work of identifying dead and injured was slow. Many were badly disfigured and lack of water made it impossible even to wash the injured. The dead were left to last

PLEASE TURN TO PAGE 2, COLUMN 4 Woodward

Summary

(By The Associated Press)

An estimated 152 persons were killed, more than 1,000 injured, and millions of dollars in property damage was caused by a tornado that ripped the northeastern Texas Panhandle and northwestern Oklahoma Wednesday night.

The toll by towns:

WOODWARD, Okla.—85 killed, 1,000 injured, guards set up to prevent looting. Fire followed tornado, but torrential rains helped firemen extinguish flames. Power, light failed, and emergency generators used. Red Cross mobilized. Streets of town (population 5,500) littered by debris. One-third of town levelled.

HIGGINS, Texas—24 killed, 150 injured. Town (750 population) levelled except for telephone exchange, bank and school building, all brick. Two blocks of business district destroyed by fire, brought under control early Thursday. Rubble blocks traffic, bulldozer sent to clear streets.

GLAZIER, Texas—8 killed, 40 injured in village (200 population), only one building left standing. Injured being treated at Canadian. Vigilantes formed.

GAGE, Okla.—2 dead, 3 injured.

WHITE DEER AND COBURN, Texas—Also hit, but no death toll.

Storm Index

(Tornado news inside)

Doctors, Medicine Flown To Leveled Area; Mighty Wind Cuts 100-Mile Path

Death snatched the lives of 152 persons as it rode a tornado path 100 miles wide through the world's richest wheat and cattle country Wednesday night.

More than 1,000 were trampled, twisted, and broken by the force of the furious wind. Estimates placed property damage in the millions.

Bulldozers and rescue crews Thursday combed the wreckage left in Woodward, hardest hit of three Oklahoma and as many Texas cities, and the known dead in Woodward reached 85 at noon.

Gage reported 2 dead; Higgins, Texas 24, and Glazier, Texas, 8. Shattuck, where many of the dead aninjured were taken, was said not to have been struck by the storm.

Early estimates indicated at least 100 square blocks of Woodward either were leveled or so badly damaged as to be unsafe.

In sharp contrast to the blackness of the storm, which struck at 8:40 p. m., Thursday's sun beamed brightly on the scenes of wreckage, while frantic survivors hurried from hospitals to aid stations and mortuaries seeking word of missing children, relatives and friends.

Planes Bring Doctors and Medicine

By noon, the scene had become orderly as the methodical search for dead and injured went on. Airplanes roared overhead to bring in doctors, nurses, medical and food supplies. Highway machinery was clearing streets. Scores of ambulances moved with screaming sirens to carry their burdens of injured to hospitals in other cities. The Red Cross was feeding rescue workers and homeless from field kitchens set up throughout the city.

The writhing, twisting tornado first dipped near White Deer, Texas, and roared northeastward through Glazier, population 200, and Higgins, population 750. Then it crossed the Oklahoma line to strike Gage and Woodward before lifting.

Stunned residents of the Texas and Oklahoma cities had almost no warning of the approach of disaster. It was first a deafening roar, cut by brilliant lightning flashes which illuminated grotesque forms of lifted buildings before they were blown apart in midair, their debris twisting and whirling with the shattered limbs of uprooted trees.

Two persons known to have been together at Glazier were lifted by the storm, and their bodies were found Thursday two miles apart, broken and twisted as the timbers of buildings which covered them.

Labor Squabble Slows Phone Repair

In the midst of the fight for open communication lines to summon aid for the stricken cities, the Southwestern Bell Telephone Co., announced it had rejected a union offer to send striking telephone operators and repair crews back to their jobs in the stricken area because the union specified as a condition that the company call off supervisory employes now manning switchboards, and that the union be left to determine what constitutes an emergency in the five-state area where the company operates.

Despite the strike, emergency long distance lines were manned, and, with aid of state highway patrol radio, cries for help from the devastated area were heard and heeded so fast that within a short time emergency forces of both Oklahoma and Texas were converging on the scenes of death and wreckage.

Using bulldozers to clear away the debris which Wednesday was the thriving center of one of the world's richest wheat and livestock producing areas, rescue crews at Woodward were divided into groups of five to dig through building wreckage for other possible victims of the storm.

It appeared certain that no accurate lists of dead and injured would be available for hours. Hospitals and aid stations were jammed, and injured victims were being sent out by train and airplane for treatment at hospitals in nearby cities.

A Santa Fe railroad special train moved dozens of the injured to an Alva hospital. A U. S. army C-54 shuttled back and forth between Oklahoma City and Woodward, bringing the most serious cases to University hospital here.

Authorities started compiling a list of known dead as frantic relatives hurried between undertaking parlors, hospitals, and first aid stations in the heartbreaking task of identifying loved ones.

Operating tables were set up in the Baker hotel. Two teams of surgeons worked without relief during the early hours of the morning.

An airplane load of doctors from Oklahoma City took off shortly after dawn to assist. Ten ambulances were dispatched by the state highway patrol from Oklahoma City and Guthrie early Thursday.

Planes filled with litter cases from the Woodward tornado area were beginning to arrive at Tinker field Thursday afternoon. At least 35 ambulance loads were to be taken immediately to University hospital.

L. J. Hilbert, Oklahoma City chief of police said police cars were standing ready to clear the way for the ambulances as they sped to the hospital.

Gov. Turner of Oklahoma, and Gov. Beuford H. Jester of Texas ordered full facilities of their respective state

President Tosses Price Issue in Business' Lap

Unless Cost of Living Is Pared, Wage Boosts Will Be Justified, Truman Says

WASHINGTON, April 10—(AP)—President Truman said Thursday the responsibility for cutting prices rests squarely with business.

"Business wanted free enterprise," he said, "now let's see them make it work. Further, unless prices come down, wage increases will be justified."

In rapid succession during nearly half an hour's news conference, the president made these additional points in discussing economic aspects of the price situation:

He feels there is no necessity for a (economic) recession.

Business wanted freedom from price controls. Now that it is free, the price problem is up to business.

It would be impractical to reimpose price controls and the people do not want them.

A buyers' strike would not help the situation but would throw a monkey wrench into the economic machinery.

He hopes strikes this year will not have the same effect as last, and will be settled.

He is not planning a message to congress on the price situation—congress is hearing plenty from the general public.

He hopes it will be possible to have group price reductions. In this connection, Mr. Truman said the justice department is studying the question of whether manufacturing concerns can combine to slash prices without running afoul of the anti-trust laws.

If a group of companies comes in and consults the department, the president said, he does not believe there would be prosecution.

Greeks Fight UN Aid Reins

Red Dictatorship Said Goal of Russian Plan

LAKE SUCCESS, N. Y., April 10—(AP)—Greece declared Thursday Russia's proposal for United Nations supervision of American aid "seems clearly designed" to encourage creation of a "communist dictatorship" in Athens.

This declaration was made in the security council by Vassili Dendramis, Greek representative, after U. S. delegate Warren R. Austin had called on the council to defer action on the soviet proposal until congress acts.

The council also heard Polish delegate Oscar Lange urge approval of the soviet resolution. Lange announced his intentions to porpose creation of a new international agency, such as UNRRA, to handle "situations like the one we face in Greece."

Weather Forecast

Showers west, showers and thunderstorms in east portion this afternoon; cooler with winds shifting to strong northerly this afternoon; clearing and cooler with diminishing winds tonight; low temperature near 40 in Panhandle to 45-50 southeast portion; Friday fair, somwhat warmer in afternoon.

Hourly Temperature

[illegible]

Driver, 70, Charged After Auto Collision

George French Downs, 70, of 1016 SW 26, suffered a neck injury and was charged with failure to yield the right of way early Thursday after his automobile collided with another at SW 36 and Robinson.

Downs was taken to Capitol Hill General hospital where attendants said his condition was not serious. Driver of the other car, Frank Kimroy, 18, of 340 SE 38, was not injured.

Truman to Fly Home For Visit With Mother

WASHINGTON, April 10—(AP)—President Truman will fly to Missouri Saturday for a weekend visit with his mother.

The White House, announcing this Thursday, said Mr. Truman will fly directly to his mother's home at Grandview. She is reported "doing nicely" after fracturing her hip in a fall several weeks ago.

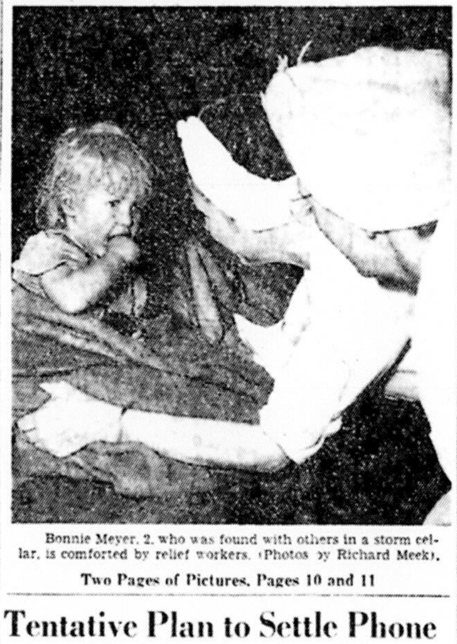

Bonnie Meyer, 2, who was found with others in a storm cellar, is comforted by relief workers. (Photos by Richard Meek).

Two Pages of Pictures, Pages 10 and 11

Tentative Plan to Settle Phone Strike Reached by Long Lines

WASHINGTON, April 10—(AP)—A proposed agreement for settling long distance lines phases of the nationwide telephone strike was submitted Thursday to the policy committee of the National Federation of Telephone Workers.

The proposal was gone over at an earlier meeting of officials of the long lines workers' organization and of the American Telephone & Telegraph Co.

John J. Moran, president of the long lines' union, and G. S. Dring, assistant vice-president of the AT&T long lines department, said the proposal was not initialed.

Moran said that as president of the national union policy committee, he was making no recommendations to that group.

One of those familiar with the proposed settlement said it calls for arbitration of four wage issues on a national level, with six other major points involved to be settled on a local basis.

He said the national issues involved are a general pay increase, differential pay, progression to higher pay scales, and classifications.

Dring told reporters the meeting with long lines union men was devoted to working out some final details that had not been settled when the proposition was agreed upon Wednesday night.

Dring confirmed the proposal involved submitting wage matters to arbitration on a national level.

Moran reiterated the proposal does not affect the entire nationwide telephone walk-out. He said the proposition has to do only with the long distance workers.

Quake Rocks Western U. S.

Damage Slight; Three States Feel Tremors

LOS ANGELES, April 10—(AP)—A deep-seated earthquake, sharp in some sectors but causing no serious damage in heavily populated areas, rocked more than 60,000 square miles of California, Arizona and Nevada at 9:59 a. m. (CST).

A few broken windows and dishes were reported but no injuries. The tremor was felt here with some sharpness, but quickly subsided into a long, rolling motion lasting nearly a minute.

Center in Desert

A shattered bank window in Glendale apparently was the most severe loss, although there were indications some damage might have occurred in remote communities on the Mojave desert, which seemed in initial checks to have been the center of the shock.

At Barstow, a Santa Fe railroad shops point north of San Bernardino, telegraph poles shook noticeably. Two tremors were felt at the desert town of Boron, about three minutes apart.

In Los Angeles, tall buildings rocked and a few persons ran into streets.

Tremor Widely Felt

Reports of tremors ranging from light to moderately severe came from Santa Barbara, on the north; San Diego, on the south; San Bernardino, Phoenix, Ariz., and Las Vegas, Nev., to the east.

It was the first quake of any severity in southern California since March 15, 1946, when Los Angeles' water supply was disrupted briefly by a heavy quake in the Owens valley, east of the towering Sierra Nevada mountains. There were no injuries in that sparsely settled area and Thursday's shock was not felt there.

Youth Discovers Father Dead, Then Hunts for Mother

WOODWARD, April 10—(AP)—A 17-year-old youth entered a funeral home in this tornado stricken city Thursday.

"Have you got my daddy?" he asked the attendant.

They looked and found daddy—A. J. Warriner—among the dead.

The lad straightened his shoulders. "Thanks," he said. "Now all I've got to do is find my mother."

Wholesale Food Index Shows Slight Decline

NEW YORK, April 10—(AP)—The Dun & Bradstreet wholesale food price index, representing the sum total of the price per pound of 31 foods in general use, stood at $6.41 on April 8, compared with $6.45 a week earlier. A year ago the figure was $4.19.

Judge Delays Rule on Refund Of Court Fine to Lewis' Union

WASHINGTON, April 10—(AP)—Federal Judge T. Allan Goldsborough Thursday postponed for two weeks a decision on whether to refund to the United Mine workers $2,800,000 of the $3,500,000 fine he imposed on the union for contempt.

In doing so, the judge said "I regret exceedingly that there hasn't been good faith" on the part of the union and its president, John L. Lewis, in complying with a supreme court mandate.

The supreme court had ordered the $2,800,000 refund provided Lewis canceled a notice terminating the UMW contract with the government. Lewis had done that.

Goldsborough said he though the matter of returning the $2,800,000 should be put off until July 1, the date on which the soft coal mines will be back in private possession.

But he granted a government request for the two week delay with this comment:

"This court doesn't see that good faith can be established in two weeks."

UMW lawyers had asked for the refund immediately, contending Lewis and the UMW had complied with court orders. The government, however, said it wanted time to determine whether there had been compliance in view of the current "safety shutdown" in some mines. **(Related News, Page 4.)**

state mental institutions. A $36 million state bond issue supported by the paper and approved by voters helped to make the reforms possible. In the same election, voters across the state rejected the repeal of prohibition. *The Oklahoman* and *Times* supported the continuation of prohibition.

A big story for *The Oklahoman* and *Times* in 1949 was uncovered by reporter Henry Burchfiel, who discovered hundreds of Oklahoma County land titles registered in fictitious names. He also learned that homes had been sold with no notice to owners that taxes were due. As a result of the papers' investigation, a grand jury was convened. Five men were indicted, including a former county treasurer who later was sent to prison. The exposé brought major reforms in state laws controlling tax resales.

Also in 1949, *The Oklahoman* and *Times* urged school children to send in their nickels and dimes to buy a new elephant for the Oklahoma City Zoo, the old one having died. More than $5,000 was raised and a new elephant named Judy was acquired. She was a star attraction until her death in 1997.

In March 1947, E. K. Gaylord went to New York City, where he accepted for WKY radio the Alfred I. duPont Award for the station's outstanding service and coverage in 1946. Some days later, on April 9, 1947, the station interrupted regular programming to provide news bulletins and to relay appeals for assistance after a catastrophic tornado struck Woodward, in northwest Oklahoma. WKY radio's mobile unit was sent to Woodward and provided a valuable communication link to the outside world.

＊

By 1949, The Oklahoma Publishing Co. consisted of *The Oklahoman* and *Times,* the Mistletoe Express Trucking Co., the *Farmer-Stockman* agricultural publication, and WKY radio. With renewed interest in television following World War II, E. K. Gaylord announced he wanted Oklahoma City to have its own television station. More than a decade earlier in 1936, when he dedicated the new WKY radio studios and office, he stated in a speech, "When television and facsimile transmission are ready for the public, WKY

E. K. Gaylord receives the Alfred I. duPont Award for WKY radio in 1947. Dr. Francis P. Gaines, president of Washington University, makes the presentation.

E. K. Gaylord reviews his notes moments before WKY-TV officially began broadcasting on June 6, 1949.

Oklahoma City residents gather on the street July 1, 1949, to watch a television broadcast in an electronics store window. Few Oklahomans owned TV receivers when WKY-TV began broadcasting.

WKY-TV transmitted a test pattern each afternoon as the new station tested its equipment before regular broadcasts began. The station received calls from viewers all over Oklahoma and neighboring states who reported they had seen the test pattern.

WKY-TV began televising football games from the University of Oklahoma in October 1949. (Courtesy Oklahoma Historical Society)

expects to serve you." He lived up to his word. On April 14, 1948, The Oklahoma Publishing Co. filed an application with the Federal Communications Commission in Washington D.C. to build Oklahoma's first television station in Oklahoma City and operate on Channel 4.

About 25 years later, E. K. Gaylord recalled that the government was begging people to apply for permits. "We were the only one to apply for one in Oklahoma City." Gaylord added: "We knew we'd lose money. . . . I expected it would take at least 90 days of red tape up there in Washington, but we

got approval almost by return mail." By mid-October 1948, a public television demonstration was conducted during the "Made In Oklahoma" exposition in Oklahoma City. Other demonstrations followed to explain and show what television was.

In early April 1949, the television antenna was installed on the WKY radio tower. By the end of April the new television station was transmitting its test pattern. The station's switchboard was flooded with calls from all parts of Oklahoma and from viewers in bordering states reporting reception. WKY-TV went on the air officially with

This photo made about 1950 looks south on Broadway from The Oklahoma Publishing Co.'s building (left) toward the Hotel Skirvin. (Courtesy Ralph Sewell)

An early view of Will Rogers World Airport in the 1950s. (Courtesy Oklahoma City Chamber of Commerce)

live and film programming on June 6, 1949. The station was on the air from 7 to 9:30 P.M., Sunday through Friday. On June 17, WKY-TV carried its first NBC television network program, "Who Said That?" It was on film since the station had not yet been directly linked to NBC. Then in August 1949, WKY-TV signed a contract to provide coverage of the University of Oklahoma home football games for the upcoming season. The first game was televised on October 1, 1949. Late in 1949, as the decade of the '40s ended, WKY-TV placed its first order for color equipment. When the equipment finally arrived, the station became the first independently owned TV station in the United States to broadcast in color.

About that time Edward L. Gaylord met Thelma Feragen Horton who worked at WKY-TV. They met on the golf course at the Oklahoma City Country Club. Dating followed and they were married on August 30, 1950. Their union produced four children: E. K. Gaylord II, named for his grandfather, and three daughters, Christy, Mary and Louise.

Chapter Nine

CHANGES IN THE '50S

The 1950 census showed Oklahoma City with a population of 243,504 and Oklahoma with 2,233,351. The future of post-war Oklahoma was looking bright, but E. K. Gaylord thought the state's education system could be better. He had a life-long interest in education. Through editorials in his papers during the '50s, he often criticized the state's educational system, believing its finances could be improved. "The whole future of Oklahoma as a state depends on the best possible education and training of our children and young people," Gaylord said. Under his watchful eyes, *The Oklahoman* and *Times* began sponsoring the Oklahoma City Science Fair to encourage promising high school students in the field. Every year The Oklahoma Publishing Co. pays the expenses of sending winning young people to the National Science Fair.

In October 1950, E. K. Gaylord hired Jim Lange as a full-time cartoonist. From the late 1930s until Lange was hired, the papers did not have a full-time cartoonist after Charles Werner left. In the interim, artists in the newspapers' syndication and art department, namely Ken Colgan and Ralph Yoes, drew occasional cartoons when the need arose. Lange began drawing cartoons full-time and won many awards. Later he became president of the American Cartoonists Association. In October 2000, Lange celebrated his 50th anniversary with The Oklahoma Publishing Co.

WKY announced plans in 1951 to construct a new office and studio building on a site east of its radio transmitter on Britton Road. The facility, they said, would house both WKY radio and WKY-TV. By then Edward L. Gaylord was supervising the operations of WKY and WKY-TV. Ground was broken for the new WKY and WKY-TV building in July, and both stations soon began broadcasting from there. WKY-TV became the first television station in the nation to establish a professional meteorological department. The station then defied a federal ban against broadcasting tornado developments by warning viewers of approaching storms. In time, they succeeded in getting the federal ban lifted.

Under Edward L. Gaylord's leadership, WKY and WKY-TV grew and provided improved service to Oklahoma City and Oklahoma. In February 1952, WKY-TV telecast the Republican State Convention from Municipal Auditorium in Oklahoma City. About two months later the station aired the Democratic State Convention from the same location. All of WKY-TV's local programming was live while network programs were on film. This changed at 7 A.M. on July 1, 1952, when E. K. Gaylord pushed a button connecting WKY-TV with NBC television via microwave relay stations. WKY-TV's on-air program schedule then expanded to more than 111 hours per week and, during 1952, viewers were able to see the national Democratic and Republican political conventions live. In 1953, The Oklahoma Publishing Co. donated $150,000 worth of television equipment from WKY-TV to the Oklahoma Educational Television Authority. The gift made it possible to start telecasting educational television programs in Oklahoma.

Meantime, E. K. Gaylord's interest in technology brought further changes to *The Oklahoman* and *Times*. The Oklahoma Publishing Co. made its greatest single mechanical improvement since 1929 as the decade of the 1950s began. It installed a $1.25 million, 12-unit Goss Headliner press, capable of printing 60,000 copies of an 84-page paper each hour. The new press produced newspapers that were easier to read. For many years they were printed with a 6¾-point Ionic type. The day the new press went into operation, a new 8-point Corona typeface was introduced. Soon after the new press was installed, both papers were among the first in the nation to use punched paper tape to operate their Linotype machines and to use photographic composition for advertisements.

E. K. Gaylord presses the button to link WKY-TV directly with the NBC television network in 1952.

During 1951, reporters Elwin Harfield and Paul Swain linked an Oklahoma County armed robbery with a missing Illinois family's car found near Tulsa. This led to the capture of multiple murderer William E. "Billy" Cook Jr.

Following the start of the Korean War, Oklahoma's 45th Infantry Division and the 20th Infantry Battalion of the U.S. Marine reserve was mobilized. *Times* reporter Wayne Mackey went with the 45th to Japan and kept Oklahomans informed. When Mackey reported the need for recreational equipment for the troops, Wally Wallis, *The Oklahoman*'s sports editor, rounded up a huge shipment of sports gear that was sent to Oklahomans serving overseas in the military. When an Oklahoma City soldier stationed in Germany was imprisoned in East Berlin, reporters from *The Oklahoman* and *Times* focused attention on the story and got the U.S. Defense and State Departments to step in. Homer Cox was freed from a labor camp. At home, reporters William Freemon and Seymour Ramsey dressed as bums in Oklahoma City and went into downtown bars to prove that derelicts were

being used to cast fraudulent votes in a city council election. Two other reporters, Jim Jackson and Bob McMillin, revealed that non-existent addresses were being used by voters. Their stories brought reforms in state voter registration laws, and ultimately led to the defeat of a veteran city council member in Oklahoma City.

Late in March 1952, E. K. Gaylord learned that his brother Lewis had died in Ventura County, California, at the age of 80. Lewis Gaylord had pursued a career in advertising in St. Louis, Detroit and New York and spent his last years in California. E. K. attended his brother's funeral services held in the Church of the Little Flowers in Los Angeles. Burial was at Grand Junction, Colorado, where Lewis was laid to rest next to the grave of his father.

When The Oklahoma Publishing Co. celebrated its 50th anniversary in 1953, E. K. Gaylord, then 80, said: "It is a matter of great satisfaction to me that most of our key men have risen to the top right here in our own organization. I am happy that my own son, Edward L. Gaylord, has shown great ability in assuming many responsibilities." As a small boy his son often

visited his father at *The Oklahoman.* "I was fascinated with the place," recalled Edward L. Gaylord years later. As he grew older, young Gaylord also worked summers on his father's Golden Guernsey Dairy located north of what is now Lake Hefner. The senior Gaylord enjoyed farming and showing his Guernsey cattle at the state fair and throughout the Southwest. At shows, one of his biggest competitors was J. C. Penney, who also owned a Guernsey dairy and showed cattle. Gaylord and Penney became good friends. Edward L. Gaylord recalled:

I remember when I was a kid during the '30s, my father told me, "I know you like farming and you are interested in this, but you'll never make more than $300,000 in your lifetime to run this farm, and you can make that much in a year at the paper." My father really didn't

push me into newspaper work. He was hoping I would get into it, but he wanted me to get into whatever I was interested in. As the years passed, I became very interested in newspapers.

Like his father, Edward L. Gaylord soon became involved in professional

A "first" for WKY-TV occurred on April 23, 1955, when the station produced a 30-minute NBC-TV network program "National Square Dance Festival" from Oklahoma City. It was the first time a color network program was originated by a non-network-owned television station.

E. K. Gaylord and his wife, Inez Kinney Gaylord, posed for this photo about 1952. He was approaching his 80th birthday.

Edward L. Gaylord works on his swing.

groups. He served as President of the Southern Newspaper Publishers Association and a director of the Bureau of Advertising of the American Newspaper Publishers Association. Edward L. Gaylord also became involved in civic work. He has since served 10 years as president of the State Fair of Oklahoma (now the Oklahoma State Fair); as director of the Oklahoma Health Sciences Foundation, Inc.; as chairman of the Oklahoma Medical Research Institute in 1997; chairman of the board of directors of the National Cowboy Hall of Fame and Western Heritage Center (now the National Cowboy and Western Heritage Museum); as treasurer, director and president of the Oklahoma City Chamber of Commerce; and as chairman of the Oklahoma Industries Authority, a position he held for more than 30 years.

✳

In 1954, *The Oklahoman* and *Times* uncovered numerous scandals in the Oklahoma City police department. Reporter Deacon New reported that the chief of detectives accepted a $5,000 loan from a city gambler and bootlegger; that jail prisoners were used to vote illegally in a municipal election; that twice as many meals were bought for jail prisoners as the total jail capacity; that a police lieutenant participated in a gambling game in which another player lost $9,000; and that an Air Force officer was beaten after he had been innocently caught in a police raid. As a result of the papers' coverage, the chief of detectives was fired, another officer demoted, and the chief of police resigned.

In 1954, *The Oklahoman* and *Times* were among the first papers in the nation to use photographic composition to create ads. That same year WKY-TV began broadcasting in color. About then OPUBCO's broadcasting

division headed by Edward L. Gaylord expanded into Florida. It purchased WTVT, a CBS affiliate in Tampa–St. Petersburg in 1956. Committed to news and informational programming, WTVT was one of the first stations in the nation to air one hour of local news and editorials. In 1959, WTVT became the first television station in America to computerize all weather information.

Back home The Oklahoma Publishing Co. continued to urge the expansion of Oklahoma City's water supply to meet the city's growing demand. The city took the first step in a $109 million project to tap southeastern Oklahoma's vast water resources. Rights were won by the city council for a half-billion acre feet of water, then five times the existing capacity of the municipal reservoirs.

E. K. Gaylord's ongoing interest in science and technology resulted in *The Oklahoman* and *Times* renewing its crusade in 1955 to upgrade science education. Editorials pointed out that Russia was training millions of scientists, while the United States had a shortage. Also in 1955 OPUBCO constructed a display building at the new State Fair grounds. Since then the Company annually brings award-winning displays and shows to Oklahoma State Fair goers each September. During 1955 E. K. Gaylord also challenged Oklahoma City to "revive the spirit of the pioneers," and to build, within 10 years, a city "larger than Dallas is now." At the time the metropolitan population of Dallas was about 600,000. A decade later Oklahoma City's population reached 585,000. When the Russian satellite, Sputnik I, plunged the world into the space age on October 4, 1957, *The Oklahoman* renewed its call to upgrade the nation's science education and research programs.

Chance of Storms
Partly cloudy, warm, chance of thunderstorms Saturday with high of 85, same as Friday.
—Map on Page 3.

THE DAILY OKLAHOMAN

(Entered as Second-Class Matter at the Postoffice at Oklahoma City, Oklahoma)

The Oil Page
See page 22. Other features:
Editorials ..... 10 Public Records ... 10
Good Morning ... 4 Sports 13, 14, 15
Markets ..... 23 Uncle Ray 23
Obituaries ..... 9 Women's News ... 8

VOL. 66, NO. 273 — TWENTY-FOUR PAGES—500 N BROADWAY, OKLAHOMA CITY, SATURDAY, OCTOBER 5, 1957 — SINGLE COPY PRICE: Daily 5c, Sunday 20c

First Earth Satellite Launched by Russians

MOSCOW, Oct. 5 (Saturday) (AP)—The Soviet Union announced Saturday it has the world's first artificial moon streaking around the globe 560 miles out in space.

A multiple-stage rocket launched the earth satellite Friday, the Russians said, shooting it upward at about five miles per second.

They said the satellite, a globe described as 23 inches in diameter and weighing 185 pounds, can be seen in its orbit with glasses and followed by radio through instruments it carries.

(Radio signals on the wavelength of the Soviet moon—sounding as a deep "beep, beep, beep"—were picked up by electronic engineers of the National Broadcasting Co., in New York.

(In Washington, the defense department said the naval research laboratory had recorded three passes of the satellite over the United States, one in the vicinity of Washington and two farther west.

In Cambridge, Mass., the Smithsonian Astrophysical Observatory said sightings of the satellite have been reported in scattered parts of the country. The first sighting was reported by a station in Terre Haute, Ind., at 8:50 p.m.

In thus announcing the launching of the first earth satellite ever put in globe-girdling orbit under man's controls, the Soviet Union claimed a victory over the United States.

The two big powers had been in a hot but mainly secret race to be first to probe the high space realms with spheres laden with instruments.

The Moscow announcement said:

"The successful launching of the first man-made satellite makes a tremendous contribution to the treasure house of world science and culture.

"Artificial earth satellites will pave the way for space travel and it seems that the present generation will witness how the freed and conscious labor of the people of the new socialist society turns even the most daring of man's dreams into reality. . ."

In a special bulletin early Saturday morning, the Soviet Tass agency said the Russian moon "is now revolving around the earth at the rate of one circuit every hour and 35 minutes."

The launching occurred just three months and four days after the opening of the International Geophysical year.

Moscow reported the satellite can be seen with the simplest kind of telescope glasses. Its velocity was given as something like five miles per second at a height of about 560 miles above the earth.

The broadcast said the Russians plan to launch several more earth satellites in the next year.

Moscow said the satellite is fitted with steel radio transmitters continuously sending signals earthward on the 15 and 7.5 meter wave lengths and easily recived by a broad range of amateur sets. Its announced weight of about 185 pounds is more than eight times the weight of a projected U. S. earth satellite.

Moscow described the signals as of about 3-10 of a second long with a pause of the same length. The two frequencies alternate in signalling, Moscow radio said.

It announced the first satellite's would appear over the Moscow area twice Saturday morning. It did not give other sighting points on the course.

The broadcast said Soviet satellites planned later will be bigger and heavier than the first sphere.

U. S. experts in Washington were amazed at the reported size of the Soviet moon. Dr. Joseph Kaplan, chairman of the U. S. national committee for the International Geophysical Year (IGY) said its 185-pound weight and 23 inch span "is really fantastic. If they can launch that they can launch much heavier ones."

The U. S. experts figured the first U. S. launching attempt would be made early next spring after an attempt to put some 6.4 inch 4-pound objects into the earth's orbit for a short time in November.

Russia had been silent on the progress of its experiments since last June 19 when a news conference in Moscow was told Russian scientists planned to launch one or more satellites during the IGY that began July 1.

U. S. spokesmen said last May the United States did not plan a secret launching and hoped the Russians didn't either.

The Moscow broadcast said Soviet scientific stations were still trying to determine the flying sphere's exact trajectory. It said that because the density of the rarefied upper layers is not accurately known there are no data to determine the points of the satellite's entry into the denser strata.

The broadcast added, however, that its tremendous velocity will cause the satellite to burn up on reaching the denser layers.

The Moscow broadcast quoted the official Tass news agency as saying:

"For several years research and experimental designing work

(Continued on Page 2, Column 3)

Hoffa Elected As Teamsters Shun Charges

Jubilant Leader Promises to Turn Union Into Model

MIAMI BEACH, Fla., Oct. 4 (AP)—Stubby-square-jawed Jimmy Hoffa Friday took over full control as president of the giant Teamsters union and pledged to turn the organization into a "model of trade unionism."

The 44-year-old target of labor scandal charges was elected chief officer of the 1½ million member union by a tremendous margin of nearly 3 to 1 over the combined vote of two opponents.

In the final count, 1,208 widely cheering delegates voted for Hoffa, 313 for William A. Lee and 140 for Thomas J. Haggerty.

Lee and Haggerty, both from Chicago, had campaigned for a cleanup of the corruption conditions charged to the union.

The delegates thus chose to ignore the charges against Hoffa, re-

Picture on Page 5.

tiring union president Dave Beck and other Teamster bosses. They had been accused of helping themselves to vast sums from the union's rich treasury and abusing union powers.

Hoffa Cries 'Smear'

The charges against Hoffa included associating with known hoodlums and racketeers.

Hoffa, denying the charges as a smear, said he and the Teamsters union "have just come through the most vicious attack any group of workers has ever experienced. Never in history has so much outside effort been exerted on the internal affairs of a free organization."

But troubles for Hoffa and his huge union are far from over. It faces an almost certain ouster from the AFL-CIO, a renewed probe by the senate rackets investigating committee headed by Sen McClellan (D., Ark.) and even a court attempt to throw Hoffa out of his newly won union office.

Sen. McClellan said in Washington Hoffa's election was "an arrogant defiance of the AFL-CIO," the federation having judged Hoffa corrupt and unfit to remain in organized labor.

AFL-CIO Silent

Secretary of Labor Mitchell, in Chicago said Hoffa's election would almost certainly lead to "repressive" labor legislation in congress.

In Washington a spokesman at AFL-CIO headquarters said AFL-CIO President George Meany would have no comment on Hoffa's election.

The first showdown on the ouster move is expected in three weeks when the AFL-CIO executive council meets to determine whether the Teamsters have rid its ranks of alleged corrupt elements.

Hoffa, in a fighting acceptance speech to the wildly applauding convention delegates, said the Teamsters want to remain in the AFL-CIO. He invited the federation to rescind its corruption finding against the Teamsters.

Hoffa said such unions as the

(Continued on Page 2, Column 2)

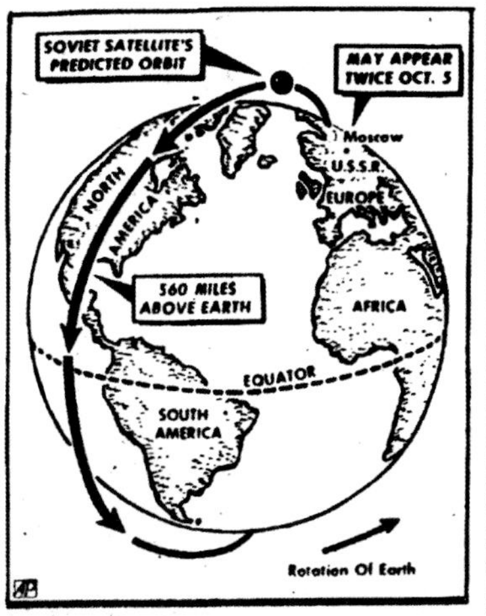
SOVIET SATELLITE'S PREDICTED ORBIT
MAY APPEAR TWICE OCT. 5
Moscow
U.S.S.R.
EUROPE
NORTH AMERICA
560 MILES ABOVE EARTH
AFRICA
EQUATOR
SOUTH AMERICA
Rotation Of Earth
AP

This global projection illustrates the orbit of the Russian satellite. The satellite is expected to pass over most of North America. The Russians say it takes an hour and 35 minutes to circle the globe at an altitude of 560 miles.

Soviet Applauded By U.S. Scientists

WASHINGTON, Oct. 4 (AP)—Quick American congratulations went to the Russians Friday night after the Moscow announcement that Soviet scientists had succeeded in launching an artificial moon.

The congratulations were extended by Dr. Lloyd Berkner, an American official of the International Geophysical Year (IGY).

The occasion was a cocktail party at the Russian embassy, given for those attending a special conference of the IGY.

Dr. Berkner, who is the reporter on earth satellites and rockets for a special committee of the IGY, said he had learned from a press dispatch of the Russian announcement.

He offered his congratulations, while Dr. A A. Blagonravov and other Soviet scientists at the party beamed in appreciation.

Dr. Berkner said American teams organized to spot artificial

Related News on Page 3.

satellites were immediately being called into action to look for the Russian moon.

IN another recognition of Soviet success, Dr. Joseph Kaplan, chairman of the U. S. national committee for IGY, said:

"I am amazed that in the short time which they had to plan—obviously not any longer than we had—I think it was a remarkable achievement on their part."

"From the point of view of international co-operation the important thing is that a satellite has been launched. They did it and did it first.

"I hope they give us enough information so that our moonwatch teams can help learn the scientific benefits."

Noting reports that the satellite was 23 inches across and weighed about 185 pounds, Kaplan said: "This is really fantastic and that if they can

(Continued on Page 2, Column 6)

Guilty Robber Wins 10 Years

Connie Gene Gray, 28, of 1415 S Indiana, one of the "Ivy league" robbery gang involved in a series of hold-ups here last month, drew a 10-year prison term Friday afternoon when he entered a guilty plea.

Gray pleaded guilty to the September 16 hold-up of the Whittaker Food store, 3629 NW 10. The gunmen took $267.61 from the store and were apprehended shortly after by Warr Acres police.

Gray entered his plea before Glen O. Morris, district judge.

The gunman is slated to make a vastly different appearance in court Monday when he is slated to be married by a common pleas judge prior to being taken to McAlester to serve his term.

Thursday, Gray and Mrs. Betty Jane White, 26, of 1303 SW 21, were issued a marriage license. John Booth, Gray's attorney, said he would ask the court for an order Monday authorizing the wedding.

Gray was given 10 years on the recommendation of William N. Mounger, assistant county attorney. Mounger told the court that Gray had co-operated with Oklahoma City police in solving the

(Continued on Page 2, Column 6)

High Speed Car Crashes in City Area Kill Two

Airman at Tinker Hits Bus and Dies; Joyride Ride is Fatal

STATE TRAFFIC DEATHS
1957 to date, 513; October, 6.
1956 to date, 493; October 1.

Two persons died in separate high speed car crashes on the outskirts of Oklahoma City Friday night. Two others were killed in an accident in Rogers county.

The highway patrol identified the dead as:

NEAL C. JOHNSON, 18, Tinker airman.

KENNETH CARSON, 15, of 2537 SW 25.

MAXINE LAUDERDALE, 34, Cushing.

ERSHEL JOHN DEAN, Tulsa.

Johnson was killed and two other Tinker airmen hurt shortly before 10 p.m. Friday when a car, reported traveling at a speed of 100 miles an hour, crashed into the side of a Continental Trailways bus at NE 23 and Douglas.

The impact knocked the heavy eastbound bus across the road. One passenger on the bus, unidentified, was reported shaken up.

Driver Hurled Out

Johnson, who was driving a 1939 souped up Mercury, was thrown out of the car. Two passengers, identified as M. L. Williams, 20, and Leonard J. Yellow Elk, 22, were hurt. Yellow Elk was reported in serious condition.

Investigating trooper Garland Richie said the northbound car ran the stop sign at 23rd street and struck the front right side of the bus.

The bus driver, Bill Elbert Leegrand, 43, of 2717 SW 48, said he tried to swerve to avoid the accident.

Williams told newsmen they were enroute to a nightspot a mile east of the scene of the collision.

"We had just left Midwest City," he said. "We crossed the railroad tracks a quarter of a mile before the wreck at 100 miles an hour. We almost had a wreck there.

Head Hits Roof

"The car bounced and threw everybody around. I was in the back seat and it bounced me so high I hit the roof with my head. By the time I straightened up the stop sign at 23rd was going past us and that's the last I remember. I don't even know what we hit," Williams said.

Police blamed speed for another accident which killed a 15-year-old boy at SW 69 and Pennsylvania shortly before 6 p.m. The victim, Carson, was killed when a car hurtled a ditch and crashed into an embankment.

He was the city's 16th traffic victim this year, compared to 12 dead at the same time in 1956.

Investigating officers C. L. Posey and Bill Lewellen said young Carson was a passenger in a 1956 model convertible which went out of control traveling 70 miles an hour.

The car was driven by Mary Suellen Huffhines, 16, of 945 SW 50, the officers said. Neither the driver nor her sister, Elena Huff-

(Continued on Page 2, Column 1)

Plight of Arkansas Viewed As 'Tragic' by Rockefeller

LITTLE ROCK, Ark., Oct. 4 (AP) — Multimillionaire Winthrop Rockefeller Friday night described the integration crisis at Little Rock Central highschool as tragic.

A friend and political appointee of Gov. Orval Faubus, Rockefeller said:

"There comes a time when every citizen of the state and country who believes in the American constitution must subordinate individual feelings to the common good and unity of the country. And that time is here now."

Rockefeller, who left New York in 1953 to make Arkansas his adopted home, has reportedly been under strong pressure to take a stand in the integration crisis. There were advance reports that he would issue a blast at Faubus and at the same time resign his position as chairman of the Arkansas industrial development commission. He did neither.

However, Rockefeller did not mention Faubus by name. And he gave every indication in his statement that he would continue to head the development commission.

Faubus appointed Rockefeller

Winthrop Rockefeller

in 1955 to a 5-year term on the commission. He was elected chairman by the other six members.

The commission's aim is to expand Arkansas' industrial economy.

Rockefeller issued his statement from his palatial farm at Petit Jean Mountain, about 65 miles northeast of here. It read:

"I believe first and foremost in the constitution of the United States and the law and order which it establishes. It is that law and order which gives the United States a position of leadership in the troubled world of today. When constitutional government was challenged in World war II, we all rose to defend it—and I spent six years in the service during that war.

"I regard the events of the past month as tragic. I respect the people of Arkansas and have faith in their goodwill and moderation. I am proud to be one of them. I firmly believe that this spirit of goodwill and moderation is beginning to assert itself and Arkansas will again go forward."

In connection with the Arkansas industrial development commission, Rockefeller said:

"I believe it will be six months before we can accurately estimate the damage that has been done—and damage there has been.

"We are not defeated. We have confidence. The commission will

(Continued on Page 2, Column 3)

Reappraisal Set For Atoka Land

State and city officials agreed at a conference in Gov. Gary's office Friday to reappraise 900 acres of state-owned land in Atoka county needed by the city for its southeastern water supply project.

The governor also disclosed that he has asked that a study be made to see if the buildings, now used by the Stringtown model prison farm, could be converted to house old persons now in mental hospitals.

He said if the state can find some use for the buildings, it would make it possible to lower the price of the land sought by the city.

Gary said the reservoir project would take all of the farm land that can be put under cultivation and would leave about $2 millions worth of buildings on 1,100 acres of rough land that is of little use for farming purposes.

The governor said Oklahoma City has appraised the land at around $90,000 and the state board of affairs has rejected the figure.

A state appraisal has placed val-

(Continued on Page 2, Column 1)

Bathing Mishap Burns Baby Girl at Stillwater

(Oklahoman-Times Stillwater Bureau)

STILLWATER, Oct. 4—A 22-month-old girl received second-degree burns over the lower half of her body in a bath-time accident F[illegible]ay.

The [illegible]d, Tommie Branson, daug[illegible] of Mr. and Mrs. Branley Bra[illegible]on, was seated in a lavatory and accidentally turned on the hot water when her mother turned her back for a moment. She was admitted to Municipal hospital.

Gary Ignores Sen. Sandlin In Job Fuss

By RAY PARR

A dispute over appointment of an Okfuskee county election board official Friday threatened to bring an open break between Gov. Gary and state Sen. Hugh Sandlin of Holdenville.

Over heated objections of the state senator, the state election board Friday, upon recommendation of the governor, voted two to one to appoint Mrs. Alice Turner, Okemah, as secretary of the Okfuskee county board.

Mrs. Turner was backed by Bennie Hill, Okemah, state representative. It was a rather unusual political alliance because county election board appointments are considered senate patronage by long standing tradition. Gary, a former state senator, has nearly always been careful to consider wishes of senators in patronage matters.

Sandlin said at Holdenville Friday, "I'm all shook up about it. This came as a surprise to me. Unless this matter is straightened out I will have a public statement later."

Gov. Gary said, "There is nothing personal between me and Sen. Sandlin."

"There is just a difference in viewpoint," he added.

At Okemah late Friday Hill defended the appointment of Mrs. Turner.

"She is the most wonderful lady in our county," he said.

Mrs. Turner was appointed Friday to succeed Huie D. Harkey, also of Okemah, who resigned. Harkey is reported to be planning to run for the house of representatives against Hill.

Harkey was named secretary last July after Mrs. Turner, who had served several years in the post, was removed upon recommendation of Sandlin.

Gary said Friday Mrs. Turner was removed without his knowledge. He said he received a number of protests over the removal

(Continued on Page 2, Column 8)

Turkey Blasts Back at Russia

ANKARA, Oct. 5 (Saturday) (AP)—Turkey Saturday sharply rejected Soviet charges of planned aggression against Syria and publicly challenged Moscow to abandon its own middle east policy.

The Turkish government released the text of a letter from Premier Menderes to Soviet Premier Bulganin claiming "subversive actions in Syria have reached a culminating point."

"This country (Syria) is arming itself speedily and far beyond its logical defensive needs," Menderes said.

"Or rather it perhaps is being turned into an armament depot eventually to be used by others.

"If establishment of the true friendship based on mutual trust between our two countries is desired as your state in your message," the Turkish leader said, "discontinuance of a policy pursued in the middle east and especially in Syria would greatly contribute to this end."

Menderes' letter was in reply to one from Bulganin September 13. Accusing Turkey of threatening to provoke a third world war by massing troops on the Syrian border for what he called an American-planned attack.

Menderes remarked it was peculiar that Soviet Russia should be taking a proprietary interest in Syria and Syrian problems while Turkey has received no message of complaint from Syria itself.

Veteran Jurist Dies

DENVER, Oct. 4 (AP)—Haslett P. Burke, veteran Colorado jurist who once turned down an appointment to the U. S. senate, died in Presbyterian hospital Friday at the age of 83.

Poland Forces Battle Student Freedom Riots

Defiant Anti-Reds Continue to Hurl Taunts at Police

WARSAW, Poland, Oct. 4 (AP)—Combined forces of Polish Red police, security troops and militiamen from worker ranks fought down a new student uprising for freedom here Friday night.

The students, still apparently untamed, taunted the anti-riot forces with shouts of: "gestapo, gestapo" (Poland was one of the first and worst sufferers at the hands of Hitler's gestapo more than a decade ago.)

The forces used clubs, tear gas and noise bombs as the violence spread beyond the student sphere to Poles of other ranks.

Others Join Riots

They broke up groups of students at the Warsaw Polytechnic school for the second straight night and smashed a demonstration outside the Communist party headquarters where the party central committee was reported in emergency session.

People from other walks of life joined the milling crowds after the first police assault on students.

The steel-helmeted riot police first released tear gas grenades to break up taunting student groups, then wielded rubber truncheons on individual students trapped in courtyards and other refuges.

Black-capped security police patroled key points throughout the city as the students gathered in the Polytechnic Great Hall for Friday night's meeting.

Paper Suppressed

Despite threats of punishment, the students massed again to protest suppression of the student newspaper Po Prostu and the rough treatment police gave them at their first rally Thursday night. The paper has been harsh in criticizing recent Communist party and government policy.

Truckloads of steel-helmeted factory militia, carrying clubs, poured to strategic spots in the city to back up the Communist police.

(Warsaw radio announced Friday night that Poland's Communist party has ordered party penalties for card-carrying communists on the banned paper's staff. The radio as heard in London quoted a communique saying the paper was suspended for printing articles harmful to the regime but did not mention student protest demonstrations.)

Tear Gas Used

The police used tear gas bombs against 2,000 students in their first protest meeting outside a school boarding house on Narutowicza square Thursday night, then loosed gas bombs twice more against hard core resistance groups.

About 20 students and 10 policemen were reported injured and another 30 students were said to have been arrested in the Thursday night melee.

It was the first anti-authority outbreak in Warsaw since Wladyslaw Gomulka returned to power as Communist party boss a year ago. Anti-Stalinist movements such as the students' had paved the way for his victory over the strict Soviet-type Communist leaders.

Despite government and college threats that the student demonstrators would suffer severe penalties the students massed again Friday night.

The first wave of students leaving the auditorium were chased into side streets. Many sought refuge in byways and courtyards. The steel-helmeted riot police went in after them with clubs.

A new wave of students massed on the steps of the gray-walled Polytechnic auditorium. A truck with Russian markings went by. The crowd whistled in derision.

The police moved in again swinging clubs and throwing tear gas and noise bombs. Students kept up their taunting cry of "gestapo, gestapo."

Several students collapsed in the road.

Crowds near the party building stretched a quarter of a mile to the skyscraper palace of culture. Riot police scattered them with noise bombs. The factory militiamen, in their steel helmets, stood in groups every 50 yards along Novy Swiat (New World) street.

The Inside Headlines

Lt. Cmdr. Michael Parker, close friend of Prince Philip of England, sued for divorce; co-respondent named. —Page 24.

Speaker tells American Association of University Women here that Little Rock case is fuel for Reds. —Page 5.

Congressman Tom Steed indicates his approval of Eisenhower's use of federal troops in integration row. —Page 4.

Lightly-clad 2-year-old girl who had been sought by 500 searchers is found shivering in Pennsylvania. —Page 11.

H. B. Groh, chamber of commerce president, reports that he found Russian people satisfied with communism. —Page 24.

Beer industries spokesman demands United Drys put up or shut up on proving charges about repeal group. —Page 16.

Lt. Cmdr. Parker

Soviet's Satellite 'Scares' Scientist

ORLANDO, Fla., Oct. 4 (AP)—The Orlando Sentinel said it checked the four earth satellite tracking stations in Brevard county, Fla.—site of the U. S. missile test center — and found none operating Friday night in an effort to track the Russian baby moon.

The stations were completed three or four months ago, the newspaper said.

The Sentinel also said the top cranking personnel of project Vanguard, the U. S. earth satellite project, expressed serious concern about the Soviet announcement.

One said, "Frankly it's enough to scare the hell out of me. If they can do that they can drop ICBM's (intercontinental ballistics missiles) on us."

Another was quoted as calling it "A tremendous scientific achievement, something you can't take lightly at all."

Death Erases Clue To Lost Bootlegger

A deputy sheriff disclosed Friday that the late gangster Gene Paul Norris once agreed to help officers locate missing Orville Lindsay Chambless, Oklahoma City bootlegger who disappeared last year.

The disclosure came during a bond forfeiture hearing Friday morning before Superior Court Judge Robert Landers in Lawton.

A witness at the hearing, E. A. "Boots" Capshaw, Oklahoma county deputy sheriff, said Norris was shot to death in a gunfight with Fort Worth officers before he could carry out his promise.

The whereabouts of Chambless has been a top mystery to law enforcement officers in Oklahoma and the southwest for more than a year. Norris had been quizzed in connection with his disappearance.

Some officers believe Norris may have assassinated Chambless for his role in assisting the FBI in an investigation of a $200,000 robbery in Fort Worth. Norris was charged with participating in the robbery.

Friday's bond hearing resulted from an application by the state to forfeit a $2,500 bond which had been posted by Chambless two years ago pending an appeal of an armed robbery conviction.

His conviction was subsequently upheld by the criminal court of appeals but Lawton officers have not been able to find Chambless.

Judge Landers ordered the bond forfeited Friday afternoon after listening to testimony from Capshaw and Chambless' wife, Mary Lou Chambless, who now lives in Texas.

Both testified they did not know the whereabouts of Chambless. Mrs. Chambless said she had not heard from her husband since his

(Continued on Page 2, Column 1)

Warm Gulf Winds Lift Rain Clouds Over Oklahoma

Cold weather disappeared from the weekend weather forecast Friday but thunderstorms stayed, as warm air moved in from the south to send Sooner temperatures up.

Four reporting points — Gage, Hobart, Altus and Fort Sill—tied for hottest-spot honors. All recorded 91 degrees. The state's coolest point was Tulsa, with 83.

A Rocky Mountain low which threatened cold weather has bypassed Oklahoma. However, southerly winds Friday brought more Gulf moisture, and scattered thundershowers are expected for the entire state Saturday. Saturday's high is expected to be in the 80s.

Hawkins, Tanya Together Again

WELLINGTON, Kan., Oct. 4 (AP)—Mrs. Tanya Hawkins was reunited Friday night with the turncoat GI she married in Red China. They met on a train and hustled off in a waiting car before newsmen could reach them.

The pretty 25-year-old white Russian woman, wife of Samuel D. Hawkins, Oklahoma City, had been scheduled to debark from the train at Wichita. But her husband and another man boarded the train here and left on the side opposite the platform where reporters and photographers were waiting.

The car, bearing a Sedgwick county, Kan., (Wichita), license plate, headed south.

Mrs. Hawkins arrived Tuesday from Hong Kong. She delayed meeting her husband by one day and went on a sightseeing tour in San Francisco.

Cool Rain
Cloudy and cooler with scattered showers. High 55 compared to Tuesday's 79. Low 42.
Map on Page 15.

THE DAILY OKLAHOMAN

TWENTY-FOUR PAGES—500 N. BROADWAY, OKLAHOMA CITY, WEDNESDAY, APRIL 8, 1959

VOL. 68, NO. 93

DAILY, FIVE CENTS

STATE GOES WET

Norick Elected Mayor; Council Pair Is Ousted

By CULLEN JOHNSON

James H. Norick, who got into the runoff by one recounted vote, Tuesday was elected mayor of Oklahoma City.

He defeated Charles R. Burba by more than 22,000 votes.

The heavy turnout of 94,000 voters also brought defeat to the two remaining councilmen up for re-election this spring.

The councilmen defeated were A. M. Bert DeBolt, ward 1, and Robert M. Constant, ward 2.

DeBolt was defeated by Harry Bell, former operator of an ornamental iron company.

Constant lost the council place he has held since 1951 to Ray Martin, insuranceman.

Wayne Speegle was elected councilman in ward 4 over Melvin Dotson and will succeed Charles Schreck, incumbent, who lost out in the primary last month.

With all 229 of the city's precincts tabulated, Norick's total was 58,648 to Burba's 35,602.

The vote by wards in the mayor's race:

Ward 1—Burba, 5,700; Norick, 12,304.

Ward 2—Burba, 7,247; Norick, 12,000.

Ward 3—Burba, 7,610; Norick, 12,344.

Ward 4—Burba, 12,116; Norick, 13,391.

The council race results:

Ward 1 (58 precincts complete)—DeBolt, 10,690; Bell 14,852.

Ward 2 (61 of 61 precincts)—Constant, 8,743; Martin, 10,938.

Ward 4 (56 precincts complete)—Speegle, 13,383; Dotson, 9,993.

Norick, who served one term as mayor and one councilman before retiring voluntarily in 1955, received results of the election at his campaign headquarters, surrounded by a flock of his campaign volunteer workers and well-wishers.

Friends Thanked

After his election was assured, Norick issued a statement thanking his friends and neighbors for their work in his behalf.

"This has not been an individual victory," he pointed out. Norick then added the promise that he will meet "head-on" the responsibilities of the mayor's office and "I will live up to my promise to be a mayor for all Oklahoma City and all the people."

"It is with deep humility and
(Continued on Page 5, Column 1)

Shawnee Jury Blasts Sheriff

Report After Quiz Urges His Ouster

By JACK SPENCER
(Daily Oklahoman Correspondent)

SHAWNEE, April 7—A Pottawatomie county grand jury, investigating county offices and election board Tuesday gave district Judge J. Knox Byrum a petition seeking the ouster of Sheriff Bruce Curtright.

The investigating panel handed down the 30-year-old verdict in its report, accusing him of willful neglect of duty and maladministration in office.

The petition, signed by Delbert Smith, jury foreman, and Harry Cady, county attorney, accused the sheriff of drunk driving, public drunkenness and accepting apparent bribes from whisky merchants.

Answer Time Set

Curtright will have until April 16 to file an answer to charges made in the civil suit. It is the first time in history a Pottawatomie county official has been requested to be removed from office.

In its petition, the grand jury said Curtright accepted $400 from Mrs. Alene Denton and Joe Cecil whom the jury identified as liquor merchants. It said one $200 payment was made by Mrs. Denton through Jake Sims, a private investigator from Oklahoma City, and two $200 payments were made directly to the bootleggers.

Whisky Confiscated

The investigating panel said Curtright allowed whisky to be sold in the Oak Ridge Terrace Supper club, where it said gambling was allowed.

The grand jury also charged that Sheriff Curtright gave a deputy sheriff, Gordon Cartwright, 17 pints of whisky on one occasion.

The jury said Curtright raided the Denton woman's and Cecil's whisky store in Macomber
(Continued on Page 5, Column 7)

Whisky Raiders Have Light Day

Oklahoma City police whisky raiders had a light day Tuesday.

Two raids were staged on walk-in-and-out liquor stores and 18 pints of liquor were confiscated.

Elmer Barnard, 62, was arrested in a raid at 2301 SW 15, and Linda Irene Lebrecht, 31, was arrested in a raid at 712 S Walker. Both paid municipal fines.

Mr. and Mrs. James Norick are pleased by results of the city's mayor's race.

German Chief To Step Aside

BONN, Germany, April 7—Under the weight of his 83 years Konrad Adenauer decided Tuesday to give up the chancellorship of West Germany and accept an easier job, the presidency.

Ludwig Erhard, economics minister who has charted Germany's spectacular postwar recovery, is the likely choice of the Christian Democratic party for Adenauer's successor. He is 62.

The chancellor is the main executive in Germany. Under the Bonn constitution he "determines the policy and bears the responsibility for it." The presidency is largely ceremonial, having powers about equivalent to those of Queen Elizabeth in Britain.

The decision of Adenauer, crusty and uncompromisingly leader of West Germany through its entire 10-year history, means he will be giving up active politics.

But Adenauer will still be at the helm when crucial east-west meetings take place this spring and summer.

It seems a foregone conclusion that Adenauer will be chosen president in the July 1 election by parliament. His Socialist opponent is a popular writer-scholar, Carlo Schmid. The incumbent president, Theodor Heuss, is retiring under a two-term rule.

A measure of the surprise at Adenauer's decision was the comment as the news spread.

"Wow," exclaimed an American diplomat in Paris.

"You're joking," said a West German parliamentary deputy.

"Marvelous," cried a caretaker newsman in East Berlin.

In Washington, it was believed
(Continued on Page 5, Column 5)

Double Sonic Booms Hand Frisco a Jolt

SAN FRANCISCO, April 7 (UPI)—A double sonic boom so powerful that it caused more damage than a recent earthquake jolted the San Francisco Bay region Tuesday.

Thousands of frightened residents thought it was another earthquake or a violent explosion.

Tall buildings shook, scores of windows were shattered and plaster fell or cracked in a 75-mile strip that included San Francisco and the peninsula cities to the south.

A sprinkler system blew up at Alameda naval air station at the moment of the boom. Officials were not positive, but said the boom might have caused a sudden change in water pressure.

Some residents reported seeing the vapor trail from a high-flying jet at time of the boom. However navy and air force bases in the area denied that any faster-than-sound planes were up at the time.

It was described as a "Wham! Whamm," double jolt with only a split second of separation. A boom of the same type but with less force hit the bay area Monday.

A police official said no boom on record has caused more "concern and consternation." An earthquake on March 1, one of the strongest since the big quake-fire of 1906, caused less damage and was not felt as strongly by residents.

There were no reported injuries Tuesday but many persons had close calls from falling glass or plaster. Windows were broken in at least 12 San Francisco buildings and others shattered in Palo Alto, San Mateo, Burlingame and other communities on the peninsula.

House Works, Votes 13 Bills

Unruffled by the excitement over the repeal election, the house put in a full day's work Tuesday, passing 13 bills.

Most of the bills were of a non-controversial nature and individual members pushed pet bills with little opposition.

The administration skipped over two key bills on the calendar to transfer functions in the public welfare commission. The bills, which will stir heated opposition, would transfer the direct relief and commodities distribution program and the Whitaker State Orphan's home and institute for colored blind, deaf and orphans.

Bills passed included a measure to authorize Oklahoma and Tulsa counties to establish retirement systems for county employees.

Without debate, the house adopted a resolution calling for an investigation of the state highway department because of road failures in Washington county.

The resolution was introduced
(Continued on Page 5, Column 1)

Daley Re-Elected Mayor of Chicago

CHICAGO, April 7—Democratic Mayor Richard J. Daley won re-election Tuesday night by defeating Republican Timothy P. Sheehan in a race that never was close.

Returns from 1,646 of the city's 3,825 precincts in the mayoral election gave Daley 255,854 and Sheehan 22,394.

Democrats, confident of victory, had hoped that Daley would top the records for total vote and plurality of candidates in mayoral contests—919,383 and 631,854—but he apparently was falling short of both marks.

Nickel Coffee Back

TORONTO, April 7—The nickel cup of coffee is back in Toronto. Restaurant owner Peter Raouil explained Tuesday recent cuts in coffee prices made it possible.

County Option Fails In Flood of Votes

Governor Asks Common Sense In Days Ahead

Drys Disappointed, Pledge Continued Temperance Fight

By RAY PARR

Gov. Edmondson Tuesday night called for the exercise of "good judgment and common sense" as Oklahomans voted to end 51 years of prohibition.

"The solemn obligation of the legislature is to write a control bill that is designed for one purpose—protection of the best interest of the people of Oklahoma and the protection of our youth and our children," the governor said.

"The interest of all Oklahomans is the same, a clear loud mandate for exercise of the best of judgment and the soundest of common sense in the days ahead."

Cannon Tells Why

The governor listened in the election returns at the home of Mr. and Mrs. D. W. Hentzel, 1930 Drury Lane. With him were Joe Cannon, public safety commissioner, who has directed Oklahoma's most vigorous liquor crackdown in history, and two of his office staff members, Sam Crossland, attorney, and John Criswell, his press secretary.

The governor said he will announce salient parts of his liquor control bill Wednesday.

Cannon declared repeal was approved for two reasons.

"The people have faith and confidence in our governor," he said. "The enforcement campaign for the first time has given the people a clear cut choice. It made those who favor repeal vote and when they did a true expression was rendered, and prohibition was repealed."

Drys Disappointed

Dry leaders expressed disappointment Tuesday night and pledged they would continue their fight for temperance.

"The people of Oklahoma have accepted a new law," said Dr. Sam Scantlan, acting executive secretary of the United Drys. "We think it is against the best interest of this state. We have not changed our opinion about liquor and liquor interest. We are unalterably opposed to its use and sale and will continue to work in the interest of sobriety and law enforcement."

Rev. Joe Shackleford, president of United Drys, blamed political pressures and a "quickie election" for defeat of the Drys.

He said the decision represents a "popular mass movement fostered by political pressures and arguments appealing to the superficial rather than the truest economic, social and moral welfare of the people."

He said lack of a dry advocate in the governor's race resulted in a campaign "weighted with wet propaganda." He said dry
(Continued on Page 5, Column 5)

Strong Support in Cities Carries Repeal to Victory By 80,000-Plus Margin

By OTIS SULLIVANT

Oklahoma voters Tuesday struck from the constitution traditional prohibition against manufacture and sale of liquor in a decisive victory for the wets which will open the way for legal sale of liquor in the state.

The amendment for repeal of prohibition was adopted by a majority of more than 80,000 votes in the first disastrous defeat for the drys who have dominated voting on liquor issues since prohibition was written into the constitution at statehood in November, 1907.

In a record turnout for a special election, the voters decided they wanted legal sale of package liquor in privately owned stores and they wanted the sale in every county in the state without any option.

They overwhelmingly turned down the proposed county option amendment which would have called for another special election May 12 for each of the 77 counties to determine whether it would permit sale of liquor. The option amendment was defeated by more than 2 to 1.

The vote was as follows:

Repeal amendment, 3,220 of 3,254 precincts, 395,242 "yes" to 313,574 "no."

County option amendment, 3,219 precincts, 467,928 "no" to 221,520 "yes."

The total vote will be about 710,000. Because of intense interest in the disturbing and emotional issue, city voters turned out enmass to express themselves on repeal and a heavy vote was recorded throughout the state.

The results of the special election means legal sale of liquor will begin in Oklahoma as soon as the legislature writes the control bill and machinery to set up under the law.

Gov. Edmondson will name a five-member Oklahoma alcoholic beverage control board to supervise the licensing of manufacturers, wholesalers and retailers and to administer the control
(Continued on Page 5, Column 2)

Hold on, Pal! There's a Law

Even in the face of repeal, Oklahoma's laws against the manufacture, sale and possession of intoxicating liquor will remain in effect until the legislature passes control laws.

That was the opinion given to Gov. Edmondson late Tuesday by Mac Q. Williamson, attorney general. The opinion was prepared by Fred Hansen, first assistant attorney.

The opinion told the governor that if adopted the constitutional amendment would in part be self-executing. However, Hansen wrote that state statutory laws dealing with intoxicating liquor would remain in effect under the police powers of the state.

The law should specify a starting time for legal sale of liquor, the governor said, so everyone will have the same opportunity. No one should be able to get a license, open a store and start sale of liquor before others have a chance to open, the governor said.

A big demand for licenses for liquor stores is expected from residents of all cities of the state. Liquor stores will be permitted in all cities and towns with population of 200 or more, and the
(Continued on Page 5, Column 3)

Bootlegger King Happy It's Over

TULSA, April 7 (UPI)—Big "Mac" McCarty, self-styled "king of the bootleggers," said Tuesday night he's going to retire and buy a used car lot.

"I'm glad it went wet," said the bootlegger in a TV interview. "I've been sick of this grind for a long time.

"The accusation that Oklahoma has been kept dry by the bootleggers is not true. A lot of us are glad it went wet. I'll be glad to get out of the business and quit dodging the police."

McCarty's wife has been going to beauty operators' school and he's planning to make an adjustment in two more apartment units in a lower East Side development. He is a strong patron for anyone who indulges himself in luxuries.

After his rent was paid, he
(Continued on Page 5, Column 2)

Funnel Reported In Lubbock Area

LUBBOCK, Texas, April 7—A pilot reported sighting a tornado funnel about 30 miles northwest of Lubbock after a threatening cloud passed over Denver City. 30 miles southwest of Lubbock, late Tuesday.

There was no word of any damage in the Lubbock area.

At Denver City, merchant Bud Roether said high wind accompanying heavy rain blew down a bowling alley which was under construction in that oilfield town.

The Inside Headlines

Alan Robert Nye, former U. S. navy bomber pilot, facing trial in Havana for alleged plot on Castro.—Page 16.

President and Mrs. Eisenhower arrive in Augusta, Ga., for vacation and more warm weather.—Page 3.

Oklahoma house passes two bills providing for continuity of government in case an A-bomb falls.—Page 5.

Tinker Air Force base will hold open house on May 16 in observance of Armed Forces day.—Page 2.

Applications will be heard today for writ of habeas corpus seeking custody of Steven Lee Rake, 6.—Page 15.

Macmillan government slashed almost a tenth off income taxes British earners will have to pay.—Page 24.

Alan Robert Nye

Features Inside

Amusements 14
Classified Ads 16-22
Comic Strips 10, 11
Editorials 8
Good Morning 1
Markets 23
Obituaries 4, 5
Oil 23
Public Records 5
Sports 12, 13
TV-Radio Today 14
Woman's Page 6, 7, 8

Snow Follows Panhandle Rain

Snow followed rain in the Panhandle of Oklahoma late Tuesday. Harry Johnson, highway department engineer at Boise City, said snow started falling there at 4 p.m. after rain through most of the day.

Johnson said 7 1/4 of an inch had fallen Tuesday night. Temperatures had dropped to 30 degrees Tuesday night. Temperatures Wednesday also are expected to be cooler with highs from near 50 in the northwest to the 70s in the southeast.

Speculating Reliefer Guilty

NEW YORK, April 7—A 71-year-old relief chiseler pleaded guilty Tuesday to petit larceny. He used his welfare pittance to play the stock market and ran a $4,000 investment into $27,000.

The canny investor, Harry Schweitzer, accumulated his original nest egg over many years mainly from the $1.16 a day he had left in welfare funds after paying his rent.

Florsheim scattered showers and thunderstorms moved across the state. Gage reported nearly an inch. The weather bureau placed the southern portions of the state under a severe weather alert as thunderstorms in Texas began moving eastward Tuesday night.

"Presumably, if he runs out of eye glasses and gray suit and repeal," a former McLarson school teacher, he came here from Poland in 1923.

Working as a hospital orderly, Schweitzer managed to put aside enough money to plunge into the booming market of the 1920s. But the 1929 crash wiped him out to the tune of $10,000.

He worked until ill health forced his retirement. Then in 1938 he went on relief. He has been receiving $11.16 a month.

But Schweitzer is a bachelor who pays $36 for a one-room apartment in a lower East Side development.

"I would have to resort to wearing gold framed eye glasses and gray suit and repeal," a former McCarson school teacher.

"I'm not interested any more," he said of the market.

He did have some advice for investors, however. He declared:

"I think we are in a period of tremendous inflation which will force the prices of stocks and real estate up.

His prediction of a bull market indicated the time was ripe for further speculation, but Schweitzer insisted:

"I would have to resort to some study of it, but I don't intend to go back."

Schweitzer is short, slightly built and nearly bald. His lawyer, Jack M. Perlamo, said.

The following year, 1958, *The Oklahoman* began printing its Monday through Saturday comics section in color, rare among North American newspapers. To accomplish this, the paper's editorial art department hand-colored the comics. The practice continues today. In April 1959, the papers reported that Oklahoma voters repealed prohibition by more than 80,000 votes, approving privately owned package liquor stores in every county. That same year *The Oklahoman* and *Times* reported an absentee ballot scheme in Wagoner County in which more than 800 votes were cast in exchange for relief checks. Probes by state agencies and a grand jury brought indictments against six persons, including a state senator who then lost his post in a special election. The senator was tried, but the jury deadlocked and the case was not tried again. The two-county relief director pleaded guilty to conspiring to defraud the state and paid

a $750 fine. The legislature tightened absentee voting laws and abolished the state relief board.

In 1959, the papers reported that after long litigation and years of delay, Lake Atoka—Oklahoma City's third reservoir—was opened in southeast Oklahoma. They also reported that construction was nearly complete on the 100-mile-long pipeline to carry water to Oklahoma City. *The Oklahoman* and *Times* had long promoted the project. Meantime, staff members from both newspapers played key roles in obtaining passage of the open meetings law in 1959, as well as amendments in 1967 and 1971, and later encouraged the state's open records law. As a result of news stories carried in both papers, an Oklahoma County grand jury in 1959 investigated sand and gravel purchased by county and city officials. Two commissioners and a council member resigned their offices to avoid ouster actions.

OPPOSITE
The front page of the April 8, 1959, issue of *The Daily Oklahoman.*

This late 1950s view looks north on Robinson in downtown Oklahoma City. (Courtesy Oklahoma City Chamber of Commerce)

Edward L. Gaylord, then executive vice-president and treasurer of The Oklahoma Publishing Co., pushes the button that starts the company's new presses on August 2, 1960. They were the first Colormatic presses purchased in the United States.

Chapter Ten

THE DECADE
OF THE '60S

As 1960 began, Oklahoma City had a population of 324,253, the metro area had 511,835, and the state 2,328,284. At the editorial urging of *The Oklahoman* and *Times,* the city council created a trust which let a contract for $43.2 million to build the 60-inch pipeline and bring water to Oklahoma City from southeast Oklahoma. As president of the Oklahoma City Chamber of Commerce, Edward L. Gaylord led the effort to increase the city's water supply. The following year Edward L. Gaylord became president of the State Fair of Oklahoma. It was on the brink of financial failure. Within a decade, he turned it around and made it one of the most profitable and successful state fairs in America. Under his leadership, the fair had major growth, with attendance going from 550,000 to just under one million, and gross receipts increased from $440,499 to more than $1.3 million annually, with increasing profits each year. It became one of the top five most successful state fairs in the nation.

In 1961, *The Oklahoman* and *Times* initiated a scholarship program for young people who delivered their papers. Carriers with a year's service, good conduct and citizenship, and few complaints were eligible. There followed more than $325,000 in scholarships to more than 3,000 boys and girls. Meantime, The Oklahoma Publishing Co. continued to keep *The Oklahoman* and *Times* on the cutting edge of technology by adding a Hoe Colormatic 8-unit press, costing more than $1 million. The new press was capable of printing 70,000 papers per hour. In another first, the Company introduced to America a German casting machine which automatically cast stereotype plates, replacing a manual process. Soon after the system was installed, the Company, which had pioneered in printing color photographs years earlier, acquired the Klischograph, a European machine that electronically made color-separated engravings. The year 1961 also saw the papers become the first in America to use a computer to set type, and The Oklahoma Publishing Co.'s *Farmer-Stockman* added a Kansas edition. Its circulation climbed to more than 440,000 making it one of the nation's largest farm publications.

When William F. "Bill" Atkinson, democrat, ran again for governor in 1962, *The Oklahoman* and *Times* opposed him editorially. On April 28, an editorial in *The Oklahoman* noted:

> The editors of this paper have no confidence in Mr. Atkinson and we opposed him with front page editorials when he was a candidate four years ago. Our adverse opinion against him is stronger than ever, and we would not support him under any circumstances. If he should happen to get in the runoff we would support his opponent, no matter which one it may be.
>
> Atkinson has done many things we consider reprehensible. Four years ago when he was then a candidate for governor, he caused to be distributed in eastern Oklahoma a dodger to which was signed the name of Howard Edmondson. It was designed to make people believe that Edmondson would reduce the number of county seats in eastern Oklahoma.

The political duel with words that followed was reminiscent of the frontier days of Oklahoma journalism when editorials contained no weasel words in expressing opinions.

The *Capitol Hill Beacon,* which supported Atkinson, replied to *The Oklahoman* in an editorial the following day:

When Edward L. Gaylord stepped down as president of the Oklahoma City Chamber of Commerce in January 1961, he needed an extra hand to hang onto his awards. He is holding a gavel and the chamber's "President's Trophy," both inscribed with his name, a plaque for "outstanding service" and a card making him a life member of the board of directors.

of his time to running against the paper and publisher, and less to the Republican nominee, than any other candidate for governor.

Atkinson lost, but a couple of weeks before the election Atkinson, the Democratic nominee, and Henry Bellmon, the Republican nominee, were holding rallies in Shawnee, Oklahoma. There were conflicting reports on the size of the crowds at each of the rallies. Both the Associated Press and *The Oklahoman* had a reporter in Shawnee. Gaylord Shaw was the night editor in the Oklahoma City bureau of the Associated Press, then located in the basement of *The Oklahoman* building on Broadway. Shaw had argued over the phone with the man on *The Oklahoman*'s state desk on which reporter's figures were correct. A bit later E. K. Gaylord called the state desk and said, "This is Gaylord. Now about these crowd estimates in Shawnee . . ." At that the man on *The Oklahoman*'s state desk, thinking it was the AP's Gaylord Shaw calling again, interrupted the caller and said, "Damn it, Gaylord, we've been through this several times," and slammed down the telephone receiver not knowing the caller was E. K. Gaylord, not Gaylord Shaw. The next day the man on the state desk learned it was E. K. Gaylord who called. The incident was forgotten.

As for Bill Atkinson, two years after he lost the race for governor, he started a daily morning paper called *The Oklahoma Journal* to compete directly against *The Oklahoman*. The *Journal,* however, continually showed huge financial losses. The paper was sold to Early California Industries for $700,000 in April 1979. It ceased publication in November 1980.

Saturday morning, in a piddling, childish editorial, the publisher of the Daily Oklahoman *attempted to pull the rug from underneath Bill Atkinson. He doesn't like Bill. He will support anyone except Bill. He harks back to four years ago when Bill or some of his supporters reputedly put out a hand bill in some of the sparsely-settled eastern counties. Bill had no knowledge of this act.*

The publisher of the Big Daily believes that he can beat any candidate with his last-minute-dirty-pool front page editorials.

The word battle continued into the fall. On October 30, *The Oklahoman* in a story written by Otis Sullivant summed up the battle with these words:

W. P. "Bill" Atkinson's efforts to make E. K. Gaylord and The Daily Oklahoman *a major issue in the governor's race is not unusual in Oklahoma politics. The publisher and the newspaper have been put at issue many times by candidates they opposed editorially. They have been "cussed" by experts in campaign oratory. Atkinson has devoted more*

✳

In 1962, The Oklahoma Publishing Co. began a scholarship program for employee's children. Grants were based on ACT test scores. The one-year grants of $1,000 for each child were renewable as long as the student maintained a high grade point average. That same year, Edward L. Gaylord headed a community-wide drive for Baptist Memorial Hospital that exceeded its goal. The $2.2 million fund made it possible to double the capacity of the hospital.

By 1962, Edward L. Gaylord was becoming the moving force behind further diversification of The Oklahoma Publishing Co.'s broadcasting division. It had already purchased WTVT in Tampa and St. Petersburg, Florida, in 1956, and in 1962 leased KTVT television, an independent station in Dallas with an option to buy. "We had an option to buy the station within 10 years for $1 million. When we gave them the check for the lease hold, the guy laughed at us. He thought we were the biggest suckers in the world. Of course today, that station is probably worth $400 or $500 million," recalled Edward L. Gaylord, who added, "We did take up our option to buy the station." In April 1999, E. K. Gaylord II negotiated the sale of KTVT to CBS for $485 million of CBS common stock. Later the stock was sold for $620 million.

Before 1962 ended, The Oklahoma Publishing Co. announced plans for a three-million dollar, five-story building at its Fourth and Broadway complex, expanding facilities for *The Oklahoman* and *Times*. The roof of the new structure became the first heliport for a downtown Oklahoma City building. Personnel from the newspapers moved into the new office building in 1963. The new facility included carpet throughout the newsroom, the first newspaper

newsroom in America to be carpeted arousing gripes from other newspapers.

"We are criticized by some of our friends in the publishing business who say they agree with everything we have done except carpets in the newsroom. Well, I believe you will live to see the day when that is an improvement other people will like to have. We don't have the floor littered with papers, cigarette butts and that sort of thing. Members of our staff are very proud to keep it looking the way it should," E. K. Gaylord said.

The growing Oklahoma Publishing Co. already included a real estate division with property investment in Oklahoma, Colorado, Arizona and elsewhere in 1963 when Edward L. Gaylord created an oil and gas division named Publisher's Petroleum. It was managed by Tenal Cooley, who had earlier built OPUBCO's personnel department. Cooley's division had much success in locating new oil and gas reserves in Oklahoma, Kansas, Texas, Ohio, Wyoming and Louisiana. After 35 years with OPUBCO, including five years as a member of its board of directors, Cooley retired in 1983. He died at the age of 75 in October 1998.

The Company made more history in 1963 by perfecting computerized type-setting tape, the brainchild of Bill Williams, manager of accounting. The Company developed the process of automatically justifying lines of type by computer and printed the first newspaper in the world using this method. The new system was a gift to E. K. Gaylord on his 90th birthday. Every line of news type in the *Times* that day was "justified"—spaced and hyphenated—by the computer's brain. The development was such a milestone in publishing history that the March 5, 1963, issue was placed on permanent display in a London Museum devoted

Edward L. Gaylord, executive vice-president and treasurer of The Oklahoma Publishing Co., in his office on Northwest Fourth in September 1963.

Three generations of Gaylords take part in the March 1962 groundbreaking for a new Oklahoma Publishing Co. building on Northwest Fourth in Oklahoma City. Left to right: Edward L. Gaylord, E. K. Gaylord II and E. K. Gaylord.

OPPOSITE
The front page of the November 22, 1963, issue of the Oklahoma City *Times*.

Jim Lange's political cartoon memorializes President Kennedy on November 24, 1963.

–And Now He, Too, Belongs to the Ages

to technology. About this time E. K. Gaylord received an honorary degree of Doctor of Humanities by the College of Wooster in Ohio. In Oklahoma City, civic leaders also honored him and described him as the "Father of Oklahoma City."

The big story of 1963 that remains fresh in the minds of many Oklahomans was the assassination of President John F. Kennedy on November 22. Allan Cromley, Washington bureau chief for *The Oklahoman,* was in the Dallas motorcade when the shots were fired. He was soon joined by reporter Jim Standard, who was dispatched to Dallas to assist in the papers' coverage. The news of President Kennedy's death came in time for a front page story in the home edition. Cartoonist Jim Lange, who had been sketching a cartoon on the upcoming University of Oklahoma and Nebraska football game, quickly pushed that sketch aside. After coming to grips with what had happened, Lange sketched an empty rocking chair and the ghost of Lincoln in the background. Above the cartoon his caption read, "And Now He, Too, Belongs to the Ages." When Jack Ruby shot and killed Lee Harvey Oswald, *The Oklahoman* published an Extra. Reporter Jim Standard was standing about 10 feet from Oswald at the time, and he provided a firsthand account. During the days that followed, the papers provided extensive coverage of the events in Dallas and Washington D.C., and the activities of Lyndon B. Johnson, the new president.

During the early '60s, The Oklahoma Publishing Co. changed its system of newspaper delivery. From the earliest days, the papers were delivered by young carriers. By the early '60s, there were 2,500 young carriers in the six-county metropolitan area and about 1,000 serving the remainder of the state. Under the new system, adult

independent contractors were used. Today more than 900 such contractors deliver *The Oklahoman* in the six-county metropolitan area. Another 500 contractors serve the remaining counties in Oklahoma and in neighboring states.

During 1964, four reporters for the papers—Bob Allen, Frank Garner, Ivy Coffey and Wayne Mackey—found unclean and rundown conditions at Miracle Hill, a children's home near Wewoka. Their stories also described how children were neglected. As a result of their stories, the home was ordered closed. Other stories that year by Jim Standard and Mary Jo Nelson tied a county commissioner to stolen goods. When the news was published, a grand jury indicted the commissioner for perjury. The commissioner resigned and left Oklahoma. The year 1964 also marked the climax of an editorial campaign that had been carried on by *The Oklahoman* and *Times* for many years. A federal court reapportioned Oklahoma's legislature giving urban dwellers equal representation with rural residents.

During 1965, the Oklahoma Supreme Court's part in a scandal involving Selected Investments surfaced. Readers were stunned when the papers reported impeachment actions against two justices, one of whom resigned from the court. The other was removed from office. Two justices, one of whom had retired, were convicted of evading federal income taxes on money received as bribes. In addition, a prominent attorney and former mayor was indicted and convicted of perjury. Later, three more judges would be implicated, although they had been cleared by the Oklahoma Bar Association.

Edward L. Gaylord continued to expand the number of broadcast properties owned by The Oklahoma

KENNEDY SHOT, KILLED DURING DALLAS PARADE

Oct. Avg.
Morning-Evening
Daily Circulation
313,289

Full Range of Trading on N. Y., American Stocks

OKLAHOMA CITY TIMES

VOL. LXXIV, NO. 240 42 PAGES—500 N BROADWAY, OKLAHOMA CITY, FRIDAY, NOVEMBER 22, 1963 FIVE CENTS

President Kennedy is slumped down in the back seat of his car Friday after being shot. Mrs. Kennedy leans over the president as an unidentified man stands on the bumper. (AP) Wirephoto)

Gunshots Turn City To Stone

A gunshot in Dallas turned Oklahoma City to stone Friday afternoon.

Mute clumps of citizens stood clustered in stunned silence around radio sets as the news of President Kennedy's shooting was broadcast.

Standing stiff and unbelieving, the Oklahoma City police chief, chief of detectives and higher echelons of the city's police department listed intently to a small radio in the detective chief's office.

'Who Would . . .'

Throughout the police station officers and office personnel shook their heads in unbelief.

"Who would do it?" an officer said dazedly, echoing his listeners' thoughts. "Who would be crazy enough to do something like that?"

At central fire station the atmosphere was the same as a dozen men, including Chief Dancy, stood intently watching a tiny transistor radio.

Newsroom Near Bedlam

The chief leaned on a file cabinet, head down and eyes nearly closed as the news of the shooting of the chief executive and governor of Texas echoed throughout the station.

In the firemen's squad room, men stood rooted listening to a large set. Downstairs the fire dispatcher and several onlookers sat quietly, listening.

The newsroom of The Daily Oklahoman and Oklahoma City Times was near bedlam minutes after word of the shooting.

Switchboard Flooded

Editors and reporters rushed to teletype printers receiving the shocking news from Dallas. Other editors and reporters were busy clearing the Times' front page for display of the news.

The company's switchboard was flooded with calls bare minutes after the tragedy became known.

In countless shops and stores across the city persons stood in shocked silence, listening to radio and TV reports.

Children Cry

In one store a woman clasped her elbows and rocked slightly when the unconfirmed report of the president's death was broadcast.

Parents held nervous children in their arms as they stood rigid, waiting for official confirmation of President Kennedy's condition.

Some small children cried, though most were awed by the tense hush evident everywhere.

Campus Is Bare

Their radios blaring, automobiles moved sluggishly through the chill afternoon, sometimes failing to heed traffic warning signals, so intent were drivers.

In Norman, University of Oklahoma students deserted classrooms. Coeds ran weeping to the nearest television sets. Young men with sober faces joined them. The campus

(See GUNSHOTS—Page 3)

Johnson Due Swearing In Immediately

DALLAS (AP) — Lyndon B. Johnson was sworn in as president of the United States at about 1:38 p.m. Friday.

The oath was administered by U. S. District Judge Sarah T. Hughes.

Johnson took the oath aboard the presidential plane at Dallas' Love Field. He was preparing to fly to Washington to take over the government.

DALLAS (UPI) — President Kennedy has been assassinated.

A single shot through the right temple took the life of the 46-year-old chief executive. He was shot as he rode in an open car in downtown Dallas, waving and smiling to a crowd of 250,000.

Vice President Lyndon Johnson, the nation's new president, was in the same cavalcade but a number of car lengths behind. He was not hurt.

Terribly shocked Johnson, who has a record of heart illness, was whisked off un-

More News, Page 3, 7, 13, 17, 30

der heavy guard to be sworn in as quickly as possible as the 36th president of the United States.

Mrs. Jacqueline Kennedy was riding in the same car with her husband. She was not hurt. She cradled her husband's head in her arms as he was sped, dying, to the hospital.

Kennedy was shot at approximately 12:30 p.m. and died at approximately 1 p.m. CST. He was the fourth U. S. president to be killed in office.

Beside Kennedy in the famous bubble-top limousine was Texas Gov. John B. Connally. He was shot in the chest. The governor was reported in serious condition and in great pain.

Mrs. Connally, also in the car, was unharmed.

The chief executive, first Roman Catholic president of the United States and in Dallas on a politicking mission for a second term, was smiling broadly as he rode through downtown streets.

"Then that awful look crossed his face," said a man at curbside only 15 feet away.

The identity of the assassin or assassins was not immediately known.

Sheriff's officers took a young man into custody at the scene and questioned him behind closed doors.

A Dallas television reporter said he saw a rifle being withdrawn from a window on the sixth floor of an office building shortly after the gunfire.

Johnson was under heavy guard. Physicians and members of the White House staff attended him.

Cityan, 21, Catapulted To Death

STATE TRAFFIC DEATHS
1963 to date 666; Nov.. 53.
1962 to date 621; Nov.. 36.

A 21-year-old woman was killed early Friday when her auto went out of control on I. H. 35 just south of the junction with I. H. 40 in Oklahoma City.

Mrs. Helen Faye Kubiak, 1717 N St. Luke, was dead on arrival at Mercy Hospital at 1:50 a.m.

Son Bruised

Scoutcar officer Powell Chick said Mrs. Kubiak's 7-month-old son, David Martin Kubiak II, received a few bruises but was not seriously injured.

Chick said Mrs. Kubiak's car apparently skidded on wet pavement, hit the east embankment of the viaduct, bounced across the highway to strike the western abutment and then veered back to hit the east abutment again.

Baby Crawling

Mrs. Kubiak was thrown from the vehicle, which ran over her.

The child was found about four feet from his mother's body and crawling from the pavement when police said Mrs. Kubiak was thrown about 35 feet.

Police said Mrs. Kubiak had been visiting her grandmother on S. Eastern and was en route to Harrah to pick up her husband, David Martin Kubiak, when the accident occurred.

Truckers Elect Chief

MIAMI BEACH (P) — John Akers, Gastonia, N. C., has been elected president of the American Trucking Association and Friday Amos, Charleston, W. Va., vice president.

Wife Slumps Across Body of President

By Allan Cromley
(Washington Bureau)

DALLAS — With President Kennedy when he died Friday afternoon was Rear Adm. George Berkley, a White House assistant.

A member of the Dallas police department said a Dallas policeman was killed in attempting to apprehend the assassin. He said the policeman was dead on arrival at Parkland Hospital.

The officer said he saw the president being carried into the hospital.

"It looked to me like the bullet just made his head explode," he said.

Mrs. Kennedy lay over her husband's body as the

'Too Horrible to Describe'
Page 16

car brought him into the hospital grounds, the policeman said.

Connally told his administrative assistant, William Stinson, as Connally was being carried into the emergency room, that he thought the shot came from behind him. Stinson said, "I asked him what happened."

"He said, 'I don't know.' 'I think they shot me from the back.'"

Connally suffered a wound in the right chest which perforated his body as well as a wound in the wrist.

Johnson, soon to be sworn in as president, slumped in the back seat of a sedan as he was taken away to an undisclosed destination.

Expressway Work OK'd

The longest section yet to be built on Oklahoma City's crosstown elevated expressway — three blocks long — will get under construction at once.

The Moore Bridge Co. of Ada was given authority to build a 1,466-foot highway-highway overpass on the expressway (I. H. 40) between Walker and Shartel. Contract price is $1,723,824.

The Ada company also has the contract for a connecting structure, a 986-foot overpass from Harvey west to Walker at $929,416.

Highway Director F. D. Coone said Friday it is estimated that construction of the 3-block section will be completed in April, 1965.

Meanwhile, the state highway commission prepared to open bids Friday afternoon for the fifth section of the expressway, a 1,466-foot high-highway overpass

Arctic Air Rolls Toward Oklahoma

An Arctic cold front moving across the state is expected to drop Oklahoma City temperatures sharply, with the mercury rising only into the 40s late Friday.

The rest of the state also will shiver. Sub-freezing temperatures are forecast for some sections.

In the Oklahoma City area, clouds are to begin clearing Friday night. Saturday is to be fair and cold, with a morning low of 35 and an afternoon high of 45 degrees.

The state forecast calls for freezing or sub-freezing temperatures Friday night and it will be cold Saturday. Saturday's highs are expected to range from 48-58 over the state, following morning lows of 22-30 northwest to 28-38 southeast.

Meanwhile, a tornado reportedly touched down early Friday in a field south of Ralston-Pawnee County, but it was not seen on the weather bureau's radarscope in Oklahoma City.

A weather spokesman said radar observations showed a storm in the Ralston area about 1:30 a.m., but that it did not look intense enough to spawn a twister.

Jim Pattison, Ralston policeman, said residents told him of seeing the twister on the ground. He said he saw it after it pulled back into the sky.

Clearing and much colder Friday night with a low near 35. Fair and cold Saturday with a high near 45. (Details, Page 22.)

Agent, Policeman Are Slain

DALLAS (P) — A secret service agent and a Dallas policeman were shot and killed Friday some distance from the area where President Kennedy was assassinated.

No other information was immediately available.

Suspect Caught In Dallas Movie

DALLAS (P)—The Dallas police department arrested Friday a 21-year-old man, Lee H. Oswald, in connection with the slaying of a Dallas policeman shortly after President Kennedy was assassinated.

Oswald was pulled screaming and yelling from the Texas Theater in the Oak Cliff Section of Dallas.

Johnson Heart Attack Denied

WASHINGTON (P) —Frank Valeo, secretary to the senate Democratic majority, told newsmen there was "no substance" to rumors that Vice President Lyndon B. Johnson had suffered a heart attack.

Valeo's statement was made after he talked by telephone with Ralph Dungan, a White House assistant.

Johnson Aide At White House

WASHINGTON (P) — George Reedy, special assistant to Vice President Lyndon B. Johnson, visited the White House Friday afternoon but his mission was not known.

What's Inside

White House Secretary Malcolm Kilduff said the president's body would be flown to Washington Friday.

The Dallas sheriff's department said a rifle had been found in a staircase on the fifth floor of a building near the scene of the assassination. It was a 7.65 Mauser. The German-made army rifle had a telescopic sight with one shell left in the chamber. Three spent shells were found nearby.

Mrs. Kennedy, who had been a tremendous hit Thursday on the first day of the 2-day visit, was seated just in front of her husband.

After the shot, her husband slumped over on the back seat and she screamed. The interior of the car was splattered with blood. Mrs. Kennedy took her husband's head in her arms and bent over him.

Mrs. Connally was kneeling

(See KENNEDY—Page 2)

Publishing Co. It obtained a license and built a new independent television station in Houston. From its tall tower KHTV had one of the strongest television signals along the Gulf Coast. Then in March 1966, WVTV television in Milwaukee was purchased by The Oklahoma Publishing Company as it continued its diversification under the leadership of Edward L. Gaylord, who that year was elected president of the Southern Newspaper Publishers Association, a position held years earlier by his father. During 1966, The Oklahoma Publishing Co. also purchased Semco Color Press and Package Engineers in Oklahoma City. Semco Color Press, which became Oklahoma Graphics, greatly enlarged the Company's printing facilities. Package Engineers became known as National Packaging. That same year *The Oklahoman* and *Times* installed more advanced computers for typesetting and for photo composition, and the *Times* introduced Action Line, a service designed to protect every citizen's right to fair treatment from government and business. More than 10,000 persons turned to the papers' new service during its first year. Before 1966 ended, E. K. Gaylord was awarded an honorary doctorate

This aerial view of downtown Oklahoma City was made during the middle 1960s. The new Stanley Draper "Cross-town" expressway is in the foreground. (Courtesy Oklahoma City Chamber of Commerce)

of laws degree by Oklahoma Christian College in Oklahoma City. Gaylord was then 93.

Even at that advanced age, E. K. Gaylord retained an intense interest in technology and science. He had the papers' editors send Alan Cromley from the Washington bureau to Cape Canaveral, Florida, to cover the Mercury and Gemini space programs which included two Oklahomans, Gordon Cooper and Tom Stafford. "It was unusual for regional newspapers to cover the space flights, but Mr. Gaylord was interested beyond the local angle," Cromley recalled, adding, "E. K. Gaylord also became fascinated with our intercontinental ballistic missile defenses and the Pentagon alertly invited him to inspect one of our then-secret Atlas sites. I'm not sure where it was, but it may have been in South Dakota. He actually was taken down into the underground complex and visited personnel there. When he got back to Oklahoma he puzzled over something that had not been explained to him— how do the underground controllers escape if the situation warrants?"

Cromley said E. K. Gaylord told him a little bit about what he had seen and asked him to find out from the Pentagon. Cromley contacted Air Force public information officers. "They were astounded that anyone should expect an answer, and their shock was compounded by my seeming to know more than I should especially because I was not a Pentagon regular from a big news organization. Mr. Gaylord had seen an exit tunnel filled with sand, and the explanation was that the sand would prevent blast from coming down the tunnel, but the sand could be removed for escape if it came to that," recalled Cromley.

In 1967, reporters Jim Standard and John Bennett uncovered more than $100,000 in checks paid to state political figures by a lobbyist for a utility firm within days of a rate increase. The stories resulted in a legislative investigation. The corporation commission chairman was ousted, and a new conflict of interest law was written for the commission and its employees. The same year reporter Jim Standard uncovered large loans by Oklahoma banks to the state treasurer. Gov. Dewey Bartlett initiated a study which was halted by the supreme court. The case was then investigated by a federal grand jury and three federal agencies. After both papers had urged court reform in Oklahoma for several years, voters in July 1967, approved restructuring the courts. The new system went into effect early in 1968, the same year the papers' computer operations were again expanded with the addition of a machine to automatically count, bundle and label newspapers for mailing and delivery. The papers were the first in the nation to create a total newspaper with computers.

The year 1968 also saw E. K. Gaylord receive the first "Oklahoma's Outstanding Leader" award from the Oklahoma City Press Club. About then a recently hired young reporter got on the elevator at *The Oklahoman* and found a spiffily dressed older gentleman. The new reporter, unaware the man was E. K. Gaylord, looked at him and commented, "My what a nice suit. I can tell you don't work here." E. K. Gaylord only smiled and said nothing.

During 1968, the papers continued their long history of supporting bond issues for advancement of the city, county and state, this time leading a campaign on behalf of the largest bond issue in Oklahoma City history. Most of the $115 million package was approved. When Oklahoma City marine Robert Franklin, touched by the suffering of thousands of homeless children in Vietnam, wrote the *Times* for help, reporter Mary Jo Nelson wrote stories that resulted in the shipment of 30 tons of baby food, medicines and supplies. When Oklahoma servicemen wrote the papers complaining about the lack of mail, the state staff collected and published their names and addresses. More than 43,000 servicemen were overwhelmed with packages, letters and Christmas greetings in 1968 and 1969. When a missionary brought a Mexican Indian girl born without ears to Oklahoma City in August 1968 for surgery that gave her hearing, stories in the *Times* resulted in $1,500 in donations to buy the 5-year-old artificial ears.

E. K. Gaylord celebrated his 95th birthday in 1968 and the Oklahoma House of Representatives passed a resolution designating him the "Dean of American Newspaper Publishers." Gaylord remained very active in the day-to-day activities of the papers and the other interests of The Oklahoma Publishing Co. The following year, 1969, WKY-TV added a $700,000 color television mobile unit to its operation. During the year, a "Compact of Understanding" and "Guidelines for Reporting" were drawn up between the Oklahoma Bar Association and Oklahoma Press Association. *Times* reporter, Wayne Mackey, was one of three journalists honored by the state bar for their work on the pacts.

In 1964, at one of their many shared birthdays, E.K. and his daughter Edith cut the cake.

Chapter Eleven

THE '70S AND A NEW LEADER

The decade of the '70s began with Oklahoma City having a population of 368,856. The metro area had 640,899, and the state 2,559,253. The year 1970 saw the death of George Katz, E. K. Gaylord's oldest friend and associate, whose New York City agency served as *The Oklahoman*'s national advertising representative from just after the founding of The Oklahoma Publishing Co. In remembering his old friend, E. K. Gaylord, then 97, recalled how he and Katz walked down the then unpaved street known as Broadway in Oklahoma City in 1910. It was then that Katz agreed to purchase some stock in The Oklahoma Publishing Co.

In the early 1970s, E. K. Gaylord's son Edward headed the Oklahoma part of a drive to raise $550,000 for the continuing education of journalists. Edward L. Gaylord, a past president and director of the Southern Newspaper Publishers Association and trustee of the SNPA Foundation, had established the foundation's program of seminars and workshops. The same year, he also headed the successful Oklahoma Christian College drive for $850,000. E. K. Gaylord had been instrumental in relocating the College from Bartlesville to Oklahoma City in 1957. Since then the Gaylord family has supported the institution extensively. Later, in 1989, Edward L. Gaylord would head the institution's "With Wings As Eagles" campaign to raise $50 million.

Gaylord Philanthropies presented the Frontiers of Science Foundation with a $120,000 gift in 1971 to form the nucleus of a scholarship fund to help students seeking medical, nursing or medical technology training. During 1971, the National Conference of Christians and Jews presented Edward L. Gaylord with its Brotherhood Award.

During 1971, *The Oklahoman* and *Times* continued to uncover problems across the state. An exposé by the state staff resulted in closing of the solitary confinement section in the women's prison at McAlester. Further investigations at the prison disclosed traffic in narcotics and drugs by prison guards as well as inmates. Stories revealing that a guard solicited a bribe from a prisoner in exchange for a trusty's job resulted in the guard's removal.

A series of stories by Robert Allen prompted a change in the law giving state grand juries authority to cross county lines in investigations. In addition, probing by the state staff was credited with prompting the governor's task force on crime, which in turn led to conviction of Rex Brinlee, an eastern Oklahoma crime figure. *Times* reporter Jim Young uncovered an attempt by Oklahoma legislators to increase their pensions, and the bill was vetoed by Gov. David Hall.

During 1972, a joint investigation by the *Kansas City Star, The Oklahoman* and *Times* uncovered a northeast Oklahoma prosecutor's part in criminal activity around the Grand Lake resort area. A federal court indicted six persons, including the prosecutor, who was convicted. Meantime, the paper's state staff reported the discovery of a six-state crime ring following a raid on a club in the Arbuckle Mountains.

After the papers reported attempts by educators to hold secret meetings, regents for Oklahoma State University, Oklahoma College of Liberal Arts, and the Blanchard and Roff school boards conducted the public's business in public.

The Oklahoma Publishing Co. gained national attention in 1972 after nearly two years of its own intensive investigation into the My Lai Massacre in Vietnam. After many stories detailing efforts of the Army to keep files secret, State Editor Jack Taylor established that basic errors had occurred in the Army's own investigation and its training command policies. Taylor also located the so-called "missing witness" in the Calley case and learned that the Army, Navy, Air Force and Marine Corps were suppressing information about war crimes investigations and ignoring allegations of violations of their own rules and the Geneva Convention. For Taylor's investigative reporting, *The Oklahoman* received national awards from the Associated Press Managing Editors and Sigma Delta Chi, the Society of Professional Journalists.

The year 1972 also saw The Oklahoma Publishing Co. continue to adopt new advancements in technology including new photo composition equipment and a new 8-unit press, with improved controls. The press cost $2.5 million, and brought total press capacity to 28 printing units. In addition, electronic conveyors and stackers were installed in the papers' warehouse. Electronic Character Recognition Machines, computers which translate reporters' copy to electronic impulses, eliminating one step in changing copy to type, were also installed. Also during 1972, The Oklahoma Publishing Co. sold the *Farmer-Stockman Magazine* to some of its executives and others who carried

The Oklahoman's political cartoonist, Jim Lange, drew this in tribute to E. K. Gaylord, who died May 30, 1974.

on its fine traditions of agricultural journalism.

When E. K. Gaylord celebrated his 100th birthday on March 5, 1973, he addressed a joint session of the Oklahoma Legislature. A little more than a year later on May 30, 1974, Edward King Gaylord, 101, died at his Oklahoma City home, shortly before midnight. He had put in a full day's work at his office. The next afternoon an editorial in the *Oklahoma City Times* read in part:

> *E. K. Gaylord was a man of awesome self-discipline and bubbling curiosity. Coupled with his innate intelligence and a marvelous, carefully husbanded physique, these qualities of mind and spirit spurred him to achievements matching the almost-double lifetime that he lived.*
>
> *A public figure in Oklahoma all of the 70-plus years he was in the state, he was the subject of countless legends, myths and misunderstandings. In later years, the total effect of his life had gained at least grudging admiration even from many of those who opposed him and his views.*
>
> *To those closer to him, his warmth, humor, and appreciation of life and the people around him were glowing and endearing characteristics. . . .*
>
> *He found it difficult to understand deviations from what he considered the clear and abiding moral standards he accepted as basic. . . .*
>
> *His business acumen was of the daring, far-sighted kind, often leading to decisions counter to the fashions of the moment—and eventually fruitful. He delighted in his daily ventures into the stock market, as much for the thrill of "guessing right" as for the money involved.*

Contrary to much of the public legend, he was neither highly directive in running his business empire nor arbitrarily adamant in decision-making, whether personal or political.

He believed in, and practiced, delegation of authority to those who worked for his various enterprises, giving gentle direction, finally, only when he thought it absolutely necessary. Defeats of political candidates or issues he backed were taken philosophically, with a silent bow in the direction of "the majority." . . .

Reserved in the rather courtly manner of an earlier time, he maintained a youthful eagerness for tomorrow. He didn't particularly like being singled out for notice because of his age.

He never, really, grew old.

Across town the competing *Oklahoma Journal*, owned W. P. "Bill" Atkinson, published a brief editorial the day after E. K. Gaylord died. It read:

No man has left a more indelible imprint on the pages of Oklahoma history. His tracks of solid accomplishments will long serve as guide marks for those who would call forth the best in their personal lives and make the betterment of their city, state and nation a constant goal. Of him it may truly be said, he shoved back the horizon for generations to come.

Four days after his death, services were held in Oklahoma Christian College's Hardeman Auditorium, and he was laid to rest next to the grave of his wife of more than 60 years, Inez K. Gaylord, in Memorial Park Cemetery. She died about four months earlier on January 16, 1974.

＊

Following his father's death, Edward L. Gaylord assumed the leadership of The Oklahoma Publishing Co. Having grown up in Oklahoma City, where he attended public schools until his senior year, he had worked part-time for the Company in the garage of Mistletoe Express in Oklahoma City during the summer of 1936. "That summer was the hottest summer we ever had. I think we had 50 days over 100 degrees," he recalled. During later summers in the 1930s, he worked in the papers' advertising and circulation departments. Edward L. Gaylord spent his senior year in high school at the Asheville School for Boys in North Carolina, where he was graduated in the spring of 1937. The following fall he

Edward L. Gaylord as he appeared about the time he was graduated from high school in 1937.

This photo of E. K. Gaylord and his wife Inez was made in their Oklahoma City home.

E. K. Gaylord (right) visits with Mr. and Mrs. Otis Sullivant at a state capitol reception following Gaylord's address to a joint session of the Oklahoma state legislature March 5, 1973. Sullivant was a long-time political writer for *The Oklahoman* and *Times*. This photo was made by Jim Argo.

went to Stanford University in California, where he studied economics and received a liberal arts education. There he worked for a short time in the advertising department of the student daily newspaper.

After he was graduated from Stanford in the spring of 1941, he went to Harvard Business School in the fall of 1941. As already related he left at the start of World War II and served in the military. Following the war, he went to work full-time in 1946 for The Oklahoma Publishing Co. Thus, when he assumed the Company's leadership following his father's death, he already had learned much from his father and had 30 years of first-hand experience in The Oklahoma Publishing Co. Edward L. Gaylord continued the Company's diversification by purchasing KSTW-TV in Seattle-Tacoma. New radio properties—KRKE-AM and -FM in Albuquerque, and KYTE-AM and KLLB-FM in Portland, Oregon—were acquired during the '70s. In 1976, however, The Oklahoma Publishing Co. sold WKY-TV in Oklahoma City in order to purchase WVUE-TV, New Orleans, and WUAB-TV, Cleveland, Ohio. Gaylord said Oklahoma City was the smallest market where the Company owned television stations. Since government regulations then limited the number of stations any one company could own, WKY-TV was sold to enable the Company to expand its television holdings in larger cities. OPUBCO retained WKY radio until 2002 when Citadel Broadcasting agreed to purchase it.

The Oklahoma Publishing Co. made its first expansion in the newspaper field outside of Oklahoma City when it purchased the *Colorado Springs Sun* in 1977. The acquisition was largely for family sentimental reasons since E. K. Gaylord had lived and worked in Colorado during his

early years. Edward L. Gaylord also moved into a new business area late in the '70s establishing the Gaylord Production Co. in Los Angeles to supply its television stations with quality programs. Its productions included the syndicated "Glen Campbell Show" and "Hee Haw" starring Roy Clark and Buck Owens, who had strong Oklahoma ties. From 1966 to 1973, "The Buck Owens Ranch Show" had originated at WKY-TV. Earlier Owens played the old Trianon Ballroom, and the Diamond Ballroom in Oklahoma City.

While E. K. Gaylord was a great businessman, Edward L. Gaylord far surpassed his father as a great business planner and forecaster in terms of buying growth properties. At the same time, like his father, Edward L. Gaylord has dedicated much time and effort toward community growth. Paul B. Strasbaugh, long-time general manager of the Oklahoma Industries Authority, credits E. K. and Edward L. Gaylord with having provided the strongest influence on the industrial development of metropolitan Oklahoma City. Formed as a corporation separate from the Oklahoma City Chamber of Commerce in 1945 with the help of E. K. Gaylord, Oklahoma Industries Authority (OIA) became a public trust in 1966, organized under state statutes to issue industrial revenue bonds. From its beginning, Edward L. Gaylord chaired OIA which has processed more than 110 projects, created 100,000 new jobs, and funded more than $1,050,000,000 for new construction. Paul B. Strasbaugh, OIA general manager, said, "Some of the more notable industrial projects are Firestone, General Motors, Hertz Corp., Unit Parts, Fred Jones Manufacturing, Little Giant Pump and Farley Foods. And there has been hospital construction for St. Anthony

Hospital, Baptist, Mercy, Deaconess and Presbyterian."

Strasbaugh added that Edward L. Gaylord "is the most important business and civic leader in the last half of the twentieth century for Oklahoma City. His father E. K. Gaylord occupied that position for the first half. Ed is a great human being, was a caring husband, is a caring father, very proud of his fine family."

More recently, as chairman of the board of directors of the National Cowboy Hall of Fame and Western Heritage Center (now the National Cowboy and Western Heritage Museum), Edward L. Gaylord helped to lead a $35 million expansion campaign to enable the museum to triple its size. A wing of the museum has since been named for him.

✳

During the 1970s, *The Oklahoman* and *Times* along with the broadcast properties owned by The Oklahoma Publishing Co. provided extensive coverage of the Watergate controversy and the resignation of President Richard Nixon on August 9, 1974. The following year they covered the space adventures of Oklahoman Thomas P. Stafford of Weatherford as commander of Apollo 18. In Oklahoma, reporter Jim Etter investigated jails throughout the state in 1976 after they were ordered to comply with strict new regulations designed to ensure the facilities were free of health and safety hazards. Etter evaluated conditions of jails in each of the state's counties.

During the early '70s, readers of *The Oklahoman* and *Times* followed the fate of Governor David Hall. During his last year in office, Hall was investigated for alleged kickbacks from contractors. Three days after he left office in 1975, a federal grand jury found Hall guilty on four counts of extortion and conspiracy to commit bribery in connection with the investment of state retirement system funds. He went to jail and served about 19 months of a three-year sentence. Among many other things, the papers also reported the election of David Boren as governor succeeding Hall. Boren campaigned for seven constitutional amendments that shortened the ballot by providing for some statewide executive offices to be filled by appointment rather than election. All seven passed. The papers supported Boren, whose years as governor were marked by substantial increases in funding for education, a drop in welfare rolls and more money for law enforcement. Toward the end of the '70s, the papers reported on the plague of grasshoppers that struck the state, the Sirloin Stockade murders, the opening of the Kirkpatrick Center in Oklahoma City, and the election of George Nigh as governor. Nigh succeeded Boren, who was elected to the U.S. Senate.

In May 1979, *The Oklahoman* carried the first story in Oklahoma announcing a federal investigation into political corruption that centered on Oklahoma county commissioners. The story told that state auditors were receiving special training, and described what they would be looking for. *The Oklahoman* and *Times* provided extensive coverage on what became a spectacular political-corruption scandal by 1984 that involved 60 of the state's 77 counties. Okscam, as it became known, resulted in 220 felony convictions during a two-year period.

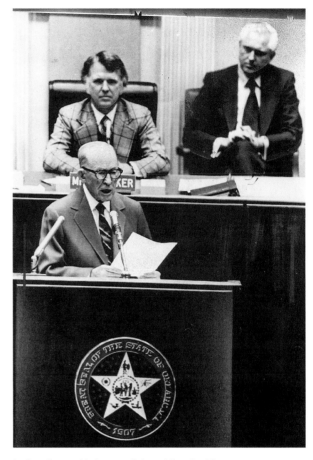

Lt. Gov. George Nigh, upper left, and Gov. David Hall listen as E. K. Gaylord addresses a joint session of the Oklahoma legislature March 5, 1973.

As the decade of the 1980s began, Oklahoma City had a population of 403,213, the metro area was 834,088, the state 3,145,585, and the decade was a period when The Oklahoma Publishing Co. made further improvements in the production of its newspapers. *The Oklahoman* became the first metropolitan daily in the nation to convert to electronic page composition, and the paper helped develop the first electronic library linked to computer typesetting and accessible to reporters on their computer terminals. More than 200 newspaper representatives from around the world came to see it.

The decade also saw its papers continue extensive coverage of local, state, national and international news. *The Oklahoman* and *Times* covered the conflict centering on the FAA academy in Oklahoma City after pilots were grounded because air traffic controllers went on strike. When Penn Square Bank in Oklahoma City failed in 1982, the papers reported the bank's insolvency and how it rocked Oklahoma and sent a jolt across the nation. The bank's collapse was the first of a string of 117 bank failures and 53 distressed mergers in Oklahoma during the 10 years that followed. During the decade of the '80s, readers also learned of a natural gas explosion that killed five children and one adult when it ripped through the kitchen of Star Elementary School in northeast Oklahoma. The papers also reported that voters had passed a wagering bill making it possible for pari-mutuel betting in Oklahoma.

Early in 1982, Vivian E. Vahlberg, assistant Washington bureau chief for *The Oklahoman,* was sworn in as the first woman president of the 75-year-old National Press Club in Washington D.C. President Ronald Reagan administered the oath of office. Using his best preacher's voice, Reagan said, "Dearly beloved, we are gathered together this evening under the slightly bleary eyes of the membership to join together this, shall we say, newsperson in unholy matrimony with the office of president of the National Press Club." As president, Vahlberg, supervised the $45 million renovation of the historic National Press Building, three blocks from the White House.

In Oklahoma, the year 1982 also saw the opening of Enterprise Square USA, a showcase for America's free enterprise system, at Oklahoma Christian University of Science and Arts. Edward L. Gaylord, his wife Thelma and The Oklahoma Publishing Co. made a gift of $1.5 million to help establish the museum and education center for economics and free enterprise. By 1982, OPUBCO's broadcasting division owned and operated 10 television and radio stations in nine of the nation's major metropolitan markets. Combined, the television stations served more than eight million homes, which was more than 10 percent of all television households in the United States. Four of the stations were independents including KTVT, Dallas–Ft. Worth, then the nation's tenth largest television market. KTVT had "Texas' Tallest TV Tower" which carried the station's signal to more than four million persons throughout North Texas and by cable into New Mexico, Colorado, Oklahoma, Arkansas and Louisiana.

KHTV in Houston was another independent television station owned by OPUBCO. Without any network affiliations the station televised top motion pictures, family oriented comedy and variety shows, and informational programming. OPUBCO's broadcasting division entered the Pacific Northwest when it purchased KSTW-TV, Seattle-Tacoma, in 1974. It also was an independent television station, the first commercial broadcast station to operate its own earth-satellite receiving station which helped it increase its news and major league sports programming.

Edward L. Gaylord and his wife, Thelma, visit with Minnie Pearl and Roy Acuff on the Opry stage in 1983.

try Music Television (CMT), and CMT Europe cable networks, the Opryland Hotel, the Opryland Theme Park, Opryland Music Group, and, later, the showboat Gen. Jackson, which plies the Cumberland River from Nashville. Early in June 1984, Edward L. Gaylord was honored in Nashville with the Spirit of America Award, the first time the award had been presented to an individual during the Olympic season by the U.S. Olympic Committee. The award recognized his very generous contributions to the financing of the American Olympic effort and his commitment to the values of the American Olympic effort, volunteerism, individual initiative and excellence.

Each of OPUBCO's television stations aired public service programs designed to meet the needs of their respective communities.

During the early 1980s, Edward L. Gaylord continued his efforts to diversify The Oklahoma Publishing Co.'s holdings with the purchase, in 1983 for $240 million, of the Opryland complex in Nashville, Tennessee. It included The Nashville Network (TNN), Coun-

In 1983, Governor George Nigh called a special session of the Oklahoma legislature and proposed a $654-million increase in state taxes to deal with a burgeoning state deficit. *The Oklahoman* opposed the tax increase as did many Oklahomans. During the special legislative session, Nigh accused the paper's publisher, Edward L. Gaylord, of using "threats . . . intimidation . . . and blackmail" on the lawmakers. "Eddie Gaylord does

In 1983, Edward L. Gaylord takes the stage at the Grand Ole Opry in Nashville to announce that The Oklahoma Publishing Co. has purchased Opryland.

Edward L. Gaylord, president of The Oklahoma Publishing Co., is receiving the Spirit of America Award on June 5, 1984, in Nashville, from Larry Hough (right), treasurer of the United States Olympic Committee.

not own George Nigh," the governor exclaimed. In a front page editorial the paper responded: *"The Oklahoman* has never made a practice of owning governors, figuring, among other things, they would make poor investments. Those cheap enough to buy would invariably be impossible to sell." The paper then published the home phone numbers of legislature members and urged voters to call the "tax hogs." On November 28, the legislature adjourned without taking action on Nigh's proposal.

In 1984, *The Oklahoman* and *Times* reported developments when House Speaker Dan Draper and Majority Floor Leader Joe Fitzgibbon were found guilty by a federal court jury on charges they participated in a fraudulent absentee ballot scheme. A federal court later overturned their convictions after seven prosecution witnesses recanted their testimony. But this was

months after their leadership roles had been filled by others. Reporters were on hand in 1984 when Oklahomans voted to legalize liquor by the drink. Oklahoma became the last state in the union to do so, and that was 50 years after Prohibition ended nationally.

❋

The national decline of afternoon metropolitan newspapers because of competition from television, changing lifestyles, and declining readership finally reached Oklahoma City in 1984. The *Oklahoma City Times,* purchased in 1916 by The Oklahoma Publishing Co., was merged with *The Oklahoman.* The *Times* had been published by OPUBCO for 68 years. Many staff members from the *Times* moved to *The Oklahoman* which intensified its efforts to serve its readers.

In 1985, after *The Oklahoman* reported the explosion at the Aerlex

OPUBCO's Edward L. Gaylord (right), chairman of the Oklahoma Christian College board of governors, makes a few comments before introducing comedian Bob Hope during Hope's visit on October 4, 1983, to Enterprise Square on the OCC campus. It was Hope's 13th visit to Oklahoma City. Hope also attended the dedication ceremonies for Presbyterian Hospital's $1.5 million Bob Hope Eye Surgery Center.

Newspaper carrier Justin Brockhaus, 13, sells Extras at the corner of Broadway and Park Avenue in downtown Oklahoma City following the August 20, 1986, post office slayings in Edmond.

fireworks factory in northeast Oklahoma that on June 25 killed 21 workers, the paper's reporters investigated problems nationally in the fireworks industry. They learned the Occupational Safety and Health Administration had never checked most of the nation's fireworks factories and were not even aware that some plants existed. *The Oklahoman* helped to inspire new federal safety regulations in the fireworks industry. Also in 1985, *The Oklahoman* became the first metropolitan daily in the nation to convert to electronic page composition by a technique developed largely in the paper's own newsroom.

During the year the paper's printing plant was relocated in its present north Oklahoma City location. *The Oklahoman* published an Extra, the first such edition published by the paper since President Kennedy's assassination in 1963. The Extra on August 20, 1986, reported that Patrick Henry Sherrill killed 14 co-workers and himself at the Edmond post office.

In 1987, Ed Martin, who had joined *The Oklahoman* in 1970, became vice president and general manager replac-

ing Howard Nicks who had retired. In 1989, Martin became chairman of the Greater Oklahoma City Chamber of Commerce, and in 1995 he was elected chairman of the board of trustees of the Southern Newspaper Publishers Association. But after 31 years of service to OPUBCO, he stepped down early in 2001. Kirk A. Jewell, who had been the newspaper's controller for 15 years, was selected as the new general manager on the business side.

Toward the end of the 1980s, *The Oklahoman* covered the opening of the Oklahoma City Zoo's aquatics exhibit in 1987, the opening of Myriad Gardens and Crystal Bridge in 1988, and the 1989 election where Oklahomans voted to shorten legislative sessions among many other stories. *The Oklahoman* also gave extensive coverage to the visit of President Ronald Reagan and a world-famous group of celebrities and entertainers at the Opening Ceremonies of the U.S. Olympic Festival on July 21, 1989, at Owen Field on the University of Oklahoma campus in Norman. The opening ceremonies marked the beginning of the largest

multi-sport athletic competition in the United States to date.

In 1987, Edward L. Gaylord was honored for his achievements and received the Golden Plate award from the American Academy of Achievement meeting in Denver, Colorado. Nineteen years earlier his father had received the same award which is presented annually to extraordinary and inspiring "exemplars of excellence" in great fields of endeavor. The following year, The Oklahoma Publishing Co. purchased the Broadmoor Hotel at Colorado Springs. The Gaylord family's Colorado heritage and love of the Rocky Mountains were responsible for the purchase, plus the resort's business potential. Since its purchase many improvements and additions have made it a world-class resort. A

ballroom, a spa, golf and tennis club, and 150 rooms have been added to what has been described as the "Grande Dame of the Rockies." The Broadmoor opened in 1918 after mining magnate Spencer Penrose decided to create the most beautiful resort in the world. He brought workmen from Italy to apply the latticework plaster ceilings that still decorate the ornate mezzanine lounge.

Penrose also imported fine marble for the curved staircase that still graces the original lobby. He ordered dazzling chandeliers that still glitter throughout the hotel, and he hired dozens of workmen to hand paint beams and ceilings. He also chose a striking pink hue for the stucco facade, a color maintained to this day. For many persons today, the drawing card is golf at the three 18-hole courses that weave their

The Oklahoma Publishing Co. purchased the Broadmoor Hotel at Colorado Springs, Colorado, in 1988.

way through white pine, Douglas fir, blue spruce, elm, maple, and scrub oak. Twelve Plexi-cushion tennis courts, two of which are covered from mid-October through May, have earned the Broadmoor a rating by *Tennis Magazine* readers as one of the "top ten tennis resorts in America." Former Wimbledon champion Dennis Ralston and his staff provide tennis instruction. Other features include six restaurants and seven lounges, three swimming pools, one lap pool, and outdoor hot tubs, riding stables, fly-fishing school, paddle boating on Cheyenne Lake, a world-class, fully equipped spa and fitness center, plus nearly 30 specialty shops, a florist, a first-run movie theater, and a car rental office.

The Oklahoma Publishing Co. also owns the Manitou and Pikes Peak Railway Co. west of Colorado Springs. Several times each day, late April through November, weather permitting, Swiss-made trains climb to the summit of 14,110-foot Pikes Peak, the mountain discovered in 1806 by American explorer Zebulon M. Pike. Using modern Swiss trains, it is not only the world's highest cog railway, but the highest railroad in North America. Its history goes back to the late 19th century when Zalmon Simmons, inventor and founder of the Simmons Beauty-rest Mattress Co., rode to the summit of Pikes Peak on a mule, partly to enjoy the view and partly to check up on one of his inventions, an insulator for the telegraph wires which ran to the Army Signal Station on the summit. It took Simmons two days to reach the summit. He was awed by the scenery but thought the views should be experienced in a more civilized and comfortable manner, like a railway to the summit. Simmons soon provided capital needed to fund the venture. The cog railway was completed by 1890 and the first passenger train, carrying a church choir from Denver, traveled to the summit on June 30, 1891.

Some members of the Gaylord family in 1991. Standing: Edward L. Gaylord and E.K. Gaylord II. Seated: Edith Gaylord (left), Thelma Gaylord and Christy Gaylord Everest.

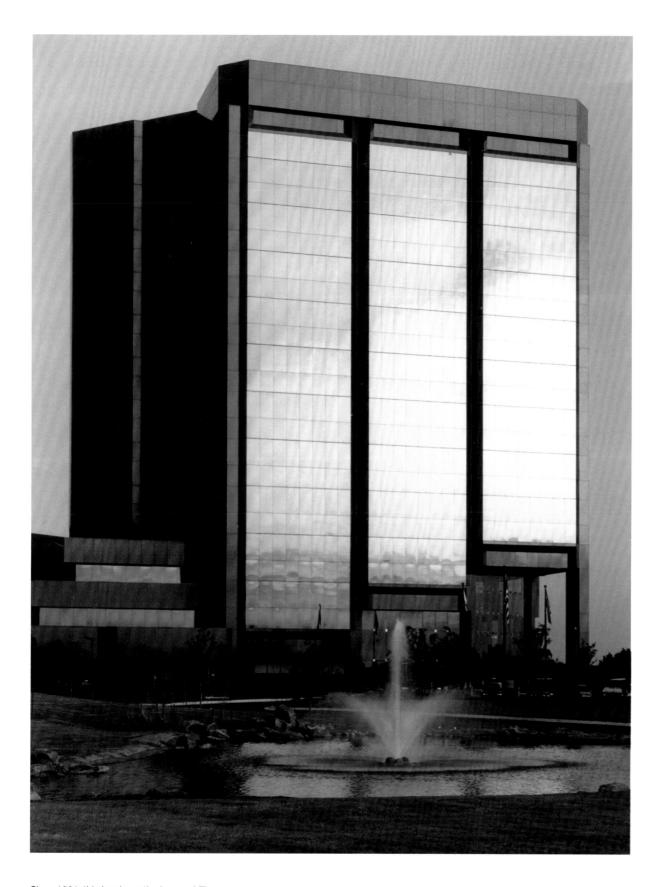

Since 1991, this has been the home of *The Oklahoman* and The Oklahoma Publishing Co. at 9000 North Broadway in Oklahoma City.

Chapter Thirteen

GROWTH WITH QUALITY IN THE '90S

As the decade of the '90s began, Oklahoma City had a population of 444,724, the metro area 958,839, and the state 3,296,040. It was a decade when *The Oklahoman* continued its aggressive reporting of news and information that affected the lives and welfare of its readers. Among the stories covered in 1990 was the establishment of a state Ethics Commission, and the opening of Oklahoma County's new $52 million jail in November and the controversy that followed when severe design flaws were discovered which contributed to a series of prisoner escapes. When the first shots in the Gulf War were fired in January 1991, the paper provided extensive coverage and published an Extra. That same year an investigation by *The Oklahoman* disclosed how the legislature in a 90-page bill passed in 1987 had included two paragraphs that abolished the existing system of state oversight of school and county cash management programs and instituted another. The paper pointed out that, under the legislation, school districts could go into debt without a vote of the people.

The year 1991 was also a big year for the Gaylord family and employees of *The Oklahoman* and The Oklahoma Publishing Co. They moved into the new 12-story tower constructed next to the paper's printing plant at the southeast corner of Britton Road and Broadway Extension. It was a grand addition to the Oklahoma City skyline. During dedication ceremonies, Edward L. Gaylord noted: "The newspaper is much more than just publishing the news and advertisements. *The Oklahoman* is mightily involved in building a city, a state and a better America."

Today those words are on a plaque inside the entrance to the new building near where a huge tapestry containing the First Amendment of the Constitution is visible to all who enter. Nearby is another plaque containing the words of E. K. Gaylord uttered 20 years earlier when at the age of 98 he was honored by the Newcomen Society. It reads: "In its entire history, The Oklahoma Publishing Co. has fought under the banner of honesty in government, progress in education and culture, high standards of morality, generosity in philanthropy, betterment of social conditions, and the steady improvement of economic conditions."

It was also in 1991 that E. K. Gaylord II joined his father, Edward L. Gaylord, in managing The Oklahoma Publishing Co. His aunt, the late Edith Gaylord, recalled the day when E. K. Gaylord asked his grandson, "What do you want to do when you grow up?" E. K. Gaylord II, then a small boy of about four or five, looked at his grandfather and without hesitation replied, "I want to be just like you." E. K. Gaylord II remembers the event. He recalled that when some of the family members began crying, "I thought I was in trouble."

From an early age E. K. Gaylord II knew it was part of the family's grand plan that he would one day run the Company. It is a challenge he welcomed. Like his father, E. K. Gaylord II has worked in different areas of *The Oklahoman,* was elected to the board of The Oklahoma Publishing Co. on November 1, 1977, and is very active in the other business enterprises owned by the company. Still, he has found time to pursue his love of horses. It is in the equine arena that he has honed and showcased his business management skills. He opened the Lazy E Ranch and Arena, located on 300 rolling acres about 30 minutes north of Oklahoma City, in 1984.

Today the Lazy E Arena is the nation's number-one western entertainment facility hosting some of professional rodeo's most prestigious events. More than 120,000 people from across the nation come to the arena to see world champion cowboys and cowgirls compete. The Lazy E Ranch also includes a 65,000 square foot mare barn and a training center constructed in 1989 four miles east of the arena. The

In 1991, E. K. Gaylord II (left) joined his father Edward L. Gaylord in the management of The Oklahoma Publishing Co.

Thelma and Edward L. Gaylord stand with a bronze of the new Oklahoma Publishing Co. office tower at 9000 Broadway. The bronze was given to the couple during a grand opening for employees in 1991. A small inscription near the bronze reads: "Edward L. and Thelma Gaylord. Thank you for providing us a bright future. Your employees of *The Daily Oklahoman* June 2, 1991."

OPPOSITE
The front page of the April 20, 1995, issue of *The Daily Oklahoman.*

training center is the headquarters for Lazy E Racing Stables. With the purchase of World Champion and World Champion sire Special Effort in 1989, the Lazy E earned recognition as one of the top Quarter Horse breeding operations in the nation. Approximately 1,500 horses pass through the Lazy E Ranch gates each year, and in 2001, the Lazy E bred more than 500 mares. Today, its thoroughbred operation, Gaillardia Racing, is centered on Gaillardia Farms in Lexington, Kentucky.

During the late 1990s, E. K. Gaylord II joined Bennie Beutler to form Beutler and Gaylord Rodeo Company headquartered at Elk City, Oklahoma, to provide stock to rodeos. In November 2000, and for the third straight year, the top 30 rodeo cowboys and bullfighters at the Copenhagen Pro Rodeo in Las Vegas, Nevada, voted Beutler and Gaylord stock as the best. E. K. Gaylord II, who was graduated

from Texas Christian University in 1979, established the E. K. Gaylord Memorial Scholarship Fund in the Ranch Management program at TCU to honor his grandfather.

Meantime new business challenges developed after his father, Edward L. Gaylord, pooled many of the resources of The Oklahoma Publishing Co. in October 1991 to establish Gaylord Entertainment Co., a publicly traded, diversified entertainment and communications company headquartered in Nashville, Tenn., which sold shares to the public. But The Oklahoma Publishing Co. retained *The Oklahoman,* the Broadmoor Hotel and the Manitou and Pikes Peak Railway Co. in Colorado, WKY radio in Oklahoma City, and extensive real estate investments in several states. In May of 1999, Edward L. Gaylord became chairman emeritus of Gaylord Communication Co. and E. K. Gaylord II became chairman, a position he held until the spring of

MORNING OF TERROR

City Struggles With Shock of Deadly Bombing

An Oklahoma City firefighter runs through rubble near the Alfred P. Murrah Federal Building after an explosion caved in the front of the building Wednesday. The blast damaged other buildings within several blocks.

Small Children Victims In Day-Care Center

By Diana Baldwin
Staff Writer

Five small children, badly injured and bloodied, and a toy doll were among the first to be removed from the Murrah Building's second floor day-care center.

"You couldn't even tell they had been little boys or little girls," said Lydia Winfrey, a licensed practical nurse, who assisted with the children wrapped in blankets and lying on the brick patio of the federal building.

One child was decapitated and others had severe head injuries,

Winfrey said. A hole in one child's head was filled with plaster pieces. The medical examiner photographed the young, innocent victims.

The toy doll, which was found near one victim, was brought out of the rubble in hopes it would help identify that victim, Winfrey said.

Dr. Kathy DeHart, a local dentist who volunteered at the southside triage center, said it appeared the blast hit the children in the face, blowing them backward.

"It was just totally devastating to

See CENTER, Page 2

A firefighter carries a child injured in the explosion in downtown Oklahoma City on Wednesday.

Scores Killed In Bomb Blast; State Stunned

By Steve Lackmeyer
and David Zizzo
Staff Writers

A thunderous bomb blast rocked Oklahoma City on Wednesday, ripping a huge slice from a federal building and killing at least 150 to 200 people, many of them children.

The bombing, felt throughout central sections of Oklahoma, shattered the downtown district and left a grieving state wondering why.

The explosion, shortly after 9 a.m. demolished about a third of the Alfred P. Murrah Federal Building, causing all nine stories, including a day-care center on the second floor, to "pancake" into a pile of rubble.

Workers in their offices tumbled out of the nine-story building to the street below. One man fell into the 30-foot wide bomb crater.

Victims fled the building, their clothes ripped off by the blast. Others wandered in a daze. Some victims with gashes on their arms and legs, or with head injuries, blood streaming down their faces, sat on curbs, quiet and shocked.

Shortly after 10 p.m., rescuers pulled a 15-year-old girl from the rubble of the building parking lot, the first survivor found in hours. The girl was listed in critical condition late Wednesday.

See BLAST, Page 3

Fresh Day in City Turns Into New-Found Horror

By Penny Owen
Staff Writer

Oklahoma City will never be the same.

This is a place, after all, where terrorists don't venture. The heartland, people kept saying. Car bombs don't kill children here.

Wednesday changed everything. In an explosion felt at least 15 miles away,

the fresh, innocent morning turned to horror. In five seconds, witnesses said, floors at the Alfred P. Murrah Federal Building "cascaded on top of each other."

Those there drew all kinds of initial conclusions: A plane crashed. An earthquake hit. Armageddon.

Once the smoke cleared,

See QUESTIONS, Page 2

Terror in the Heartland

Coverage of the bomb blast and its aftermath is on **Pages 4, 5, 7-9, 11-14, 21-22** and in a Special Section on **Pages 15-20.**

Inside

Features

Prayer for Today

WHEN life gets weary, Lord, remind us to count our many blessings you give us every day. Thank you for helping to ease our fears of heartaches. Amen.

2001. Today he serves on the company's board of directors.

During the 1990s, E. K. Gaylord II also broke into the film industry, co-produced the movie "My Heroes Have Always Been Cowboys," and served as co-executive producer of a Bonanza sequel that was aired in 1994 on NBC. His business responsibilities in these areas grew in March 2001 when The Oklahoma Publishing Co. obtained Pandora Films, Gaylord Films, Gaylord Sports Management, Gaylord Event Television and the Gaylord Production Company from Gaylord Entertainment Co. E. K. Gaylord II has since purchased Gaylord Films / Pandora from OPUBCO. Its operations are headquartered at Warner Brothers Studios in Burbank, California. More recently he served as executive producer for the Hollywood film, "The Divine Secrets of the Ya-Ya Sisterhood," a classic Southern tale of life, love and family that follows a group of lifelong friends. In January 2002, he was executive producer of another film, "A Walk to Remember," a coming-of-age love story based on the best-selling novel by Nicholas Sparks. The film starred Shane West and Mandy Moore.

Publicly owned Gaylord Entertainment Company included the Grand Ole Opry; the Acuff Theater; Ryman Auditorium; Opryland Hotel; Opryland Theme Park; the General Jackson Showboat; a 40,000-song country music publishing house; Gaylord Syndicom, a television distributor whose programs included "Hee Haw"; The Nashville Network (TNN) and Country Music Television (CMT) cable networks; television stations in Seattle-Tacoma, Houston, Milwaukee and Fort Worth; three radio stations; cable television systems in California and North and South Carolina; and other related businesses.

In Nashville, Gaylord Entertainment Co. expanded Opryland Hotel making it the largest combined hotel and convention center under one roof anywhere in the world. It has 2,884 rooms and 600,000 square feet of meeting space. During the '90s the company also spent $8.5 million in renovating Ryman Auditorium in Nashville as a performance hall and museum. It also purchased a minority interest in the Bass Pro Shops headquartered in Springfield, Missouri. In October 1997, Edward L. Gaylord and E. K. Gaylord II held meetings with Michael Jordan, then CEO of Westinghouse, which led to Gaylord Entertainment Co. trading The Nashville Network (TNN) and the Country Music Television (CMT) cable networks in the U.S. for one and one-half billion dollars in Westinghouse stock in a tax-free exchange. Gaylord Entertainment Co., however, retained ownership of Country Music Television International which launched a cable channel in Argentina in November 2000 and another in Brazil early in 2001.

✳

On October 14, 1993, *The Oklahoman* learned that Governor David Lee Walters had been secretly indicted. Prosecutors asked that the story not be printed. Governor Walters said the story was not true. Editors debated whether to run the story. As is occasionally necessary, they sought a decision from publisher Edward L. Gaylord. He reviewed the facts and told them to run the story, and the following morning, October 15, 1993, a large front page headline in *The Oklahoman* read: "Governor Secretly Indicated." Six days later reporters watched as Governor Walters stood before a judge in a late-night session and pleaded guilty to one misdemeanor campaign violation. Eight felony counts were dismissed as part of a plea agreement.

Near the end of 1993, *The Oklahoman* gave full coverage to the approval by Oklahoma City voters of a penny sales tax for the Metropolitan Area Projects Plan (MAPS), the multimillion-dollar project to bring a ballpark, river canal, and other improvements to downtown Oklahoma City.

On April 19, 1995, the new 12-story tower housing The Oklahoma Publishing Co. and *The Oklahoman* on the northern edge of Oklahoma City shook at 9:02 A.M. when the Alfred P. Murrah Federal Building in downtown Oklahoma City was bombed. The crime killed 168 persons. From the newsroom at *The Oklahoman,* everyone could see the black smoke swirling over downtown Oklahoma City. Ed Kelley, managing editor, dispatched as many people as he could to the scene, knowing from the early television pictures that there likely

would be hundreds of dead and injured. Eighty minutes after the explosion, the paper's editors met. They realized the story was too big to leave to the city desk to handle. The normal organization of the newsroom was discarded. Top editors were assigned specific areas of coverage. One editor was assigned to handle the crime. Another was charged with handling the damaged building. Still another editor assumed the responsibility of reporting on the dead and injured, and another editor was assigned the task of covering the many downtown buildings that were destroyed or damaged. Then one person was given the responsibility to maintain the casualty list. By then it was obvious there were going to be many casualties.

Kelley and others toyed with the idea of publishing an Extra to come out in mid-afternoon, but the decision was made to wait and to throw the paper's resources, including an extra

Jim Argo of *The Oklahoman* took this photograph on the morning of April 19. It appeared on the paper's front page the following morning.

The OPUBCO board of directors on March 28, 1994. Seated (left to right): Edith Gaylord, Edward L. Gaylord and Thelma Gaylord. Standing (left to right): Eugene Katz, Glenn Stinchcomb, Christy Gaylord Everest, E.K. Gaylord II and Martin Dickinson.

six-page section, into the next morning's paper. Three members of the paper's staff had been in the area of the explosion. One reporter was across the street at the post office obtaining a passport. She was injured. Another was in a nearby building with officials from a county grand jury. She was badly shaken. The third, a graphic artist, carried two young children including his year-old son, out of the YMCA day care center. They were not injured. The paper's efforts to cover the story and its impact on the city, state, nation and world stretched from long hours into many long days as the world focused on Oklahoma City.

Aside from the first day, the biggest day of the paper's coverage was on the following Sunday, when President Bill Clinton and Mrs. Clinton and Rev. Billy Graham came to Oklahoma City for a prayer service. During the five months following the bombing, *The Oklahoman* published more than 3,400 stories about it and its consequences. In addition, the paper published more than 750 photographs and dozens of graphics. *The Oklahoman* also turned to some nontraditional ways to tell the story and to help the community. The paper used its audiotext system, giving callers access to the lists of how to help and how to get help and other coverage highlights. Within the first six weeks, the paper received about 65,000 calls. The paper also put a temporary home page on the Internet providing information on the bombing. Edmund O. Martin, who was then vice president of The Oklahoma Publishing Co. and general manager of *The Oklahoman,* recalled that the bombing probably cost the newspaper $1 million in overtime, extra newsprint and lost advertising revenue.

The Oklahoma City bombing damaged the YMCA building. Within a short time The Oklahoma Publishing

Co. gave its old building and property on Broadway to the YMCA to replace their damaged building across the street from the bombing site. The Company's $4 million gift included renovation of the building and a new day care center.

Edward L. Gaylord received the Adam Smith Award in October 1996, awarded by Hillsdale College at Hillsdale, Michigan, to honor individuals and institutions which have substantially advanced the cause of free enterprise through education, investment or industry. In receiving the award, Gaylord joined a select group of individuals, including former President Ronald Reagan, Bill Buckley and Bill Simon.

Robby Trammell and Randy Ellis, reporters for *The Oklahoman,* went after a big story with important consequences for Oklahomans in 1997. They got ahead of the official investigators and dug up more information about bid rigging, altering of documents and official lying. Their work fueled and expanded a state investigation that led to 10 indictments. For their work, and that of other reporters, *The Oklahoman* won the 1997 Associated Press sweepstakes award.

In July 1998, Gaillardia Golf and Country Club opened on 253 acres in northwest Oklahoma City. It was created by the OPUBCO Development Co. It was the first phase of a mixed-use development where one can live, shop and work in a unique master-planned community. The Gaillardia course hosted the final official money event of the 11th annual PGA Senior Tour in 2001, and the event was scheduled to be played annually at Gaillardia through 2004.

In September 1998, Edward L. Gaylord was honored for his contributions to the Oklahoma State Fair and the state by the unveiling of a statue

The family gathers in 1998 to honor Edward L. Gaylord's contribution to the State Fair of Oklahoma and the state during his long career. With Edward L. and Thelma Gaylord are their children, (from left) Louise Bennett, Mary McClean, Christy Everest and E. K. Gaylord II. The statue of Edward L. Gaylord, in the background, was dedicated shortly before this photo was taken.

Edward L. Gaylord and the statue of him dedicated at the State Fair of Oklahoma in 1998.

of him. Paul B. Strasbaugh, general manager of the Oklahoma Industries Authority, recapped the history of the Fair and told of its financial difficulties before Edward L. Gaylord was elected to its board of directors in 1955 and became president in 1961. Strasbaugh recalled, "By the end of Ed Gaylord's first year as President, the State Fair earned $82,063 and has not lost any money since. The last year of Ed's term [1971] the Fair earned $429,306, over the 10-year period $2,479,545 was realized. . . . While we recognize Ed Gaylord today for his contributions to

The Oklahoma Publishing Co. began construction of Gaillardia Golf & Country Club in far northwest Oklahoma City in 1998. Late in 2002, it was sold to Herrington Inc. of Little Rock, Arkansas.

the State Fair of Oklahoma, they are but a microcosm of his total contributions to this city, state and nation. They span the broad range of economic development, health care, education, cultural institutions, community development, entertainment and public welfare."

In early May 1999, tornadoes struck central Oklahoma including the Oklahoma City area leaving 40 persons dead. President Bill Clinton visited the area to offer his sympathy and federal assistance. *The Oklahoman* provided extensive coverage of the tornadoes

and the recovery efforts that followed. About five months later *The Oklahoman* reported the death of Thelma Gaylord, Edward L. Gaylord's wife of nearly 50 years. She died on October 27, 1999. For the Gaylord family, the end of the decade was devastating.

CLOCKWISE FROM TOP LEFT

E. K. Gaylord (top center) listens to President Harry S Truman.

E. K. Gaylord shaking hands with President Richard M. Nixon.

Edward L. Gaylord listening to President Lyndon Johnson.

Edward L. Gaylord with President Ronald Reagan. Gov. Henry Bellmon on the left.

Edward L. Gaylord (right) with President George Bush and then-Sen. David Boren.

Chapter Fourteen

THE NEW CENTURY

As the year 2000 dawned, the census reported the population of Oklahoma City had climbed to 506,132 while the metropolitan area had 1,083,346 residents, having grown more than 13 percent since 1990. But the state's population had dropped. The census figures caused Oklahoma to redraw its congressional districts. Y2K fears spread as some people believed computers might cause massive problems because they would not accept the 2000 date. Many Oklahomans purchased extra supplies of canned food, batteries, bottled water and stocked up on blankets should they be needed. But nothing materialized. The start of the new year was calm.

The Oklahoman, of course, provided full coverage of these and countless other stories including the death of former House Speaker Carl Albert on February 4. He was 91. Albert, known as the "Little Giant from Little Dixie," had been in frail health for years. He had served six years as House Speaker, including the turbulent times of President Richard Nixon's downfall. Twice he was within a heartbeat of the presidency; once when Vice President Spiro Agnew resigned in 1973, and when President Nixon resigned and Gerald Ford became president on April 9, 1974. Albert retired in 1977 keeping a public promise he would not run for re-election after reaching age 70. He returned to Oklahoma to live with his wife Mary on a quiet hillside near McAlester at Bugtussle where he had been born.

Early in 2000, Gaylord Entertainment Co. began constructing another Oprylandstyle hotel near Orlando at Kissimmee, Florida. In the fall of 2001 the Gaylord Entertainment Co. renamed its Opryland convention hotels as Gaylord Hotels including Gaylord Opryland in Nashville and the $450 million Gaylord Palms Resort and Convention Center in Florida. It opened on February 2, 2002, a 2.1 million-square-foot facility located on 65 acres. It includes an atrium that resembles the lush tropical views found at St. Augustine, the Old Hickory Traditional Steakhouse surrounded with moss-laden cypresses like those found in the Everglades, and an area that resembles Key West with cabana-striped gift "tents," a lagoon and a 60-foot sailboat that serves as one of several bars. The Gaylord Palms has 1,406 guest rooms, including 106 suites and nine presidential suites. Its 3,180-square-foot Osceola Ballroom can seat more than 3,500 guests for dinner. The convention area, with 400,000 square feet of meeting, exhibition and other space, can accommodate a convention with 5,000 attendees. Within the Gaylord Palms is another hotel called The Emerald Tower which includes 362 guest rooms boasts 26 luxurious suites with a Caribbean theme, plus a dozen break-out rooms, two executive boardrooms and many other amenities. In addition, the world class facility teamed up with Canyon Ranch for a spa, and La Petite Academy Kids Station to provide an on-site, supervised, accredited program of activities for children. Gaylord Palms Resort and Convention Center is only five minutes from the gates of Walt Disney World.

In June 2000, Gaylord Entertainment Co. broke ground between Dallas and Fort Worth, Texas, for another hotel, Gaylord Opryland Texas. When completed in 2004, the entrance will be lined with rolling pastures, ponds and grazing longhorn cattle. Canyon walls will rise to a dramatic hotel entrance. Inside, the hotel will capture both Texas mansion grandeur and the feel of a working ranch. Its centerpiece will be a 4-acre atrium of gardens and waterscapes that replicate Texas, with the Rio Grande, the governor's mansions—actually two bed-and-breakfast inns—and the wide Texas plains. The $400-million Opryland Hotel Texas will employ 1,700 and attract an estimated two million visitors annually.

Also in 2000, The Oklahoma Publishing Co. began developing Querencia, a private 350-unit luxury golf course community, located on 700 acres in Los Cabos on the Sea of Cortez at the southern tip of Mexico's Baja peninsula. Querencia boasts a golf course designed by Tom Fazio, a stocked lake for fishing and small watercrafts, and the Querencia Village and Spa.

*

By May 2000, reporters for *The Oklahoman* were providing extensive coverage of a federal investigation into a scandal in the Oklahoma Health Department. Brent Van Meter, 46, was arrested by FBI agents, May 2, following a day in which federal and state agents served 12 federal search warrants at the health department and elsewhere in Oklahoma City. Van Meter was charged with soliciting bribes from nursing home owners in exchange for regulatory favors. The FBI had first launched its investigation in 1996 after several individuals approached the agency with allegations of corruption within the nursing home licensing and regulation section of the department. The paper also provided extensive coverage of "ghost" employees in state jobs.

On March 29, 2000, The Oklahoma Publishing Co. sold the historic 21,000-acre Greenland Ranch in Douglas County, Colorado, to The Conservation Fund of Boulder, Colorado, assuring that this largest undeveloped tract of land remaining in the Front Range region of the Rocky Mountains would be preserved. OPUBCO did retain a large percentage of the water rights. The sale was largely funded by a private donor. The Conservation Fund, a national nonprofit organization dedicated to protecting the nation's outdoor heritage, planned to maintain the property as a working ranch. The ranch has eight miles of frontage on both sides of Interstate 25 between Colorado Springs and Castle Rock, Colorado.

Many painful memories returned April 19, 2000, on the fifth anniversary of the Oklahoma City bombing. Its National Memorial was opened by President Bill Clinton, Oklahoma Governor Frank Keating and numerous local officials, just north of the site of the Alfred P. Murrah Federal Building. Behind the memorial's "Gates of Time," with portals marking "9:01" and "9:03," are 168 empty chairs, each having the name of a person who died in the bombing. There, also, are the Survivor Tree, the Survivor Chapel and the Children's Orchard. *The Oklahoman* provided extensive coverage before, during and after the dedication ceremony, and continued to report on events surrounding Timothy McVeigh, who ended his appeals and asked U.S. District Judge Richard P. Matsch in Denver to set his execution date for having bombed the Alfred P. Murrah Federal Building in 1995. McVeigh was executed on June 12, 2001, in the federal prison at Terre Haute, Indiana.

Dry conditions that began in many areas of Oklahoma in 1999 intensified in 2000. By July, Gov. Frank Keating had extended a ban on all outdoor burning to 29 more counties. In all, 35 Oklahoma counties, most south of Interstate 40, were affected. Thirteen deaths in Oklahoma were attributed to the heat and drought. Wildfires kept many fire departments busy into November. By then, reporters from *The Oklahoman* were providing coverage of the steep increase in the cost of natural gas on the heels of an increase in gasoline prices. The paper also covered the political campaigns, the November election, and the Florida presidential vote counting that continued through much of December.

Oklahomans agonized over hanging and dimpled chads. The Florida recount ended with the election of George W. Bush as president.

On December 27, 2000, *The Oklahoman* and Oklahoma City television station KWTV (Channel 9) announced that they were joining forces in a multimedia project. Because the OU Sooner football team had had a spectacular year, E. K. Gaylord II said, "We wanted to match the climax of the season at the Orange Bowl by offering Oklahomans stories whenever they want to read them or watch them. Oklahomans read about the team in *The Oklahoman,* watch live telecasts from Miami on News 9, and there will be 24-hour coverage on our Web sites at 9online.com and Oklahoma.com." David Griffin, president of KWTV, added: "We're both Oklahoma-owned companies, and we care about what happens in our state. The Orange Bowl is the perfect opportunity for us to showcase the best of television, newspaper and Internet leading up to and during this championship game." Oklahomans watched and read as the Oklahoma Sooner football team won in the Orange Bowl on January 3, 2001, over the Florida Seminoles 13–2. It was their seventh National Championship.

The Oklahoman and KWTV soon expanded their venture that included a regular column in *The Oklahoman* by KWTV meteorologist Gary England, and in August 2001 merged their Internet Web sites to create NewsOK.com, an online information powerhouse including video clips, Gary England's weather, wall-to-wall news stories and photos, columnists from the paper, and all of the community information available. NewsOK.com combined the two organizations' resources to provide better in-depth news and readily available information on television, in print and online. The news media

convergence of *The Oklahoman* and KWTV is truly a pioneering venture. They were among the first organizations to do so in the nation. When NewsOK.com began, it averaged 50,000 hits per month. There are now more than one million hits per month.

When New York City and Washington D.C. were struck by terrorists on September 11, 2001, NewsOK.com provided continuous coverage on the nation's most deadly day since the Civil War. The following morning the headline in *The Daily Oklahoman* read: OUR NATION SAW EVIL, and the paper provided extensive coverage of the tragic events and how they affected Oklahoma, Oklahomans and the nation.

✳

On Sunday, January 28, 2000, Edith Kinney Gaylord died in Oklahoma City at St. Anthony's hospital, where she had been born 84 years earlier. Three days later, memorial services were held in Hardeman Auditorium at Oklahoma Christian University in Oklahoma. David Boren, president of the University of Oklahoma, where she received an honorary doctorate a few years earlier, gave the eulogy and noted that Edith Gaylord was a true pioneer journalist who helped to open the door for women in the profession. "She will be most remembered as Oklahoma's 'quiet philanthropist' who often made gifts anonymously to help those in need."

Edith Gaylord, who had served as corporate secretary and member of the board of directors of The Oklahoma Publishing Co., had supported education, women's causes, the arts and the environment with her time and her financial resources. She established several endowments at the University of Oklahoma and at Colorado College in Colorado Springs, where she also received an honorary doctorate.

In 1982, she established the Inasmuch Foundation—the name was taken from a biblical passage in Matthew—as a vehicle to support charitable and educational projects, and that same year she also established the Ethics and Excellence in Journalism Foundation to support projects to improve the quality and ethical standards of journalism media.

After Edith Gaylord's death, it was announced that she had provided a $500,000 endowment to the University of Oklahoma to provide an annual $20,000 prize to a faculty or staff member, or student who exhibits "keen perceptivity." The award was named the Otis Sullivant Award in honor of *The Oklahoman*'s chief political writer. Sullivant joined the paper in 1927 and became one of the state's most influential journalists. He retired in 1968 and died in 1974. Edith Gaylord wanted the award to go to a person "who manifests intuitiveness, instant comprehension, empathy, is observant and interprets from experience." She wanted the term "perceptivity" to be broadly understood and not limited strictly to the results of academic scholarship and research.

A few weeks after Edith Gaylord's death, the national media joined reporters and photographers from *The Oklahoman* to cover the dedication of the Oklahoma City National Memorial Center Museum on February 19, 2000. President George W. Bush and first lady Laura Bush attended the noontime ceremonies, along with a distinguished list of other speakers, to open to the public the museum located in the old *Journal-Record* building.

In late March 2001, Lee Allan Smith, chairman of the Oklahoma Heritage Association, announced that "through a very generous $3-million donation by Edward L. Gaylord," the Association would purchase the Mid-Continent

Life Insurance Building built in 1927. Located at 1400 Classen in Oklahoma City, the four-story neoclassical building, listed on the National Register of Historic Places, would house the Oklahoma Hall of Fame Galleries, the Oklahoma Sports Hall of Fame and the Jim Thorpe Museum. Edward L. Gaylord said he "wanted to help the Oklahoma Heritage Association obtain suitable headquarters for its operations and for the Oklahoma Hall of Fame." He added that the building should meet the Association's needs for many decades into the future.

On October 24, 2001, voters across the state made Oklahoma a right-to-work state by a vote of 447,072 to 378,465. *The Oklahoman* published front page editorials supporting right-to-work. The election was a rematch of one held 37 years earlier when Oklahomans defeated a right-to-work proposal. *The Oklahoman* continued to cover local, state, national and international news as 2002 began, and before the year ended they reported on Middle East problems, the arrest of the Washington D.C. area snipers, and the November elections that saw the Republicans regain the U.S. Senate and continue to control the House of Representatives. Those elections saw Democrat Brad Henry elected governor of Oklahoma replacing Frank Keating, who had served two terms. Voters also made cockfighting illegal in Oklahoma and citizens celebrated the completion of a dome on the state capitol building in Oklahoma City.

During 2002, the weekly Oklahoma City newspaper, *Friday*, asked a panel of about 200 community leaders from across Oklahoma to choose the "25 Most Powerful Oklahomans." Panelists were asked to cast their ballots from a list of 38 possible nominees, plus write-ins. Edward L. Gaylord received 167 votes and was named the

Edward L. Gaylord, chairman, editor and publisher of The Oklahoma Publishing Co., posed for this photo in a portion of the OPUBCO Production Plant pressroom located on the southeast corner of Britton Road and the Broadway Extension on October 7, 2002.

most powerful man in Oklahoma. His son, E. K. Gaylord II, was selected as the 23rd most powerful man in the state. His interests in the film and horse industries saw him step down as president of The Oklahoma Publishing Co. in early December 2002 after serving in that position for eight years. The board of directors chaired by Edward L. Gaylord then elected Christy Gaylord Everest as president. The board also elected Mary Gaylord McClean as vice president, a position her sister Christy had held. E. K. Gaylord II said he would remain an active member of the OPUBCO board.

＊

As The Oklahoma Publishing Co. celebrated its centennial early in 2003, it proudly looked back at its successes and accomplishments. Since the Company was formed, *The Oklahoman* has been on both the winning and losing sides at times, but in ferreting out corruption and abuses by government officials, citizens have been kept informed. Changes have been made in laws and in people holding public offices. Edward L. Gaylord and his son, E. K. Gaylord II, were firm in the belief that *The Oklahoman* and The Oklahoma Publishing Co. should continue on the same course set by E. K. Gaylord early in the last century in spite of occasional and often unfair criticism. The Gaylords know well that some Oklahomans swear by *The Oklahoman* while others swore at it. They know that Oklahomans have never been afraid to speak their minds, and *The Oklahoman* is part of that tradition.

Politicians through the years have denounced the newspaper for its strong editorial position, but editorials are a strong tradition with *The Oklahoman* as they are with all major metropolitan newspapers in America. The policy of The Oklahoma Publishing

During the summer of 2001, Edward L. Gaylord (right) vacationed with his children at OPUBCO's Broadmoor Hotel in Colorado Springs. Left to right: E. K. Gaylord II, Louise Bennett, Christy Everest and Mary McClean.

Co. is to always clearly label editorials so readers will know that they are reading opinion rather than news. Reporters are instructed to cover the news honestly and accurately regardless of the opinions expressed in their paper's editorials. *The Oklahoman* has historically taken strong positions, sometimes in front page editorials. For instance, a sampling of E. K. Gaylord's views can be gleaned from the following editorial excerpts taken from *The Daily Oklahoman*:

CANDIDATES (1967)

The most reliable candidates are the few who are straightforward in their statements and who will not attempt to malign their opponents with unfair and groundless charges.

CITIES AND TOWNS (1968)

Everyone likes to live in a live town. Live towns are ones which constantly make improvements, bettering living conditions and upgrading their economy.

CONGRESS (1969)

Some greedy Congressmen and Senators who already have stuffed their own purses with a 41 percent increase in salaries plus a non-taxable expense account now want

to soak every homeowner in the land
with an increase so as to give them
still more money to squander.

COURTS (1968)

It is imperative that our courts must
all be established by laws that will
absolutely prevent judges being
bought like sheep.

DEFECTS (1968)

The best way to cure defects is
to expose them and every citizen
is entitled to know the exact
conditions.

DEFENSE (1940)

Can't somebody in Washington get
the idea how big this country is
and how much it takes to defend it?
Congress is approaching its task
with a tack hammer instead of
swinging a sledge hammer.

EDUCATION (1968)

The whole future of Oklahoma as
a state depends on the best possible
education and training of our children and young people. Our present
educational system is not accom-
plishing this.

FREEDOM (1970)

Freedom in America is a lighted
candle which can be snuffed out
in the fraction of a second.

GOVERNMENT (1969)

The first and most important duty
of any government is to protect the
lives, the safety and the freedom of
its citizens.

LAW AND ORDER (1907)

This paper has always insisted upon
the maintenance and enforcement
of all laws. It abhors anarchy and
despises hypocrisy.

TAXES (1969)

It ought to be illegal for a national
government to tax any local government, just as it is illegal for a state
or city to tax post offices or any
other property of the federal
government.

UNIONS (1964)

Most union members are under the
thumb of union bosses. Our constitution guarantees freedom of
speech but many union members
dare not speak their minds.

Many of these views have been held
by Edward L. Gaylord and his son,
E. K. Gaylord II. They have been con-
sistently reflected on the editorial
pages of *The Oklahoman*.

When a free-lance Texas writer
sold an article to the *Columbia Journalism Review* published at Columbia
University in New York early in 1999
calling *The Oklahoman* the worst
newspaper in America, the Gaylords
ignored the attack. But J. Leland Gourley, publisher of *Friday*, a competing
weekly newspaper in Oklahoma City,
did not. In an editorial January 22,
1999, Gourley described the article as a
"scurrilous, totally false and malicious
attack" and "gutter journalism at its
worst." Gourley added: "You can bet
your bottom dollar, the writer, Bruce
Selcraig, and the magazine that was
suckered into printing the lying, pre-
judicial, trashy article would not have
done this had our state's daily newspaper been a newspaper with a liberal,
left wing editorial policy." Gourley
pointed out that *The Oklahoman* is one
of the last home-owned metropolitan
newspapers in America, the others
being owned by newspaper chains and
absentee owners.

About seven months earlier, *Insight*
magazine consulted media watchdogs
and compiled a list of the nation's 10

top newspapers from both ends of the political spectrum. On May 25, 1998, *Insight* magazine reported that *The Oklahoman* was picked as one of the top five conservative newspapers in America along with the *Wall Street Journal,* the *Washington Times, New York Post,* and *Manchester* (N.H.) *Union-Leader.* The top five liberal newspapers ranked by *Insight* were the *New York Times, Los Angeles Times, Washington Post, Boston Globe,* and *Chicago Tribune.*

Edward L. Gaylord's views have not imposed in the daily news columns of *The Oklahoman.* Some readers fail to realize that it is impossible for one person, even the publisher, to impose his viewpoint throughout the paper. Most decisions are made by editors at a different level, and they strive to be as fair and objective as any paper strives to be. As a newspaper, *The Oklahoman* cannot escape criticism because it chronicles events. It provides the day-to-day history of Oklahoma City, the state, nation and world. It is the *messenger,* reporting news and information that affects the lives, welfare and interests of its readers, and not all readers like what they read. Some blame the messenger for bad news or for opinions in editorials, columns and other readers' letters with which they disagree. History shows that *The Oklahoman* has never pulled any punches when stating opinions. It has fought for good schools, industry, water supplies, roads, highways, a strong national defense, lower taxes and a strong economy.

As E. K. Gaylord spoke his mind, so has his son, Edward L. Gaylord, not only through the editorial page of *The Oklahoman* but in casual conversation. Edward L. Gaylord has been a strong believer in a bright future for Oklahoma, especially he noted, because the state now has "right-to-work." When asked what he saw in the future for The Oklahoma Publishing Co., he said, "More growth with quality."

✶

Through the years *The Oklahoman* has carefully avoided the commonly voiced criticism that newspapers across the nation are controlled by the business offices. In spite of the financial successes of The Oklahoma Publishing Co., the Gaylord family has never lost sight of the privilege their newspaper has in leading public thought, guiding the readers into ambitious and worthwhile projects, and staying ahead of the public in enterprise thinking. The practices established by E. K. Gaylord nearly a century ago continue today. As E. K. Gaylord wrote in 1953: "An attempt is always made to select persons [employees] not for ability alone, but for character and sincere purpose." Edward L. Gaylord has continued his father's practices in building and maintaining a careful and efficient organization of loyal employees with much ability at The Oklahoma Publishing Co. The same is true of the public corporation, Gaylord Entertainment, Inc. Both corporations have grown into highly successful companies worth several billion dollars.

In Oklahoma, however, *The Oklahoman*'s efforts to build a better city and state go beyond reporting and investigating the news, expressing editorial opinions, and selling advertisements. The paper and its employees also seek to serve fellow Oklahomans. The pages of *The Oklahoman* reflect this, and behind the scenes employees are encouraged to help their community. They can be found serving in numerous leadership positions and in supporting worthy causes in Oklahoma City and the state. Like his father,

The Gaylord family posed for this 2002 photograph on the University of Oklahoma campus. Clay Bennett (left), Louise Gaylord Bennett and E. K. Gaylord II are standing. Sitting on the Thelma Gaylord Memorial Bench are Jim Everest (left), Christy Gaylord Everest, Edward L. Gaylord and Mary Gaylord McClean.

Edward L. Gaylord and his son, E. K. Gaylord II, believe employees have an obligation to help their community, and they lead by setting the example.

During the last half century the Gaylord family has quietly contributed tens of millions of dollars to dozens of philanthropic causes. Most family contributions are personal and done quietly without fanfare. But occasionally their giving does make headlines. On April 30, 2000, University of Oklahoma President David L. Boren announced that Edward L. Gaylord and family was donating $22 million to build a "world class" college of journalism and mass communication at OU. The University's program was elevated to a free-standing college and was named for the Gaylord family. A portion of the money was earmarked for the construction of a new journalism and mass communications building to be called Gaylord Hall. Edward L. Gaylord's daughter Christy Gaylord Everest, an OU Regent, said she was excited to see that the gift will help elevate the journalism school's status.

Three months later, in July 2000, Edward L. Gaylord announced that

he was providing a $40 million gift—$2 million a year for 20 years—to Oklahoma Christian University, the largest single gift by a living individual ever given to a college in Oklahoma. The gift is being used to advance the University's academic programs, build the endowment, and fund capital projects such as renovation and expansion of student housing. Upon hearing of the gift, former President George Bush said: "Barbara and I have enormous respect for Ed Gaylord and were not at all surprised when we heard of his very generous gift to Oklahoma Christian University. He is a very giving person, and once again, he is demonstrating his great generosity and his willingness to help other people."

In May 2002, Edith Gaylord's Inasmuch, and Ethics and Excellence in Journalism foundations combined to contribute $2 million toward the construction of Gaylord Hall housing the Gaylord College of Journalism and Mass Communication at the University of Oklahoma. The Edith Kinney Gaylord Library and Research Center in the building will honor her contributions to journalism. As a pioneering newswoman, she was inducted into the Oklahoma Journalism Hall of Fame in 1989.

About five months later the Gaylord family provided a gift of $12 million to OU to help the University complete an expansion of Oklahoma Memorial Stadium. The family came to the University's aid after the city of Norman refused to tax residents to cover the remaining cost of the stadium's expansion. By then the family had given more than $50 million to OU. To honor them, President David L. Boren said the words "Gaylord Family" will be prominently displayed in appreciation for their contributions along with the words "Oklahoma Memorial Stadium" on the edifice, and a monument will be erected at the stadium carrying the names of family members and acknowledging their generosity.

A century ago E. K. Gaylord was like many other pioneer newspapermen and other business people in countless communities in the West providing the leadership needed to build frontier towns and territories into large cities and states. The tiny acorn that E. K. Gaylord planted when he moved to Oklahoma City in 1903 has grown into a mighty oak tree with many branches but deep roots in Oklahoma. E. K. Gaylord's original investment of $5,000 in The Oklahoma Publishing Co. has grown into an enterprise worth billions of dollars thanks to the business acumen of E. K. Gaylord, his son Edward L. Gaylord, grandson E. K. Gaylord II, granddaughters Christy Everest, Mary McClean, and Louise Bennett, and the dedication of countless employees. Oklahoma born, it remains an Oklahoma company even though its diversification has spread beyond the borders of the state. The Oklahoma Publishing Co. has not wavered from its original goal established by E. K. Gaylord to help shape the growth of Oklahoma City, the state and nation.

Christy Gaylord Everest, a member of OPUBCO's board since December 31, 1975, was elected president late in 2002. "As the leading provider of information in Oklahoma, we will continue to put out the best product and provide our readers with relevant news and information," she said, adding that one of her goals is to see the company more involved in the community and with the Chamber of Commerce. Early in 2003 she was named, "Oklahoma City's Person of the Year 2003" by the newspaper *Friday*.

Christy Gaylord Everest lives in Oklahoma City with her husband Jim. They have two children: Tricia Louise

and Mary Christine. A third child James Christopher died of cancer in 1992 at the age of 17. Christy Gaylord Everest also serves on the board of directors of Gaylord Entertainment Co. In addition, she currently serves on the University of Oklahoma Board of Regents, as director of the Metro Youth Development and Education Foundation, Children's Medical Research Institute Board, as a driver for Mobile Meals, and as a trustee and member of the Grants Committee of the Presbyterian Health Foundation. She is past chairman of the board of trustees of Casady School, an Episcopal College Preparatory Day School, and was honored with the distinguished graduate award in 1994. In 1998, she and her husband jointly received the Dean's Award for Distinguished Community Service from the OU Medical Alumni Association and Outstanding Philanthropist Award from the National Society of Fund Raising Executives, Oklahoma Chapter, 1998. In 2000, she was honored as the Woman of the Year by the Redlands Council of the Girl Scout's of the United States of America. She is an avid golfer and has made six holes in one.

Mary Gaylord McClean, who was elected to the OPUBCO board on June 9, 1998, and now serves as vice president, is married to Jeff McClean. They breed and show American Saddlebred horses and Hackney ponies on their Golden Creek Farms at Simpsonville, Kentucky, near Louisville. They have won 137 world championships with their horses and ponies. She is well-known in the national horse community and is the recipient of the Audrey Guthridge Award in 2000, the highest honor a horsewoman can win. In addition to supporting community activities in Kentucky, she supports many horse related issues including

Mary Gaylord McClean (left) poses with artist Gwen Reardon in front of Reardon's bronze statue of Mary McClean's multiple world-champion horse Santana Lass. The statue is located across the street from the Shelby County Fairgrounds in Kentucky. A likeness of Mary McClean is atop the horse. (Photo by "Avis")

The employees and management of The Oklahoma Publishing Co. posed for this photo in celebration of the company's first century.

the United Professional Horsemen's Association (UPHA) Exceptional Challenge Cup which is a competition for handicapped riders. She is also the recipient of the UPHA Distinguished Service Award.

Also steeped in the Gaylord family traditions is Louise Gaylord Bennett, who was elected to the OPUBCO board on March 5, 2001, and serves as secretary. She and her husband Clay have three children: Mollie Inez, Christine Marie, and Gaylord Graham. Their family lives in Oklahoma City, where Louise is very active in business, civic and charitable activities. She serves as an officer and shareholder of Dorchester Capital, a diversified private investment company formed in 1990. Like her sister Christy Gaylord Everest, Louise is a member of the board of trustees of Casady School. She is also a member of the board of directors, and president in 2003, of Care Center, a non-profit organization that serves abused children. She is a lifetime member of the board of directors of Free-to-Live, a non-profit animal sanctuary created to provide a lifetime home for abandoned and abused dogs and cats. Her other voluntary activities include serving on the board of Westminster Presbyterian Church, Mercy Health Center Foundation, and the Jasmine Moran Children's Museum in Seminole, Oklahoma. She is a former board member of the Mental Health Association of Oklahoma County and the Oklahoma City Zoological Society. In 1997, she received the Volunteer Fund Raising Award from the Oklahoma Chapter of the National Fund Raising Executives Association for providing extraordinary leadership in non-profit fund-raising.

E. K. Gaylord II, a longtime member of the OPUBCO board, also serves as a board member of Gaylord Enter-tainment Co., is chairman of Gaylord Films, and is a board member of the Broadmoor Hotel and Golf Club in Colorado Springs. He also serves as a director of the National Cowboy and Western Heritage Museum, the Oklahoma State Fair, the Breeder's Cup Board, and is very active in the thoroughbred industry. In Oklahoma City, E. K. Gaylord II is involved with Children's Hospital, Children's Medical Research, the Leukemia Society, the Arthritis Foundation, and the United Way. Of his eight years as president of OPUBCO, E. K. Gaylord II said: "During my tenure, I recruited top management professionals and focused our business on our core assets. I created and helped implement our convergence with News 9 TV, brought about the merger of oil and gas assets with Rick's Exploration and instilled a collaborative culture that is flourishing today. We also improved the campus of the OPUBCO headquarters, added a state of the art fitness center for our employees and built a superior child development center for our employees' children."

If the record of the twentieth century is any indication, the future of The Oklahoma Publishing Co. will be secure under the leadership of Edward L. and Thelma Gaylord's children and will undoubtedly continue to grow with quality during the 21st century. The foundation for a dynasty, laid a century ago by E. K. Gaylord and enhanced by his son, Edward L. Gaylord, is solid. The names Gaylord and The Oklahoma Publishing Co. will continue to be synonymous with building an empire, building a state, and building a city. The saga continues, and Oklahomans can be proud of the accomplishments and contributions of the Gaylord family and The Oklahoma Publishing Co. as they enter their second century.

Bibliography

A great many sources were consulted in researching and writing this centennial history of The Oklahoma Publishing Company and the Gaylord family. Census figures for 1980 and 1990 came from the Oklahoma City Chamber of Commerce; census figures prior to 1980 were found in *The Oklahoman*. Each chapter contains material that may be found in old copies of *The Oklahoman* and *Times* on or about the dates cited in the text. Additional material came from the following anniversary supplements (listed chronologically):

Fifty Years of Progress. A 40-page supplement to *The Daily Oklahoman*, March 1, 1953.

This Is OPUBCO. A 32-page supplement to *The Sunday Oklahoman*, October 20, 1963.

Growing with Pride. A 23-page supplement to *The Daily Oklahoman*, March 11, 1973.

75th Anniversary. A 24-page tabloid published by The Oklahoma Publishing Co., 1978.

Eightieth Anniversary. A 24-page supplement to *The Sunday Oklahoman*, November 14, 1982.

The Oklahoma Publishing Co. Celebrating 85 Years of Service to Oklahoma 1903–1988. 24-page supplement to *The Oklahoman*, [1988].

The Daily Oklahoman, April 24, 1994. The Centennial Edition containing five sections.

Famous Front Pages from The Oklahoman & Times. N.d. Thirteen front pages from *The Oklahoman* and *Times* published between 1907 and 1963.

The chapter by chapter summary below lists additional sources consulted in specific chapters.

CHAPTER ONE

Carter, Ed. *The Story of Oklahoma Newspapers.* Muskogee, Okla.: Western Heritage Books, 1984.

Gaylord, E. K. Typed copy of remarks made by E. K. Gaylord in an impromptu speech, November 1970. Four pages.

CHAPTER TWO

The Gaylord genealogy is well documented in family records. Much of the early family history is contained in: William Gaillard, comp., *The History and Pedigrees of The House of Gaillard or Gaylord in France, England, and the United States, With a View of Chateau Gaillard, in Normandy; a View of Gaylord's Ville, in Connecticut; a Portrait of the Author, with the Family Arms, and other Portraits.* Self-published, Cincinnati, Ohio, 1872.

Family Search, the Web page providing Internet users access to the genealogy files gathered by the Church of Jesus Christ of Latter-day Saints, http://www.familysearch.org/.

Other Sources Consulted:

Atchison (Kans.) Champion, July 7, 1876.

Brockett, L. P., and Mary C. Vaughan. "Mrs. Lucy Gaylord Pomeroy." In *Woman's Work in the Civil War: A Record of Heroism, Patriotism and Patience.* Boston: R. H. Curran, 1867.

Eldridge, Shalor Winchell. *Publications of the Kansas State Historical Society Embracing Recollections of Early Days in Kansas.* Topeka: Kansas State Printing Plant, 1920.

Gaylord, E. K. Personal four-page typed letter to his son, Edward L. Gaylord, dated May 30, 1968, containing his childhood recollections and family genealogy.

———. "The Strange Divorce of the King of Cripple Creek," *Empire Magazine, The Denver Post,* July 23, 1972. Gaylord, writing at age 99, recounts his own experiences and the story of the divorce case of Albert E. Carlton.

Martin, George W. "A Chapter from the Archives." In *Collections of the Kansas State Historical Society, 1911–1912.* Topeka: Kansas State Historical Society, 1912.

CHAPTER THREE

Several stories pertaining to early Oklahoma City were related by E. K. Gaylord in a talk to an Oklahoma City men's organization about 1970. They are included in a 12-page unlabeled and undated transcript of his remarks in the files of Edward L. Gaylord.

Scott, Angelo C. *The Story of Oklahoma City.* Oklahoma City: Times-Journal Publishing Co, 1939.

CHAPTER FOUR

The Daily Oklahoman and *Times* as cited in the text.

Gaylord, Edith. Interviews with the author, April 1998.

Johnson, Edith C. *The Story of My Life.* Oklahoma City: Oklahoma Publishing Co., 1940. A 24-page booklet.

CHAPTER FIVE

The Daily Oklahoman as cited in the text.

Gaylord, Edith. Interviews with the author, April 1998.

Gaylord, Edward L. Interview with the author, March 6, 1998, and subsequent conversations.

Harrison, Walter M. *Me and My Big Mouth.* Oklahoma City: Britton Publishing Co., 1954. A 515-page book containing the recollections of a longtime managing editor of *The Oklahoman* and *Times.*

CHAPTER SIX

The Daily Oklahoman and *Times* as cited in the text.

Gaylord, Edith. Interview with the author, May 1, 1998.

Harrison, Walter M. *Me and My Big Mouth.* Oklahoma City: Britton Publishing Co., 1954.

Johnson, Edith C. *The Story of My Life.* Oklahoma City: Oklahoma Publishing Co., 1940.

CHAPTER SEVEN

Allen, Gene. *Voices on the Wind: Early Radio in Oklahoma.* Oklahoma Heritage Association, Oklahoma Horizons Series. Oklahoma City: Western Heritage Books, 1993.

Cronkite, Walter. *A Reporter's Life.* New York: Alfred A. Knopf, 1996.

The Daily Oklahoman and *Times* as cited in the text.

Gaylord, E. K. "Supplement to History of WKY." Three-page legal-size mimeographed document containing remarks made at a banquet dedicating new WKY studios and offices in the Skirvin Tower Hotel, Oklahoma City, April 13, 1936.

"An Outline History of WKY AM, FM and TV." Seven-page legal-size mimeographed outline of the history of the WKY stations from 1920 through 1952.

The Story of The Oklahoma Publishing Company: Men, Methods and Machinery. Oklahoma City: Oklahoma Publishing Co., [1939]. An 18-page pamphlet.

WKY files, Oklahoma Historical Society.

CHAPTER EIGHT

The Daily Oklahoman and *Times* as cited in the text.

Gaylord, Edith. Interview with the author, May 1, 1998.

Gaylord, Edward L. Interview with the author, March 6, 1998, and subsequent conversations.

"An Outline History of WKY AM, FM and TV."

CHAPTER NINE

The Daily Oklahoman and *Times* as cited in the text.

Gaylord, Edward L. Interview with the author, March 6, 1998, and subsequent conversations.

Los Angeles Times, March 31, 1952. Funeral notice, Lewis Gaylord.

CHAPTER TEN

Cromley, Alan. Correspondence with the author, March 17, 2001.

The Daily Oklahoman and *Times* as cited in the text.

Prestridge, Sharon. "The Gaylord Image." January 1969. A 35-page research paper by a University of Oklahoma journalism student.

Shaw, Gaylord. Correspondence with the author, February 6, 2001.

CHAPTER ELEVEN

Cuff Stuff: The Magazine of The Oklahoma Publishing Co. June 1974. 17 pages. Summarizing the life and death of E. K. Gaylord.

The Daily Oklahoman and *Times* as cited in the text.

"Final Rites Held for E. K. Gaylord." *The Daily Oklahoman,* June 4, 1974.

Gaylord, Edward L. Interview with the author, March 6, 1998, and subsequent conversations.

Gaylord, E. K. "The Oklahoma Publishing Company." New York: The Newcomen Society in North America, 1971. Remarks delivered by E. K. Gaylord, March 25, 1971, when he was honored in an Oklahoma City banquet. 28 pages.

——. *Quotations.* Oklahoma City: Oklahoma Publishing Co., 1973. A 24-page booklet containing quotations made by E. K. Gaylord during his lifetime.

Pitts, Teresa C. "The History of E. K. Gaylord from 1950–1970." May 1972. An eight-page research paper by a University of Oklahoma journalism student.

"Simple Rites Honor Gaylord." *The Oklahoma Journal,* June 4, 1974.

Stewart, Richard L. "A History of E. K. Gaylord and His Press." December 1974. A 26-page research paper by a University of Oklahoma journalism student.

Strasbaugh, Paul B. Correspondence with the author, June 19, 1998, and subsequent telephone conversations.

CHAPTER TWELVE

American Academy of Achievement. 1987 Banquet of the Golden Plate. Phoenix: n.p., 1987.

The Daily Oklahoman and *Times* as cited in the text.

Gaylord, Edward L. Interview with the author, March 6, 1998, and subsequent conversations.

Kaye, Susan. "Resort of the Month, Grande Dame of the Rockies." *TravelAmerica.* March/April 1998. A two-page article on the Broadmoor Resort Hotel in Colorado Springs.

CHAPTER THIRTEEN

The Daily Oklahoman as cited in the text.

Gaylord, E. K. II. Interview with the author, July 7, 1998, and subsequent conversations.

Kelley, Ed. Copy of his remarks on the Oklahoma City bombing coverage delivered at the annual convention, Southern Newspaper Publishers Association, Colorado Springs, Sept. 19, 1995.

CHAPTER FOURTEEN

The Daily Oklahoman as cited in the text.

Gaylord, Edward L. Interview with the author, March 6, 1998, and subsequent conversations.

Gaylord, E. K. II. Interview with the author, July 7, 1998.

Gaylord, E. K. II, Christy Gaylord Everest, Mary Gaylord McClean, and Louise Gaylord Bennett. Conversations with the author, fall 2002.

Oklahoma City Friday, January 22, 1999.

Russell, Keith. "Rating the Top 10, Left and Right." *Insight,* May 25, 1998.

Index

Gaylord, Edward Lewis, 6, 7, 54, 101, 103–4, 109, 110, 117ff, 123ff, 128, 136, 137; birth, 63; college, 89; compared to father 120–1; editorial opinions, 144ff, 147–8; military service, 89, 99, 117ff; most powerful Oklahoman, 144

Gaylord, Elizabeth, 22

Gaylord Entertainment Co., 132, 134, 141, 149, 151

Gaylord Event Television, 134

Gaylord Films, 134, 151

Gaylord, George Lewis, 19–22; street named for, 25

Gaylord Golden Guernsey Dairy, 67–8, 103

Gaylord Hall (OU), 148

Gaylord Hotels, 141

Gaylord, Inez Kinney (Mrs. E. K.), 59, 63, 103, 119

Gaylord, Joseph, 19

Gaylord, Lewis, 23–7; death, 102

Gaylord, Louise, 99. See also Louise Gaylord Bennett

Gaylord, Lucy Ann, 20

Gaylord, Martin Luther, 20–2

Gaylord, Mary, 99. See also Mary Gaylord McClean

Gaylord, Nicholas, 19

Gaylord Opryland Texas, 141

Gaylord Palms Resort and Convention Center (Fla.), 141

Gaylord Philanthropies, 92

Gaylord Production Co., 120

Gaylord, Ruth, 19

Gaylord Sports Management, 134

Gaylord Syndicom, 134

Gaylord, Thelma (Mrs. Edward L.), 99, 123, 124, 128–36, 137; death of, 138

Gaylord, Virginia, 54, 65

Gaylord, Willis Edward, 19

Gemini space program, 114

General Jackson Showboat, 134

General Motors, 120

Glen Campbell Show, 120

Gloomy Gus Show (WKY), 72

Golden Creek Farms, 149

Golden Plate Award, 127

Gourley, J. Leland, 146

Graham, Rev. Billy, 136

Grand Junction (Colo.), 25, 102

Grand Junction News, 26

grand juries, 117, 121

Grand Lake (Okla.), 117

Grand Ole Opry, 124

Grant, Whit M., 16

Greenland Ranch (Colo.), 142

Griffin, David, 143

Grubb, Gayle, 78, 85

Guggenheim, Benjamin, 49

Gulf War, 131

Gunnison (Colo.), 24

Guthrie (Okla.), 13, 29, 32, 36–7, 39–40, 42, 46–7, 49

–H–

Hall, Gov. David, 117, 121

Hall, F. C., 78

Hamon, Jake, 65

Hardeman Auditorium (OKC), 119, 143

Harding, Warren G., 65

Harfield, Elwin, 102

Harlow's Weekly, 66

Harlow, Victor, 66

Harreld, John W., 65

Harrington, B. R., 11–12

Harrison, Walter M. "Skipper," 57–8

Harvard Business School, 89, 120

Haskell, Gov. Charles N., 39, 42, 46

Hee Haw Show, 120, 134

Hegler, Burns, 44

helicopters, 92, 111

Henry, Gov. Brad, 144

Herrington Inc., 138

Hertz Corp., 120

Hillsdale (Mich.), 136

Hillsdale College (Mich.), 136

Hitler, Adolf, 86

Holloway, William J., 74

Hoover, Herbert, 70

Hope, Bob, 126

Horton, Thelma Feragen, 99. See also Thelma Gaylord

Hough, Larry, 125

Houston (Texas), 12, 134

Howell, J. Owen, 73

Huckins Hotel (OKC), 10, 74. See also Lee-Huckins Hotel

Hudson, Clark, 29, 36

Huerta, Victoriano, 53

Hughes, Charles Evans, 58

Hull, Earl C., 68–70

Hull, Jack, 89–90

–I–

Inasmuch Foundation, 144, 148

Indians, 22

Indian Territory, 16, 39

Indian Territory Illuminating Oil Co., 70, 73

Industries Foundation, 89

Insight magazine, 146–7

–J–

Jackson, Jim, 102

Japan, 35–6, 89, 90, 91

Jarret, Walter, 80

Jasmine Moran Children's Museum (Seminole), 151

Jennings, Al, 53

Jewell, Kirk A., 126

Jim Thorpe Museum (OKC), 144

Johnson, Andrew, 13

Johnson, Cullen, 61

Johnson, Edith, 43, 49, 51, 65, 74–5

Johnson, Pres. Lyndon B., 112, 139

Johnston, Gov. Henry S., 73

Jones, Dorothy Dayton, 67

Jordan, Michael, 134

Journal-Record building (OKC), 144

–K–

Kaltenborn, H. V., 91

Kansas City (Mo.), 12, 14, 32, 70, 80

Kansas City Star, 13, 70, 117

Kansas Pacific Railroad, 24

Kansas Territory, 20

Kansas Valley Bank (Atchison, Kans.), 20

Katz Advertising Agency (N.Y.), 31, 117

Katz, Eugene, 136

Katz, George R., 31; death, 117

Keating, Gov. Frank, 142, 144

Kelley, Ed, 61, 135–6

Kennedy, Pres. John F., death, 112–13, 126

Kerr, W. F., 44

KFJF radio (OKC), 70

KHTV (Houston), 114, 123

Kimball, Capt. Jesse, 19

King George V, 73

Kingman, Samuel A., 22

Kinney, Inez, 54–5

Kinney, James, Jr., 54

Kiowa Indians, 22

Kirkpatrick Center, 121

Kirkpatrick, E. E., 80

Kissimmee (Fla.), 141

Kitty Hawk (N.C.), 55

KLLB-FM (Portland), 120

Klondike gold fields, 17

Knickerbocker Magazine, 19

KOMA radio (OKC), 70

Korean War, 102

KRKE-AM/FM (Albuquerque), 120

KSTW-TV (Seattle-Tacoma), 120, 123

KTVT (Dallas), 111, 123; sale of, 111

Ku Klux Klan, 66

KWTV (OKC), 143

KYTE-AM (Portland), 120

–L–

Lake Atoka, 107

Lake Hefner, 89, 103

Lake Overholser, 59

Land, J. T., 44

land run, 11, 45

Lange, Jim, 101, 112, 118

Langley Field (Va.), 89

Las Vegas (Nev.), 132

St. Joseph (Mo.), 9, 29
St. Joseph Dispatch, 9, 27
St. Louis (Mo.), 9, 45
St. Louis Post-Dispatch, 15, 58
stock market crash (1929), 75
Strasbaugh, Paul B., 120–1, 137
streetcar workers' strike (OKC), 48
Sullivant, Otis, 61, 120
Swain, Paul, 102
Syracuse (N.Y.), 19

–T–

Tacoma (Wash.), 134
Taft, William Howard, 49
Taylor, Jack, 117–18
Teapot Dome scandal, 65
Teller County (Colo.), 26
Tennis Magazine, 128
Texas (state), 15, 75, 89, 123
Texas Christian University, 132
"Texas' Tallest TV Tower," 123
Thelma Gaylord Memorial Bench (OU), 148
The Oklahoman, 6, 9ff, 28ff, 39ff, 65, 67, 75, 77,
   80–1, 85–6, 89ff, 101ff, 117ff, 121, 123, 126,
   144–5, 147; action line, 114; audiotext, 136;
   carpet, 111; cartoonists, 78, 101; comics in
   color, 104–5; computerized type-setting, 109,
   111, 114, 118; delivery, 112 (*see also* Mistletoe
   Express); Linotype machines 29, 43, 45, 81,
   101; news coverage, 9ff, 31–3, 35–6, 39, 44ff,
   49ff, 53–4, 57, 61, 63, 65–7, 72–5, 78ff, 89, 90–1,
   95, 102, 104, 107, 109–10, 112ff, 115, 117, 121,
   123ff, 126, 134–6, 141, 142ff; "Pennies from
   Heaven" campaign 85–6; political policy, 57;
   printing presses, 17, 29, 35, 39, 43, 101, 107,
   109, 118; Pulitzer Prize, 78; Red-headed
   Daily, 35; scholarship programs, 109, 111;
   technological advances, 101, 104, 118, 123, 126;
   Washington (D.C.) bureau, 61, 114
The Oklahoma Publishing Co. (OPUBCO), 6,
   7, 29ff, 55, 57, 66, 75, 77ff, 92, 97, 98, 101ff, 111,
   117ff, 123ff, 134, 145, 149, 151; broadcasting
   division, 104, 111, 123; fiftieth anniversary,
   102; holdings: (1949), 95; (1991), 132; incor-
   poration, 29–30; oil and gas division, 111;
   real estate division, 111, 132, 136, 146
Tinker Air Force Base (OKC), 90
Tinker, Maj. Gen. Clarence, 90
Tishomingo (Okla.), 39
Titanic disaster, 48, 50
tornadoes, 77, 78, 94, 101, 138
tractors, 55
Trammell, Robby, 136
Trapp, Martin E., 66
Trianon Ballroom (OKC), 120
Trotter, Pat, 73
Truman, Pres. Harry S, 91–2, 139
Tucker, H. H., Jr., 42

Tucker, Howard, 42
Tulsa (Okla.), 66, 85
Tulsa World, 46, 82

–U–

Unassigned Lands, 11
underground railroad, 21
Union-Leader (N.H.), 147
United Appeal, 66
United Fund, 66
United Press, 61
United Professional Horsemen's Assoc.
   (UPHA), 143, 151
United Way of Metro Oklahoma City, 151
Unit Parts Co., 120
University of Kansas, 22
University of Nebraska, 112
University of Oklahoma, 66, 85, 99, 112, 126,
   143, 148–9; football, 85, 97, 99, 112, 143;
   Gaylord College of Journalism and Mass
   Communications, 148; medical alumni
   assoc., 149; memorial stadium, 148
Urschel, Betty, 80
Urschel, Charles F., 80
U.S. Army Air Corps, 89
U.S. Dept. of Commerce, 68–9
U.S. House of Representatives, 74
U.S. Olympic Committee, 124
U.S. Olympic Festival (Norman), 126
U.S.S. *Oklahoma City,* 91
U.S. Volunteers (Union Army), 21

–V–

Vahlberg, Vivian E., 123
Valley Forge (Pa.), 19
Van Meter, Brent, 142
Ventura County (Calif.), 102
Vera Cruz (Mexico), 53
Vietnam, 115; My Lai Massacre, 117–18
Vinita (Okla.), 36

–W–

Wake Island (Pacific), 90
"Walk to Remember, A" (film), 134
Wallingford (Conn.), 19
Wallis, Wally, 102
Wall Street Journal, 147
Walt Disney World, 141
Walters, Gov. David Lee, 134–5
Walton, Jack C., 65–6
Ward, Perry, 73
Warner Brothers Studios (Calif.), 134
Washington (D.C.), 14, 20, 22, 59, 61, 88, 89, 112
Washington Post, 147
Washington Times, 147
Watergate, 121
Waynick boardinghouse (OKC), 45
WDAF radio (Kansas City, Mo.), 70

Weatherford (Okla.), 121
Weekly Oklahoman, 48, 67
Wells, Clifford, 73
Wells, Willie, 73
Werner, Charles, 78, 86, 101
Westinghouse Corp., 134
Westminster Presbyterian Church (OKC), 151
West, Shane, 134
Wewoka (Okla.), 112
Whalin Brothers' Band, 72–3
Whalin, Kermit, 73
whisky, 31
Whitewater (Colo.), 25
Wichita (Kans.), 11, 22, 36, 89
wildfires, 150
Williams, Bill, 119
Williams, Robert L., 61
Will Rogers World Airport, 88, 106
Wilson, Thomas E., 59–60
Wilson, Pres. Woodrow, 61, 66, 68
"Winnie Mae" (airplane), 86
"With Wings As Eagles" campaign, 117
WKY radio, 68–70, 72–3, 75, 77, 78, 82, 85, 89,
   95, 101, 132; mobile unit, 85; sale of, 120
WKY-TV, 96–7, 99, 101, 102, 103, 104, 115; mobile
   unit, 102; sale of, 120
woman suffrage, 65
Women's National Press Club, 59
Woodward (Okla.), 39, 94
World Champion (quarter horse), 132
World War I, 61
World War II, 59, 89, 90–3, 118
Wright, Orville, 55
Wright, Wilbur, 55
WTVT (Tampa–St. Petersburg), 104
WUAB-TV (Cleveland), 120
WVTV (Milwaukee), 114
WVUE-TV (New Orleans), 120
Wyoming (state), 65

–Y–

YMCA, 136
Yoes, Ralph, 101
Young, Jim, 117
YWCA, 54
Yukon (Okla.), 14